Ascension Numerology

Ascension Numerology

Michael Hersey
with Sanhia

Illustrations by
Ulla Lindgren

WWW.LIGHTSPIRA.COM

Published by: LightSpira, Sweden
www.lightspira.com

ISBN: 978-91-86613-29-7
First edition, 2016

Author:	Michael Hersey
Illustrations:	Ulla Lindgren
Cover & Book layout:	Ulla Lindgren, Marie Örnesved
Digital design:	Marie Örnesved
Editing:	Stella Hansen
Authors cover & Biography photos:	Anna-Malin Saluna Andersdotter
Ascension Guidance:	Sanhia

Copyright © 2016, 2018 by Michael Hersey and Ulla Lindgren.
www.channelswithoutborders.com

CONTENTS

0.	Introductions	8
1.	Ascension	28
2.	Numerology	36
3.	How to use this book	44
4.	The Numbers	52
5.	Motivation	76
6.	Karmic Number	86
7.	Personality	96
8.	Stress Number between Motivation and Personality	104
9.	Integrated Self	138
10.	Life Path	162
11	Stress Number between Motivation and Life Path	174
12.	Cycle	204
13.	Pinnacle	212
14.	Personal Year	220
15.	Ascension Number	232
16.	Table of Intensification	244
17.	Plane of Expression	250
18.	Now what?	268
19.	Computations	274
	Appreciations	291
	Biographies	295
	Index	296

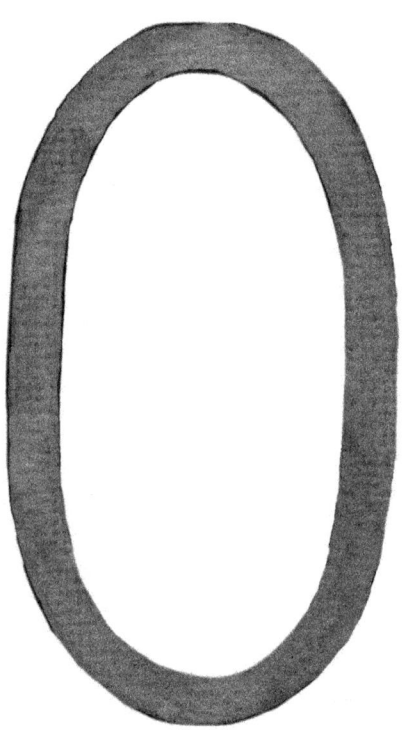

INTRODUCTIONS

SANHIA &
MY LOVE LETTER FROM MY HIGHER SELF

I have been channeling the ascended master Sanhia since 1985. Sanhia ascended as an Apache Indian in pre-Columbian America. Previously he was Thomas, the disciple of Jesus. One morning, as I was on my daily walk, Sanhia told me that we were going to write a NUMEROLOGY book together. I let Sanhia know that the idea of writing a NUMEROLOGY book bored me. Now, I have been reading NUMEROLOGY CHARTs since 1977. I do enjoy reading NUMEROLOGY books, but they are like textbooks and the thought of writing one felt tedious. Sanhia said, and I quote him, "This is not your father's NUMEROLOGY book." *He went on to let me know that it would be titled "ASCENSION NUMEROLOGY" and was not designed as a reference book, but as a way for people to access their own information from what he calls your LOVE LETTER FROM YOUR HIGHER SELF.*

Sanhia teaches that before we were born we had a preplanning session with our higher self, other significant souls who would join us in our new incarnation, and spirits that would support us through our trip on planet Earth. The information from this preplanning is encoded in our birth name and birthday. After birth we forget about the plan, our intentions, and the truth of who we are. Sanhia's goal was that this book would become a tool an individual could use to rediscover the plan and use it. Sanhia defines ASCENSION as the direct realization of the truth of who we are as divine beings. We are divine immortal beings of unconditional love and unlimited creativity. Our preplanning was undertaken with the intention that we would realize our ASCENSION in this incarnation. In order to accomplish that, we learn to accept the perfection of everything that happens in our life, receiving everything as a divine gift designed only to help us realize our ASCENSION. We also begin to let go of judgment of ourselves and others so that we can see our and their divinity. This is all facilitated by our willingness to take full responsibility for everything in our life, surrendering the tendencies toward blame and victimhood. Above all we forgive, forgive, forgive.

I agreed to do the book. Sanhia suggested that I begin it by introducing myself, letting my spiritual story be accompanied by a few references to my NUMEROLOGY CHART. All capitalized words are terms that are defined elsewhere in the book and listed in some form in the index.

I was raised as a Catholic. I tried to be a good Catholic, but I usually fell short and lived with a lot of guilt. I don't blame the Catholic Church for this. I'm pretty sure I brought the guilt with me (KARMIC TWO and KARMIC SIX). I would have found a home for my guilt in any religious dogma. Once when I was about ten a thought came flying into my head out of nowhere, "What if somebody just made up the New Testament?" I immediately let God know that I wasn't responsible for that idea, that I had no idea where it came from, and that I disavowed it. I was certainly concerned about the fires of hell. That, by the way, was my introduction to Sanhia — as he informed me over 25 years later; it was he who sent me that message, which I came years later to find was mostly true. He has one hell of a sense of humor.

Sanhia says that the main reason that we created having other people in our world is to help us see ourselves more accurately.

During junior high a young priest tried to lead me toward a priestly vocation. I was a little flattered (not a very spiritual response) but was way too interested in the opposite sex to consider going down the road of celibacy. This priest saw something in me that I was absolutely incapable of seeing. I was kind of a typical guy (meaning I didn't have a clue), though a very shy, socially clumsy one, and I didn't feel like I fit in anywhere (SEVEN FIRST CYCLE). Though I was a top student, I didn't think of myself as smart. I did however love math (MENTAL SEVEN) and was the best at it in my class in high school. What nobody knew was that I got what I would now call a "spiritual excitement" or an "aha experience" when I came to a new mathematical understanding, following a period of intense confusion. I played with numbers the way that someone else might knit or dribble a basketball.

During my senior year, in the midst of the Vietnam War, my Sunday school teacher invited a young man to class who spoke about being a conscientious objector and a pacifist, based on the teachings of Jesus. He did not change my mind, but a small chink appeared in my Catholic spiritual foundation (FOUR MOTIVATION). Another Sunday, in response to our laconic attitudes, this teacher challenged us about why we even bothered coming to church. "Do you think that God will send you to hell for not coming," she asked. My answer would have been in the affirmative if I had been brave enough to voice it. "Well God doesn't work that way," she countered. "Do yourself a favor and don't come back until your heart draws you here". I took her advice and decided to take a little time off. I thought it would be just a temporary lull. It wasn't.

Later that year I talked at length with a Christian Scientist girl I met at a party. She explained about how they trusted their health to God. I was blown away. I don't think I had ever been exposed to real faith before. Surrender all attachments; let go and let God. I felt tremendous energy racing up and down my spine (INTUITIVE THREE).

I had felt an energy like that once before during junior high when I slept over one night with three friends from different churches. We stayed up late into the night in the dark talking about our religions. My fantasy of going to college included a lot of similar late night talks. This did not fully materialize, but I did begin to learn how to question everything. I also began to experiment with drugs. First it was marijuana, then psychedelics. I wasn't a heavy user, but my consciousness simply changed through the use of drugs. I am not advocating the use of drugs. They have certainly proved to be highly destructive in many lives. On the other hand Sanhia teaches that "destruction" is an illusion, that nothing that is real can ever be destroyed, or even hurt.

My family moved after my freshman year in college. I found myself alone, very alone, separated from all my friends, and the girl I thought I would marry had broken up with me. I was beginning the real task of learning my NINE LIFE PATH lesson. Sitting on a small hill one evening, stoned, I was looking at a beautiful starry sky through the tall oaks, but enjoying none of it. A voice came into my head out of nowhere and said, "You know that Jesus would never approve of killing for any reason." This was an absolute non sequitur. I thought about it for a little bit and realized that I totally agreed. When morning came, I was still a pacifist. I realized that I was no longer in support of the Vietnam War and that I was no longer a political conservative, but I had no idea what I now was. This was the second time that Sanhia found his way into my thoughts.

Sanhia continued to nudge me. Since I didn't know who I was, what I believed, or where I was going, he dropped little hints. I can't say just how I formed these notions, but I started to trust that I was being led to things. If a friend recommended a book or an album, I trusted that there was information in it meant for me, personally. I read Herman Hesse's Siddhartha, which opened up to me all of eastern mysticism and the idea of ASCENSION or enlightenment.

I went through two majors and finally settled on Economics. I somehow thought I could be happy as a certified public accountant working with numbers. When I returned my junior year, I found that I had absolutely no interest in the Econ class I was required to take, that I no longer had any idea why I was in school. One night, unable to find a single friend to talk to, in my confusion and my misery I wandered off to my fall-back friend the woods with a tab of mescaline. That night I talked with a fly who convinced me to drop out of school. Sanhia was preaching to the choir. I finally felt a peace, and a calmness come over me after weeks of confusion and anxiety.

There was nothing brave about me taking off two weeks later with my thumb up in the cooling fall weather. I really didn't feel that I had any other choice. I couldn't stay in school. There was absolutely no warm, nurturing energy waiting for me at my parents' home. I had no other place to go. But I was walking away from my security blanket (NINE LIFE PATH). I was leaving behind the illusion of financial safety that a professional degree seemed to offer. Sanhia teaches that the only real security comes in trusting the universe, in listening to spirit—to inner guidance. I had absolutely no idea where to go. So, I followed a loose combination of desire and chance. Call it listening to guidance if you like; I did feel that something wiser than me knew which direction to go. Sanhia says that everything that happens is perfect, that it is impossible for the wrong thing to happen to anybody, and that all choices are correct. I couldn't remember the last time I had been truly free to set my course each day. I headed for the Pacific Ocean. Spirit narrowed that down to San Francisco.

It seemed that everyone I met in San Francisco in 1969 was on one spiritual trip or another. Mostly they were newly on their path and, like many a spiritual neophyte, they were eager to proselytize. I was the perfect fit because I was eager and willing to listen to one and all. I talked to Nichiren Buddhists, Southern Baptists, Scientologists, agnostics, Wiccans, TM meditators and more. I also found books magically appearing for me including classics by Napoleon Hill and Dale Carnegie, which got me thinking about the power of positive thinking, as well as an obscure little book called *I Am*, by Freedom Barry — which opened my mind to the power of thought in manifesting reality (MENTAL SEVEN). Finally, a friend turned me on to the book Summerhill, by A.S. Neill. Neill ran a private school in England where children were not forced to take any classes, but were instead encouraged to find what truly drew them. I wondered how my life might have been different if I had had more choice as a child. The spiritual excitement energy was running rampant again. I felt I had found my purpose. Off I jumped into the fields of psychology and alternative education.

One thing that I was slowly learning to understand was that just because spirit led me off in a direction, it might not have a lot to do with where I ended up (FIVE STRESS NUMBER between MOTIVATION and LIFE PATH). Sanhia says that the goal has very little importance, that it is the process in the now, the listening to inner guidance and following it without question that is important. I never ended up teaching in an alternative school. I learned a great deal studying the great psychologists, especially Carl Rogers. I studied Zen and Taoism (MENTAL SEVEN). By my early twenties I knew what I wanted to do with my life. I wanted to do what Jesus had done. I wasn't so much concerned with miracles, and definitely not with crucifixion; what I wanted was ASCENSION (FOUR

MOTIVATION). I wanted to get off the wheel of reincarnation. I wanted this to be my last time around. I wanted enlightenment. During this time I took the Silva Mind Control course, which taught me how to visualize intended outcomes, to deal with health challenges, and to find a safe, relaxing center that I could always go to. I had a fair amount of success with "programming", that is with visualizing desired outcomes and then watching them manifest. But it was a little disconcerting to me, I think, because I wasn't sure what was the best thing to ask for; I was fearful of being powerful.

Sanhia wants me to warn everybody that ASCENSION is not an easy path. He wants me to let people know how miserable and unhappy I often was, that pain was a major motivator for not wanting to be born again. A memory I have is of me at around ten years old, standing in front of the full length mirror in the upstairs hall looking at myself and saying silently, "I want to burn this moment into my memory. When I am an adult and a biographer asks me about my childhood, I want to remember to tell him that it was unhappy". As I studied Buddhism and "the void", I found myself feeling utterly alone in the universe, unloved and hopeless. A few years later I would sometimes walk the ridge tops near my West Virginia cabin at night asking for a UFO to beam me up. I just wanted to get out of Dodge. Funny, though, I never considered suicide. I guess I didn't feel that intentional death would make things any better. I figured that I would just end up with a new body and the same old shit. Plus I would have to endure another childhood. I wanted a dramatic change and it seemed that the only way to accomplish it was by ascending. The downside of ASCENSION is that it requires a willingness to let go of absolutely everything, and one might very well have to pay up on that willingness. That's why many of us who choose ASCENSION have already lost so much that a willingness to lose the rest seems like a small price to pay for peace.

During my early to mid-twenties I had a series of losses. My father died when I was twenty-three (NINE LIFE PATH). As a boy I was sometimes terrified of him; he was a physically and mentally powerful man. As a young man, I began to speak up for myself. I realized that I wanted to be my own person, but there was nothing I desired more than his approval. On top of the debilitating grief I felt at the news of his death, I realized that now I could never get that approval. My only grace would come from my own self-approval. That was going to be an awesome challenge. In the following several years I found myself being divorced by my first wife, losing another significant lover, having my dreams of creating a rural free school dashed, and ending up as the only remaining resident of a rural commune we had begun. I found myself in the deepest of depressions.

Enter Jacqueline Robertson-Swann, Australian numerologist. On my 28th birthday, Jacquie read my CHART. I was not a dream subject. Because of my skepticism I tried to give her no help, no smiles, no nods of agreement. She talked for two hours. I was blown away. For the first time I actually understood what had been going on in my life (LOVE LETTER FROM YOUR HIGHER SELF). It made sense. I realized that I was a unique person; that I wasn't meant to be like others, that I was me. I understood what all the loss was about (FOUR FIRST PINNACLE). Jackie was willing to sit with me for another couple of hours and told me how she had constructed the CHART and about the books she recommended as sources.

The next day I purchased my first three NUMEROLOGY books and I studied and then practiced on friends for the next two years (FOUR PERSONALITY). I had a bag with all of my NUMEROLOGY books, notes and CHARTs that I often hauled around with me. One evening when I arrived home I started to grab the bag out of my car, but then decided to leave it since I wasn't planning on doing anything with it that night and would just be carrying it back out, up the hill in the snow the next morning to do a planned reading. I woke up that night to a wall of fire. That bag, my guitar, my long johns, and down booties were all that survived of my worldly possessions. I lost all my clothes, everything I had written, my "library" of read and unread books, my memorabilia, my cash, my identification, my furniture, my kitchen stuff, every damn thing. And this is the part that might seem weird. I felt that spiritual high feeling. I was free! It was as if I were being allowed to let go of all that had been weighing me down. I had a clear message from spirit (INTUITIVE THREE). I was to continue doing NUMEROLOGY. I guess I was supposed to keep plunking away on the guitar, too. Interestingly, the songs I had written were all in the case. My old Dodge Dart had not been starting reliably that winter. I decide that if it wouldn't start that next morning I would throw the key over the hill, grab my NUMEROLOGY bag and guitar and hitchhike to Texas. The engine turned right over, so I spent another year in an even smaller cabin learning NUMEROLOGY. I was beginning to learn how to accept my NINE LIFE PATH.

The message came to me to stop working at jobs that were not in my heart to do (INTUITIVE THREE). Spirit said to accept money for doing NUMEROLOGY readings. I had already read for everyone I knew and their mother for free in West Virginia, so it looked like it was time to move again, and Austin was calling to me.

As soon as I arrived in Austin, I took off for the International Silva Mind Control convention in Laredo. At lunch the first day at the hotel dining room I was offered the only free seat at a table otherwise filled with nuns and priests. This was the closest I had come to the Catholic Church in over ten years. The nun across from me asked me what I did. I gulped, clenched my fists, and mumbled apparently audibly (and for the first time publicly) that I was a numerologist. She didn't bat an eye, just asked what I charged. This was a subject I hadn't thought about. The first thing that came to mind was twenty dollars, so I said that and she reached into her purse, threw a twenty down on the table, looked me in the eye, and said, "When are we, going to do this?" Before the weekend was over I had done a reading for everyone at the restaurant table as well as several others. My career was launched.

One of the workshops I attended in Laredo was entitled "Right Livelihood". It confirmed the information I had received intuitively about committing my life to purpose rather than working to support myself (EIGHT INTEGRATED SELF). A few weeks later I saw a flyer for a speaker on "prosperity consciousness", which looked like a different take on Right Livelihood, so I went. Not long after that, I found myself headed to California to take a week-long leadership training with the speaker. Even though the workshop required an investment of half the money I had built up to finance my transition to Austin, a voice in my head said to do it.

I began speaking out more about the ideas of Right Livelihood and began working with several new age businesses as a "prosperity consultant". I combined my spiritual knowledge with my economics and psychology backgrounds to help them run their businesses. Two friends asked me to co-lead a group they were starting called The Winners' Circle, which was mostly composed of people wanting to support themselves doing the work they felt guided to do. I was terrified at the thought of speaking before a group, having just barely begun to master doing a reading for a single stranger. I survived the first evening, but was definitely not in my comfort zone. After the second gathering, one of my partners backed out. Two weeks later the other friend bailed on me, too. I suspect that most of you are all smelling Sanhia's handiwork in this. I decided to organize a second Winners' Circle. It filled up. Eventually, I was leading two or three circles on different days of the week and I was sending out a short monthly newsletter to a growing mailing list (EIGHT INTEGRATED SELF).

I started out holding the circles in my living room, but they were outgrowing that space, not to speak of my neighbor's patience. I decided to find a house to buy that would accommodate my family and the business. What Sanhia says about our guides and angels is that they are always here to help us. All we have to do is ask by stating our intention. They do the heavy lifting. My realtor called and said she had found the perfect place, but that it cost a little more than what we had been looking for. I asked her how much more. She said to just come look first. The sticker price was over twice the amount that we optimistically thought we could handle. I went inside (myself, that is, not the house) to see what spirit had to say. "Go for it", I heard. "I don't even have the down payment," says I. "If you had it, would you go for it?" "Sure" I thought, thinking that was certainly a safe bet. I had nothing in the bank. Then a friend called. He had just sold his store and had a bunch of extra cash and got this intuitive message to call me to see if I wanted to borrow money for something. Guess who was getting those chills running up and down the old spine. Then the realtor offered to loan us her commission so that we could close the deal. I had asked nobody for money, but the down payment had appeared. I was stuck. I had made my deal with the devil (Sanhia) and now I had to dance. However, I still lacked a loan. My bank turned me down, so the owner said that she would finance it herself. What's a fellow on the path supposed to do? Spirit had delivered. Scared shitless I signed on the line (ZERO STRESS NUMBER between MOTIVATION and PERSONALITY). I crunched the numbers and realized that it would require a doubling of my income flow to be able to pay the mortgage. The short story is that the flow did double, or at least I never missed a payment, for a couple of years.

I also began writing a column on prosperity consciousness which appeared in the local new age newspaper as well as in a half dozen or so similar publications around the country. The basic ideas were that:

1. You create your own reality through your thoughts and emotions.
2. You have a purpose that you came here to do, that you love doing, and that you deserve to be doing.
3. If you act purposefully, the money required for survival will be there.

All of this was bringing me some level of notoriety, not exactly rock star famous, but a level of being recognized by strangers that was not easy for me to handle (KARMIC TWO). Not only was the old shyness still there, but deeper reservoirs of unworthiness and fear of my private life becoming public were being tapped into.

Sanhia brought something else into my sphere of awareness. Channeling was introduced to me during my early twenties through a book about Edgar Cayce. I was more than a little skeptical, but also strangely attracted. Then I found the Seth books by Jane Roberts. The information was so good that I gave up my skepticism. I never could have explained or justified how the whole channeling thing worked, but the fruits were obvious. I had never come across any information that made more sense to me. I simply trusted it, though I would discuss it only with the converted or at least the interested. A few years after devouring all of the Seth material, I came into contact with A Course in Miracles. Seth and ACIM seemed totally aligned to me. The path to ASCENSION was beginning to make more sense.

In Austin I experienced channeling directly through a number of different people. One acquaintance began channeling an entity named Sanhia, an ascended master whose last incarnation was as an Apache Indian. I was both drawn to Sanhia and wary of the channel. Let me mention that I am very much a FOUR in my NUMBERs. Honesty, truth, and reliability are very important to me. I am basically slow to change, but solid once I get there. That first Sanhia channel had a mental breakdown while on a vision quest. After he recovered he became a fundamentalist Christian, rejecting all the new age things that he had done as being the work of the devil. Another person began channeling Sanhia, and I went to her a couple of times. I felt a little more trusting of her energy. Then, she chose to stop channeling. Nothing as dramatic as the first channel, but she also became a fundamentalist Christian. Dum-de dum-dum.

During this whole period of time I did not have any conscious desire to become a channel, nor did I believe that I had the ability to do so. Despite my success with NUMEROLOGY, I was convinced that was much more a left brained than a right brained process. I didn't think I was particularly "psychic"; I was just good at understanding NUMBERs and had mastered the ability to quickly interpret and blend the different VIBRATIONs during a reading.

One Saturday during a break in the midst of an all-day monthly workshop I was leading for Winners' Circle graduates, I was relaxing in a room by myself. I began to feel a pressure in my head, not so much a headache as a feeling as if something wanted to burst right through the crown of my skull, like Athena bursting forth fully matured out of Zeus's head. As the pressure increased, I asked silently, "What is this?" I heard a voice respond (again silently), "Do you want to let me come through?" At this point I felt like I was in the old Bill Cosby "Noah" routine and wanted to say, "Riiiiiiight." Instead I asked, "Let who through?" "Who do you think it is," was the reply. I was silent for a while and then said the first name that came to mind, though I said it as a question, "Sanhia?" "Right," was the reply, "so do you want to let me through?" "You mean to channel you?" I asked. "Yes," he said. "I don't know how to channel", I said. "You are doing it right now", he said. "Yeah", I replied, "but this is just going on inside of my head and nobody else can hear it." "So, just open your mouth and say what you hear", was the response. "Okay, then", I surrendered, "I'll give it a shot."

When the group reassembled, I told them what had transpired and asked them if they wanted me to attempt a channeling. And so it began. I don't remember anything Sanhia talked about that afternoon. I know that when I talked I found myself using a louder voice of a different timbre and accent than my own. I was totally conscious and could have recalled any of it. This wasn't the way that most channels I knew of operated; usually they were unconscious, went somewhere else, and had no recollection of what had been said through them. I was pretty skeptical of the whole thing. So apparently was about half the group. They didn't return the next month. But there were just as many people present. People began to request private sessions (TWO SECOND PINNACLE).

Let me tell you more about what I know about Sanhia. This is from what he has said to others. He ascended as a pre-Columbian Apache Indian. I was with him in that lifetime, as were some of the others present in that early group. He said that nobody ascends without assistance and that our support was invaluable to him, so he was there for us now from the other side to offer support in our

ASCENSION process. He is also here to assist anybody who gives intention for ASCENSION. He said all it takes to manifest anything is to state your intention. Then it is only a matter of time. Time is an illusion. So it actually happens as you ask for it. There is nothing else you have to do, but the illusion of time passes faster if you don't spend it in doubt and worry. Sanhia said that previous to the Apache lifetime, he was Thomas, the disciple of Jesus. Yes, he says, "doubting" Thomas, the author of The Gospel of Thomas. He likes to talk about that experience and about the teachings of Jesus. He has an incredible sense of humor, is enormously supportive and warm, and absolutely non-judgmental. At the same time, he will say exactly what it is that is perfect for me to hear and will give me the occasional well directed kick in the ass to do whatever it is that I want to do, but am afraid to. He is not forceful, does not want followers, and is willing to talk as often or as little as a person chooses. He is all about free choice. But, the bottom line on the choice is whether or not we will choose what we came here to choose.

Channeling Sanhia marked the beginning of the end of my short period of fame and success in Austin. I was still living in a lot of fear. Though I had found success in the relatively large Austin new age community, I was terrified of the mainstream. I was afraid of being judged and/or persecuted. I was afraid of the wrath of Christians for my beliefs and especially for being a channel. My ego was all wrapped up in this, too. I wanted to be admired; I wanted to be a "success". That awesome challenge of self-approval was far from being realized. Sanhia had always taught through me to follow passions. He differentiates between "lower" and "higher" passions, not that there is anything wrong with "lower" ones, but the "higher" ones are where our higher self is speaking to us. He encourages us not to worry about the quality of the desire, that the following of any and all desires will all lead to the same place, that place called ASCENSION.

My desire at that time was to move from being an Austin personality to being a national one. A friend expressed a desire to write a book about me and so the die was cast. I was having mixed feelings about the direction the book was moving in, so I began work on one of my own in addition. Sanhia gave me the outline for it. The book was titled Being, Doing, Having: A Manual for Right Livelihood. It was neatly divided in a numerological sense into three sections, each containing three sections with names like "The Having of Having", "The Doing of Having", "The Being of Having", "The Having of Doing", and so on. I had no sooner begun work on the book when I was contacted by a man who was an independent agent, had read my columns, and wanted me to consider writing a book which he would help me market. The spiritual chills ran rampant; I saw everything playing out beautifully.

Not quite. My friend, who was working on his book, became quite upset that I was also pursuing a book, and we had a falling out. As my book was moving ahead strongly, my agent called to inform me that he was getting out of the business to do something else. I ended up with a completed book and no idea of what to do with it. I printing out copies on my dot matrix printer and sold them at workshops. Somewhere out there are about twenty copies. Meanwhile, the rest of the empire began crumbling. I ran into zoning issues and was forced to find spaces to rent, while the numbers of attendees began to drop off. I was finally forced to put the house up for sale. By the time the house had sold, I was deeply in debt and had no idea how to climb out. I eventually spent a frustrating year trying to sell mutual funds and term life insurance as well as keeping some of my former work happening. I was back in the deepest of depressions (NINE LIFE PATH).

I made the decision to move to Mesa, Arizona to join a spiritual community where some of my former Austin friends were living. The next year was probably the most difficult of my life. The community considered itself to be a spiritual boot camp. I was verbally attacked, ripped up, chewed up, and spit out day after day. I had no control over my living quarters, money, clothing, or food. I was told not to channel, that I would be taught the "right" way to do it. They maxed out what remained on my credit cards and did nothing to handle my debts. Telephone calls from creditors became a regular part of my life. I was in fear, guilt, helplessness, impotence, and rage. The community did their best to tear my marriage apart. Finally, after fifteen months my wife and I called friends and relatives and begged enough money to rent a U-Haul trailer and get out of town. The place that was open to us was rural Kentucky. It was beautiful, green, and lush after the heat and aridness of the southwest. We were led to a subsidized apartment and to food stamps. I began delivering pizza and substitute teaching. Nobody had any idea of my past life. The healing process began. We thought we might spend a year there and then move on to greener pastures.

It is so easy for me to look back now and to see how every step of the way was perfect. I had asked for ASCENSION and life was presenting me with every opportunity to help me let go of whatever it was that stood in my way. Sanhia could not have led me to a better place. Unlike Austin, there was no counter culture, no new age community. There was nobody I felt comfortable sharing my spiritual understandings with. Nobody knew I channeled or did NUMEROLOGY. I was afraid of letting those cats out of the bag. As it turned out I didn't have much to fear. Nobody ever expressed any curiosity about me, about where I had come from, or why.

One year turned into many years. I had no draw to stay, but I had neither the means nor the reason to go anywhere else. Creditors were still on my back, but I was losing my fears around debt and money. What Sanhia had told me for years was true. Whatever was required to get through each day was always there. I began to stop worrying about money for the first time in my life. I started teaching full time in a middle school (PHYSICAL SIX). I was able to buy a big old house. I channeled regularly for my wife and occasionally for old friends on the phone or when we traveled. Year by year I healed my fear of living in Middle America. I raised my five children (SIX SECOND CYCLE/SIX THIRD PINNACLE).

After ten years in Kentucky, an old friend suggested that I come down to McAllen, lead a group channeling with Sanhia and do some personal sessions. Sanhia encouraged me to go ahead if I wanted, but suggested I keep my head out of the money side of it. Sylvia rented a meeting room in a fancy hotel downtown and put ads in the paper. I was terrified — terrified that nobody would show up, but even more terrified that they would. They did. Over forty of them. I had never channeled before that large a group, and this one was mostly full of strangers. The rest of the weekend was wall to wall readings. I agreed to come back once or twice a year. I also began channeling or doing straight NUMEROLOGY readings for a handful of people in Kentucky.

Soon after that Sanhia suggested I watch him do a NUMEROLOGY reading. I was blown away. Where I spent at least two hours presenting a CHART (not to speak of the time preparing), Sanhia had me prepare only the top part of the CHART, requiring maybe five minutes and then he delivered the reading in no more than an hour. AND....it was a superior reading. He got right to the point. Above all he did not shy away from telling people things they didn't want to hear. I was always afraid of rejection and tended to soft peddle things that I felt might be upsetting to people. As a conscious channel I could and did block information from coming through for this very reason. Sanhia began to teach me how to get out of the way. It took years. A few other venues began to open up to me in other cities to do channeling and NUMEROLOGY. I retired from teaching.

The past three paragraphs covered twenty years. Not much to report. Not much drama. The pain and suffering were relatively insignificant because they were gradually lessening. Sanhia says to put this simply. So here it goes. Twenty-five years ago I thought was ready to be a spiritual teacher. I had the mental understanding. I look back at the book I wrote then and would make only a few minor adjustments. But I didn't know it in my body. I didn't understand it on a cellular basis. It took me twenty-five more years to realize that my ASCENSION was here. Now. Not in the future. I didn't have to be able to walk on water. My challenge was to always trust, to surrender attachment to outcomes, and to be willing to act fearlessly wherever I was guided. My intention was to love myself unconditionally. I learned how to become my own support, my own approval system. I found that I am not alone, have never been alone, and could not ever be alone. I truly realized that there was no death. I was guided to let go of all judgment, to give up the idea of right and wrong. I was learning to relax into the joy and the perfection of the moment, day in and day out. I slowly discovered how to walk away from situations when I was out of balance, when I was in fear rather than in love, so that I could find my balance and only then to come back to the situation (EIGHT ASCENSION NUMBER). I was becoming the eternal, innocent child of God. It took twenty-five years of practice for me.

I would expect that most of you could do this faster if you really set your mind on it, but the twenty-five years are like nothing now. As are the twenty-five years that came before that. My passion may guide things, but my passion is aligned with the will of my higher self. It always has been. It just took me a while to get it. It took me a while to be able to hear the voice inside. It took me a while to surrender to that voice. It doesn't matter that my voice calls itself "Sanhia". It never asks me to do anything that is not in my heart to do, anything which is not mine to do. It is not all perfectly easy. I have my moments of fear and of self-destructive thinking. But it never lasts long; it may just be part of being in a body. Non-perfection is perfect.

Over these same twenty-five years I ever so gradually recognized that my marriage no longer supported me or my purpose. It was not an easy understanding for me to arrive at. I traveled to Sweden to visit Ulla Lindgren, the person who had become my closest friend over the past dozen years, though that friendship had all been experienced over the phone or through e-mail. After three days we both had a deep awareness that our relationship was something we had planned before this life (FIVE THIRD CYCLE). However, we could not have realized the relationship until we first each passed successfully through preliminary challenges. We learned to love ourselves and not to need another to be complete. We had each reached a point where we were willing to accept never having a relationship again. We are now a partnership in every way, but the foundation is our mutual commitment to ASCENSION. The support we give to each other allows us each to surrender more fully into our divinity (EMOTIONAL TWO). We co-lead workshops and do parallel work with individuals, sometimes working together in a session. Ulla has drawn the images you will see as you continue reading.

So, Sanhia has asked me to write this book (THREE FOURTH PINNACLE). I am pretty much finished with talking about me, now. I think it is time to bring in our friend NUMEROLOGY. Sanhia is going to take over for a while. I think he will have a bit more to say. Well, let's go find out.

ASCENSION

WHY YOU ARE HERE

ASCENSION means the experiencing of your divinity. It is the full conscious realization that you are the creator of everything you experience, that you cannot be a victim, that you always exist, and that nothing outside of love is real. *The possibility of realizing your ASCENSION is the major reason for your present incarnation.*

Michael says that he is passing me the baton and the rest of the book is my responsibility. He introduced ASCENSION to you, but there is a bit more left to say. As for NUMEROLOGY, well, all in good time. NUMEROLOGY is quite valuable, but its worth, as far as we are concerned, is as a tool to be used in realizing your ASCENSION. So, first things first.

WHO ARE YOU?

Let's start with some truth about who you are. You are. You always have been. You always will be. You are not your body. What is truly you, can never be hurt, can never be damaged, and can never be killed. Sometimes we refer to this eternal part of you as your higher self. Part of your task is to realize that you are one with your higher self, that is, to realize your divinity while you are in the body that you are now using. This is called ASCENSION. You start by choosing ASCENSION on a mental level, as an idea. ASCENSION is realized as this choice becomes internalized, as it vibrates in each cell of your body, as you develop certainty. NUMEROLOGY is a gift that assists you in this process.

You are a Child of God, an innocent Child of God. You may have the belief that you are here to be redeemed, that you are guilty of crimes against God that you need to atone for. This is an illusion. God does not judge. God loves you unconditionally. Your sins are just illusions. When you decide to let them go, they are gone. It is only the power of your mind that keeps them in place. You are the god that judges and condemns you. The Old Testament tells the story in Genesis of the Garden of Eden. Adam and Eve represent you. The truth of you is not male or female, nor does God have gender. The fruit that was eaten in the story was of the tree of the knowledge of good and evil. It is this belief in good and evil, in judgment, that keeps you unenlightened and in pain and suffering. This belief is what gets you kicked out of the garden. God does not judge. You are created in God's image; you an immortal being of unconditional love and of unlimited creativity.

WHY ARE YOU HERE?

So why *are* you here? There are two primary reasons, and they are intertwined. You are here to realize this truth of who you are as a divine Child of God. In other words, you are here to ascend. You share this purpose with every other person on the planet, whether you or they are conscious of it or not. You are also here to express your individual uniqueness. The Children of God are, at the same time, one and separate. You are different from every other entity. You have a highly individual part to play; you are an irreplaceable piece of the whole. Nobody can tell you what you should be doing here on planet Earth. You discover your purpose by listening to your own inner voice.

You also discover your path by paying attention to and trusting what life presents to you. Everything is perfect. That bears repeating. Everything is perfect. Everything that happens to you in your life is perfect. All is unfolding exactly as it should. Part of your task is to learn to trust. Before this incarnation you participated in pre-life planning sessions with your higher self, significant other souls with whom you would share your incarnation, and other guides or angels. You planned for specific events or certain energies to be presented to you to encourage your development in desired directions. You did this because you were fully aware that when you crossed the threshold and took on a physical form you would forget all of the preplanning and forget the truth of your divinity. To resist what is happening is to be at odds with this plan, to be at war with your higher self. To resist what is, is a losing proposition, a denial, a daily and ritualistic pounding of your head against the cosmic wall. There are no victims. You are the power in your life.

HOW MANIFESTATION HAPPENS

You create everything that you experience in your "reality" on earth. You do this either consciously or unconsciously. Because you are an infinitely creative Child of God, whatever you choose to create comes into being. If you are pretending not to be what you in fact are, then you may pretend not to be powerful. Pretending doesn't stop the power; it merely keeps it hidden from you. If you have a strong belief in your powerlessness, you will create situations to prove yourself right. It works like this. The universe is powered by love. When a Child of God thinks about something, the love which is the nature of its being brings the thought into physical reality. But let's say that the Child of God is denying its divinity and is living in fear and victimhood. The thoughts are still powered into existence, but take the form of an undesired outcome. Fear (the absence of love) creates negative experiences. Even when a person is consciously trying to manifest a desired outcome, perhaps through affirmation, if the baseline emotion is one of fear then the manifestation will not succeed. The manifestation process works when the individual is in a state of love, at peace, at one with the universe. So the process is to face the fear, the devil, until the unreality of it becomes obvious, until only the truth of love remains. As you are remembering how to be a Child of God, it is best to give up attachment to results. Go ahead and affirm, but trust spirit to bring you what serves you best in the moment.

GIVING UP ATTACHMENT

Attachment can be a major barrier to experiencing your ASCENSION. Attachment means believing that specific outcomes are important. It means giving reality to illusions. Examples of attachment are needs for success, for money, for relationships, for self-worth. You are fine just as you are. You have no need of anything to complete you. Whatever things you use in this life are there for your enjoyment and support. They are easily replaced. They are the means and not the ends. To be attached to them makes ASCENSION temporarily inaccessible. We call this temporary insanity. No true damage can happen to you because of attachment. So, eventually, you just give it up.

LIFE IS JUST A PICTURE SHOW

It is easier to give up attachment when you realize that none of this is real. Your life is no more real than a movie. All things that have caused you pain are just illusions. If it is not about love, it is temporary, temporal, and nothing more than a good (or bad) story. And it gets better. You are the author of the story. You are the director, the casting director, and the protagonist. The other actors are merely following your directions. It is all you. So how are you enjoying the show so far? Not having a good time? Just change the channel. Or turn the damn thing off. Or leave it on and experience from truth, from the point of view of it not being real, of the character not being the real you. This is all ASCENSION is, the realization that what has been happening and that what is happening is not any more real than the last show you watched on television. The drama only exists so that you can love yourself and everybody else. And I call that ASCENSION.

There is a reason why you have such a large cast in your movie. Each one represents a different part of you. When you find yourself judging another, it is really you that you are judging. I call this the "mirror" effect. The other is reflecting a side of you that you don't want to look at (because you would judge yourself seriously if you were aware of it). When you become aware of the mirror process and embrace it, your ASCENSION path becomes immeasurably easier. Now you know what to forgive in yourself. You might say that you would never murder or physically torture another. Well, you have done it in another lifetime and you have not forgiven yourself. Remember, the truth of another can never be hurt; the murder or torture was and is an illusion. It was and is not real. Through your mirrors you also know where you love yourself; these are the places and ways where you love others.

THE ASCENSION PATH

The ASCENSION path is truly quite simple. The first step is for you to consciously choose to realize your ASCENSION. As soon as you state that intention, the universe moves in to support you in co-creating your realization. Now, it is only a matter of time. If you wish to be proactive and speed up the process, here is what you can do. Choose love over fear at every step. Fear has many names: doubt, anger, hatred, judgment, blame, paralysis, competition, lack, victimhood, inability, pride. We are only getting started. Love had only one name, but it implies trust and faith. Love knows that only love is operating at all times. It knows that God is love, that all that is real is love. The ASCENSION path is one of always choosing love. It is one of always rejecting whatever is not love. The beauty of it is that all false choices are not real. You cannot choose wrongly. It's kind of like the GPS system for your car. No matter what choice you make, life will recalculate and send you the next best opportunity for ASCENSION. You get infinite opportunities. When you choose illusion instead of truth, nothing really happened, because illusion is just that—illusion. It is not real. Only love is real. There is no judgment for choosing illusion. It just takes you longer to get "there". And time is an illusion, so it doesn't matter how long you take. What is certain is that you will get "there". It is certain because you are already "there". All that is lacking is your awareness that you are "there", that here and now is "there".

NUMEROLOGY

A LOVE LETTER FROM YOUR HIGHER SELF

Welcome to your body and to planet Earth. You have been planning this adventure for a long time. During the preplanning with your higher self, your guides and angels, and the fellow travelers who have agreed to incarnate with you and play major roles in your story—you set things up to encourage the likelihood of you realizing your ASCENSION. You gave yourself certain attributes and skills that you had developed in previous lifetimes. You knew that you would forget the truth of your divinity when you entered the physical realm. That is what happens. So, you planted some time capsules along the way, events that might trigger your awareness. You also created a special map to help you understand the plan you have created. I call this map a LOVE LETTER FROM YOUR HIGHER SELF. It can also be called your NUMEROLOGY CHART. *You will recognize the "you" that emerges from your CHART. That recognition supports you in accepting, and then, in being yourself. It also helps you accept what you are drawing into your life.*

NUMBERS AND WORDS

The Ascended Master Lao Tzu said that the Way that can be explained is not the true Way. Words can only approximate truth. However, NUMBERS don't lie. NUMBERS are truth, but, the words used to explain those NUMBERS are not. NUMBERS have a reality of their own. They are a pure form of information, as are sound and color. The ultimate reality of the universe can be expressed as a mathematical reality. NUMEROLOGY deals with fundamental harmonies and disharmonies. It yields a great deal of information. This resource is negative entropy; that is, it adds energy; it is energy.

ALL CHARTS ARE LOVE LETTERS

There is no such thing as having a good or bad CHART. Yours is perfectly in line with your pre-life intention. The information is not always comfortable to receive, but it is rarely truly surprising. Seek the truth, for it shall set you free. Receiving a reading is like being fed the proverbial fish. It will feed your spiritual growth for today. As you become conversant in the numerological language you will be able to feed yourself forever. There are many paths to truth and they are all blessed. This one I love because of its simplicity: nine VIBRATIONs, twelve MAJOR POSITIONs, three MINOR POSITIONs, and three SPECIAL RELATIONSHIPs. The VIBRATIONs or NUMBERs, you are familiar with in their counting capacity, the NUMBERs ONE through NINE. Their spiritual significance will be described in Chapter 4. The POSITIONs and SPECIAL RELATIONSHIPs are introduced here but you will come to know them in Chapters 5 through 17.

VIBRATIONS AND POSITIONS

Each NUMBER VIBRATION has an essence about it. Words can attempt to give you a verbal understanding of that essence, but ultimately it is a truth that is felt. The same is true of the various POSITIONs that a numeric VIBRATION might manifest in a personal NUMEROLOGY CHART. The true meaning of that POSITION can be implied, but never fully explained. The real truth of the NUMBER in that POSITION can only be intuited, as can the RELATIONSHIPs between VIBRATIONs in different POSITIONs.

Why is all of this important? It is valuable because it is a way that divine wisdom, your higher self, or universal guidance can speak directly to you. Your CHART is a LOVE LETTER FROM YOUR HIGHER SELF. It is a coded message reminding you of the plans that you had for this incarnation. This is not predestination. This is the planet of free choice, but there are no accidents in the universe. The name you were given represents the truth of who you are in this incarnation and what you came to do. Your birthday tells about the events that your higher self is creating so that you can realize your purpose on Earth.

The energy of the NUMBERs is not written in stone, it is written in flesh. It does not command, it only informs. The wise pay attention and learn from all that they create. Know yourself through NUMEROLOGY and you can open yourself to a realization of your divinity.

SECTIONS OF THE CHART

Your CHART is divided into two sections comprised of various POSITIONs. The first group is called NAME NUMBERs, which, obviously, are derived from the letters of your name. These VIBRATIONs talk about who you feel yourself to be. The second group is called BIRTH NUMBERs, and are calculated from your date of birth. These NUMBERs talk about what is happening in your life, seemingly outside of your control. There is one COMBINED NUMBER that draws energy from both groups. There are also PLANEs OF EXPRESSION, derived from the letters in your name, which describe your day to day dialogue with life. In addition, there are SPECIAL RELATIONSHIPs that describe certain qualities that some NUMBERs have for you, as well as the way different POSITIONs in your CHART might interact. Finally, there are a few MINOR POSITIONs, which can add some subtle understandings to your LOVE LETTER. These POSITIONs and RELATIONSHIPs are listed on the following pages. Take some time to look at the icon for each one, while reading the short explanation.

TWELVE MAJOR POSITIONS

NAME NUMBERS

 MOTIVATION — the INNER you

 PERSONALITY — the OUTER you

 INTEGRATED SELF — the whole of you

BIRTH NUMBERS

 LIFE PATH — what is happening to you

 CYCLE — a subset of the LIFE PATH

 PINNACLE — spiritual growth inspired by the CYCLE

 PERSONAL YEAR — what energies are influencing this year

COMBINED NUMBER

 ASCENSION NUMBER — your ultimate goal and expression

PLANES OF EXPRESSION

 PHYSICAL PLANE — your relation to the physical world

 EMOTIONAL PLANE — your feelings and creativity

 MENTAL PLANE — how you think

 INTUITIVE PLANE — your relationship to the unseen worlds

SPECIAL RELATIONSHIPS

 KARMIC NUMBER — past life imbalance with a specific VIBRATION

 STRESS NUMBER — the interaction between two different VIBRATIONs

 TABLE OF INTENSIFICATION — your relative strength and weakness with each VIBRATION

THREE MINOR POSITIONS

ANTI-NUMBER
your resistance to your Life Path

PERSONAL MONTH
what energies are influencing this month

PERSONAL DAY
what energies are influencing this day

HOW TO USE THIS BOOK

A FEW SUGGESTIONS

You are literally of two minds. One of these I call the brain-mind. You might think it is the only one you have. It does your thinking, is connected with male/yang energy, and is located in your head. Most books are written primarily to the brain-mind. This one isn't. Your other mind I call your belly-mind. It is your intuitive center, is connected with female/yin energy, and is located in your abdomen. The unconditionally loving belly-mind is intended to take the lead as you unravel your spiritual path in a body. I will give your brain-mind enough information about the NUMBERs, the POSITIONs, the NUMBERs in the POSITIONs, and their (inter) RELATIONSHIPs to get you started. The book is designed for you to take that basic understanding and use your intuition to develop it to a much deeper and more usable level. You might do this through meditation or reflection. The symbols and icons are designed to speak directly to your belly-mind. They can serve as a focus for contemplation. Your belly-mind can communicate to you through messages, visions, or dreams. You may also gain insights through talking with others. If something isn't clear to you, try jumping back to another part of the book to see what you read about yourself or a term there. *Let your brain-mind be responsible for understanding, but be sure to free your belly-mind to go wherever it might in bringing you greater insights. Your fullest understanding of your LOVE LETTER FROM YOUR HIGHER SELF will be interpreted by your belly-mind.*

BEING YOUR OWN NUMEROLOGIST

NUMEROLOGY is an intuitive science. The intuitive and the scientific halves have equal weight. Faith and intellect operate in balance. You cannot be a proficient numerologist without a thorough understanding of the nine VIBRATIONs and the twelve MAJOR POSITIONS (plus three other SPECIAL RELATIONSHIPS and three MINOR POSITIONS). But knowledge is not enough. The knowledge is there to help you to open to your intuitive knowing. Insights will come to you. Trust them and more will follow. It is analogous to playing a musical instrument. You learn how the instrument operates and perhaps a bit about music theory. The true playing happens though when you let your mind go, and feel the music playing through you. Some have more of a natural gift for this, but if you have the desire and you give the effort, you will become a proficient numerologist for yourself. Your NUMEROLOGY will be eclectic and evolving. This instruction is only a beginning or, for some, a continuation in this process. As a numerologist, you will be unique and your process will be your own. The truth of the NUMBERS does not change, but the way that they will speak to you will continue to surprise you. Your CHART continues to present gifts to you throughout your life. There is no end to the insights it may present and no bottom to the depths to which it may lead.

At the end of the book is a chapter on "COMPUTATIONS" (see page 274). You will be shown there how to compute your personal NUMBER for each of the MAJOR POSITIONS. You can assemble your own CHART, building it piece by piece. There is a model of a blank CHART there available to copy, or you can go to the website[1] and download it. There is also a completed CHART for Gandhi in that chapter which you can use as an example. If you only desire the instructions for the chapter you are reading, the page number for those directions is listed in the "More About" section at the end of that chapter.

You may have noticed that some words are capitalized. These are terms that are important for you to understand as you are reading. If you are unsure of a meaning or want to expand your comprehension, you may go to the index at the back of the book and locate the page where the term is defined or explained.

---

1) www.channelswithoutborders.com

WORKING BY YOURSELF

I suggest that you work through the book in order, but you are welcome to jump around if you prefer. Some things may make more sense to you, though, if you are following in the sequence that is given.

- With each chapter, begin by reading the introductory page to get a feel for the POSITION.

- Then read the offered interpretation for your VIBRATION. It is not intended for you to read all of the readings in the chapter, only the one(s) that are connected to your CHART. However, you can feel free to read anything else that draws your attention. Other readings might help put yours into perspective.

- As you are reading, you might choose to replace each "you" with "I" and each "your" with "my".

- Let it sink in. Think about it, and feel it.

- Return to "THE NUMBERS" on page 52 and read about your VIBRATION for the POSITION.

- Let that sink in.

- Finally, read the "More About" section at the end of the chapter.

As you are taking these steps, you are encouraged to take notes on the insights and reflections that come to you. Pages are included in this book for that purpose. Journaling like this can assist you in realizing your ASCENSION, perhaps speeding up the process. This is your book. Treat it like a workbook: highlight, underline, or write in the margins.

Do the same with each succeeding chapter, but also take time to think about how the POSITION you are now looking at ties in with what you have already thought about from the previous chapters. It is recommended that you take some time between chapters when you begin your personal reading (with Chapter 5). A week or two to assimilate and work with what you have just added to your CHART could assist you in the integration of your NUMBERS into a seamless whole. This might work best if you take daily time to focus on your CHART. You will know when it is time to move on.

Always keep in mind that what you read in this book is only half of the process of doing your reading. The other half comes from using your intuition, your inner guidance. Ideas will come to you.

Insights and connections will be made. Your LOVE LETTER FROM YOUR HIGHER self is written to you. You are the one who can best interpret it. Nobody knows you better than you know yourself. The readings within this book are only suggestions; they are only starting places. Go deeper.

The reading never stops. Once you have learned what to do, you will continue to mine your CHART for more profound understandings of yourself and of your purpose. An annual birthday reading is a wonderful gift to give yourself, using it as a guide to help you focus on your new year.

Remember that the goal is to realize your divinity and the perfection of you. Treat yourself lovingly. There is no such thing as a good or a bad CHART.

WORKING WITH A GROUP

It might be more fun and even more productive to do your reading with a friend or friends, with your partner or your workmates. This is particularly powerful if your friends have a similar spiritual drive to yours. They know you well and can act like "mirrors" for you, helping you in seeing yourself more accurately and with more divinity. The focus of the group is to lovingly support each other in using the LOVE LETTER to help each of you to know yourself and your purpose on a more profound level.

A group of three or four might be the best, though you can certainly do it with one other person, such as with your partner. Groups larger than four can become unwieldy. It is not suggested that you attempt to do the whole reading at one time. You might wish to set a time limit of between two and three hours for each gathering. It might take three or four sessions to complete everyone's CHART. When doing the readings together, it might be best to have everybody's CHART computed in advance, though there is no reason you can't do that together. If you decide on the latter, it will probably mean taking one additional session together to complete the readings.

When working in a group or with a partner, there are many possibilities of how to do things. It is again suggested that you work chronologically through the chapters. For each POSITION, look at each person's VIBRATION. Read everything out loud, beginning with the introductory box. Take turns reading as you wish. When individuals' personal information is being read, they can choose to read it themselves or have it read to them. After reading for an individual, that person can share how it feels. The group can then discuss how they see that VIBRATION and POSITION demonstrating in that person's life. Your friends will have insights about you. They will sometimes tend to hold you in a higher light than you hold yourself in and see more of your potentialities. You can also support each other in getting a greater feel for each POSITION and for each VIBRATION. As you are taking these steps, you are encouraged to take notes of the insights and reflections that come to you. Pages are included in this book for that purpose.

When working with others in such a personal, vulnerable and revealing manner, it is good to set some ground rules. Confidentiality is a good place to start, agreeing that whatever is discussed in the group stays in the group. Work out whatever agreements you would like to have in order to feel safe, cooperative, and empowered.

You might even wish to participate in this way with more than one group. The process of a group reading can pull you closer to your friends or partner. You may learn to know each other in a deeper and more accepting way.

This is not intended to be a tool for group therapy. If you choose to use it in that way, it is suggested that you first use it for self-discovery, and only when all members are comfortable with those understandings would you want to use it as a tool for problem solving or group/relationship dynamics.

Be clear about your intentions and have a mutual goal of the highest most loving result.

ASCENSION is the goal, no matter how this information is used. The purpose of the LOVE LETTER FROM YOUR HIGHER SELF is to realize your own and others' personal divinity and to use that awareness to pursue your individual purpose on planet Earth.

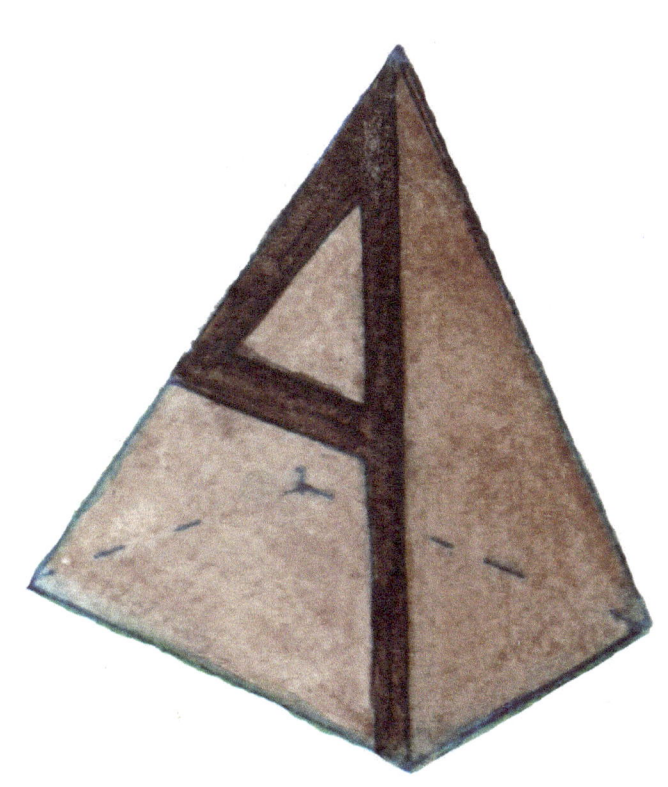

THE NUMBERS

THE STARS OF THE SHOW

Now it is time to introduce the stars of the show, the NUMBERs 1 through 9, and, of course, ONE insists on going first. As has been mentioned before, NUMBERs tell absolute truth—a truth that words can only approximate. We will use words in the beginning to explain a NUMBER until you develop an inner knowingness when a NUMBER is revealed to you. There are certain NUMBERs that play a greater significance in your personal life, but you deal with all the VIBRATIONs (in this book the terms NUMBER and VIBRATION are interchangeable) at various times. *A NUMBER does not stand alone, but is always connected to a POSITION in your CHART. The book will deal with the POSITIONs one at a time – but first we will look at each of the nine VIBRATIONs giving a sense of what the truth is that they tell, explaining what they feel like when they are out of balance, and looking at how they may be brought further into balance.*

Ascension Numerology

As we look at the NUMBERs, much can be intuited by noting the shapes of the symbols. First of all, think of four horizontal lines drawn through the NUMBERs, as shown above. The bottom line represents the physical world; the middle lines represent the emotional and mental worlds; and the top line represents the spiritual world. Each NUMBER resides in all four worlds. You can pay attention to the type of shape that is found in each world for the NUMBER, as well as the way that the different worlds are connected within that NUMBER. For example, notice how the energy for 9 seems to hang out between the mental/emotional and the spiritual worlds, whereas for 6 the focus is between the mental/emotional and the physical worlds. 1 does not hang out in any world, but simply moves up or down between them. Suggestions for interpreting the NUMBER in this way will be included as a part of the description of each VIBRATION in this chapter.

Different shapes can be interpreted in specific ways. Horizontal lines within a symbol represent feminine energy, as in the 2, 4, and 5. Vertical lines represent masculine energy, as in the 1 and 4. Angles stand for change, as in the 4 and 7. Curves show consciousness as in the 2, 6, and 9. A semicircle represents the unconscious as in the 3. A circle represents the super-conscious, as in the 6, 8, and 9. Again, we'll point out specific application of these ideas with each NUMBER symbol explanation in this chapter. Notice that there are different ways that NUMBERs can be drawn. For example, 4 is sometimes represented with two vertical lines between the mental/emotional and spiritual worlds, rather than having one line angled and joining the other in the spiritual world. 7 can be drawn with a short vertical line on the mental/emotional worlds. Consider what effects these changes might suggest. Computers and other electronic devices tend to remove all of the curves in the VIBRATIONs. What might you infer from that?

In timing, ONE represents beginnings. We talk about VIBRATIONs being feminine or masculine. As in discussions of yin and yang we are not talking about the qualities of a woman or a man; we are talking about energies that are more introspective and self-focused (odd NUMBERS/yang) as opposed to energies that are more extroverted and take the other into consideration (even NUMBERS/yin). These qualities can be present in men or women.

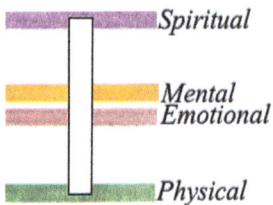

ONE is the most masculine/yang of the nine VIBRATIONs. It is the phallic symbol. Symbolically we have a vertical line (masculine) traversing from the spiritual world to the physical world (and vice versa), screaming nonstop through the mental/emotional worlds.

This is how the ONE acts. It is unaffected by everything around it, referring only to self and divine inspiration for its actions and its choices. Therefore ONE is a leader, but a leader who neither requires nor even desires followers. ONE begins new things. New things cannot be started by listening to others. Others know only of the old ways. They can do little more than to try to discourage, dissuade, or at least slow down the ONE. It is only the ONE who is guided to this new direction, to the frontier, to the unknown. ONE has more integrity than any other VIBRATION. It is also the most independent. ONE children can be quite a challenge to raise, as they always feel capable of choosing for themselves and resent any intrusions on their will. The ONE expresses courage, daringness, self-respect, self-reliance, inventiveness, forcefulness, a fiery disposition, and enthusiasm. ONE is spirited, forthright, and determined. It has high aspirations.

Be careful in looking at imbalances of the ONE (or of any VIBRATION) to be sure the imbalances are not in the eye of the beholder. TWO might see ONE as overly aggressive and uncooperative. THREE might see ONE as boastful, while FOUR could find ONE to be stubborn. FIVE might see impulsiveness, and SIX might find ONE to be egocentric and pushy. If SEVEN didn't find ONE interesting, it would probably simply ignore it. EIGHT might find ONE to be arrogant, domineering, and overly ambitious. NINE might feel ONE to be selfish. When ONE is powered by love (truth), it manifests as was expressed in the previous paragraph. When ONE is powered by fear or other negative emotions, it tends toward one of two poles of imbalance. At one extreme, the ONE is like the lion in The Wizard of Oz—loud and intimidating, covering its fear with bravado, yet unable to take the decisive action required of it. The other extreme might find ONE withdrawn in a self-centered world of inactivity, unable to take the steps that the inner voice demands.

What is to be done when fear overwhelms and freezes the ONE? The answer is always found in love. It is always found in going within and calling on guides, on angels, on higher self, or the Divine until the place of self-love and self-acceptance is found. It is in knowing that the support for your actions will never come from the outside, so it must come from within. It is in knowing that there is purpose in being guided in the direction to which you are being propelled. You see, the ONE is not gifted with the vision of seeing the end, it sees only the beginning. The ONE is being asked to step off into the unknown, into the abyss. Great courage is called for. Without ONE, nothing new can happen; the world and your life are stuck in old patterns.

If ONE is a major VIBRATION in your life, I wish you to know that you are blessed with great courage and to remind you that life is but an enormous game, one that is more fun when you totally throw yourself into it. You are ONE with the divine. For the rest of you, honor ONE whenever its time comes in your life and honor it in those who shine with that independence.

A VIBRATION on the MENTAL PLANE

In timing, TWO is a period to bring things into balance. TWO is the VIBRATION of sensitivity. Where the ONE is self-focused, the TWO is outwardly directed. Like all even NUMBERS (which have TWO as a factor) there is always an attention towards others. With the TWO, this outward focus is paramount; the TWO acts not out of inner drive but out of reaction to the immediate environment—always operating to bring things into balance. In the natural rhythm of timing the ONE sets a new course, then the TWO attempts to bring a new balance to the world that has been upset by the somewhat bullish movement of the ONE. If the world had no ONE, nothing new would happen; there would be no progress. If the world had only ONE, nothing would ever be completed. It would be a world of one night stands and failed attempts.

So what does the TWO do? Look at the symbol. There is a sensitive feminine horizontal line on its base in the physical world. Above that are two connected curved lines or semi-circles representing the unconscious which connect to the mental/emotional worlds, and from there to the spiritual world.

TWO listens; it pays attention; it gets feedback; it reflects; it nurtures; and it supports. TWO has no real goals for itself other than to be in a partnership; it wants only a pleasant, peaceful environment. TWO is the feminine/yin energy. It is the reflective moon to the ONE's sun. The ONE has planted the seed. The TWO makes sure the growing plant has enough water, light, nurturance, quiet, and warmth. It is aware of subtleties. It is emotionally and spiritually sensitive to the challenges others face. The other's success is the TWO's success. The TWO has no compulsion to be seen as the primary actor; the background is just fine. TWO is patient, helpful, and gentle. TWO pays attention to details and is orderly and meticulous. TWO can be the great diplomat and peacemaker because it is cooperative, compromising, tactful, understanding, agreeable, adaptable, fair minded, and persuasive. Though TWO is passive and sacrificing, it is also quietly tenacious.

The TWO has the potential to act on a very high spiritual level. This gives the capacity to be highly intuitive, clairvoyant, inspirational…. an "awakener". However, if the TWO is out of balance (coming from fear rather than love), this energy can turn dark and schizophrenic. If imbalance is realized, focus on self-love, calmness, and forgiveness.

Judgments of the TWO are likely made by one who is out of balance with the VIBRATION. ONE might find that TWO is overly dependent and vacillating. THREE could perceive TWO as timid or shy. FOUR might see TWO as deceptive or spiteful while FIVE could find insecurity. SIX could perceive TWO as hypersensitive and moody while SEVEN might see a passive-submissive energy. EIGHT might find TWO petty while NINE might see an apathetic nature. Because the TWO is so sensitive, it can take on the negative emotions of others as its own. It is important that the TWO be in an emotional state of love. Fear can lead to either of the extreme imbalances, on the one hand being hypercritical and on the other hand being hypersensitive. TWO is served by learning techniques for finding inner peace and how to "shake off" or quickly release the negative emotional energy of others.

If TWO is a major VIBRATION in your CHART, then you are a person who truly lives in the present. That present can be heaven or hell depending upon whether you are in love or fear. Always take time for your own inner peace. You are the loving, nurturing energy that can make every moment not only livable but heavenly for everyone in your sphere. Take care of yourself, not only because you deserve it, but also because the world so wants your energy. You are the divine peacemaker. For the rest of you, there is always a time to listen, a time for patience. A TWO will come into your life to let you know when that time is for you. Pay attention.

A VIBRATION on the EMOTIONAL PLANE

In timing, in that sequential movement from ONE to NINE, THREE represents the time for visualization. The ONE has set a new course, the TWO has worked to reestablish a balance, and now the THREE's job is to picture the perfect destination for the voyage. THREE, therefore, brings with it a lessening of demands and responsibilities, a space for playfulness and dreaming, and a playground that provides the fertile soil that creativity thrives in. By the end of a THREE period of timing one has a clear picture of where one is going, is excited by it, and can't wait to dig in and get to work manifesting the dream.

THREE is the child and what you get when you combine the masculine (father) ONE and the feminine (mother) TWO. THREE is the VIBRATION of creativity. It is the VIBRATION of expression. Like most children, the THREE is not particularly concerned with others except as audiences, playmates, or providers. The THREE is in the moment, worried about neither the past nor the future. The THREE is buoyant, usually up, but when it is down the thunder is booming, the lightening is flashing, and the rain is pouring down. Not to worry, the storm is usually brief and then the sun bursts through again.

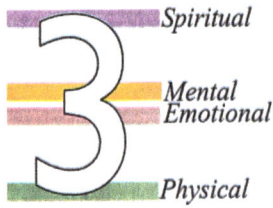

Notice the shape of the THREE. It is made of two "unconscious" curved lines, one connecting the physical world to the mental/emotional world, and a similar curve connecting the mental/emotional worlds to the intuitive world. There are no masculine or feminine lines. It is truly the creative, impractical child.

The THREE is supposed to be somewhat self-centered and childish. The "serious" world does not reward creativity, because it does not seem to be practical. The THREE is the space cadet. They are the ones who find fun and joyfulness in everything around them. The THREE's job is to remind themselves and others to always visualize the highest dream and to refuse to settle for less. The THREE intuitively understands that we are what we believe we are. THREE is not limited by logic or practicality or "maturity" into believing that there are duties that everyone has and that it is its responsibility to grow up and to face them. THREE, like Peter Pan, is not growing up, but if we pay some attention to THREE then our loads can become lighter and our goals can be set higher.

It is the duty of the THREE to point out to us the potentials of life on Earth. THREE is the artist, and the artist's job is to inspire, to show what can be. Sometimes this is through poking fun at what is, but the final job is to show us the truth of who we are, to show us our divinity whether the demonstration comes through music, movement, visual arts, invention, the written and spoken word, or drama.

The THREE is talented, charming, and naive. THREE is outgoing, humorous, and imaginative. It is optimistic, youthful, and joyous. The THREE is quick, witty, and amusing. It is elegant, tasteful, and effervescent. Seeing THREE out of balance is likely to be out of the judgment of the beholder. To ONE, THREE can appear impulsive, while TWO might find it to be inattentive. FOUR could perceive THREE to be unreliable and insincere, while FIVE is more likely to see THREE as extravagant, flirtatious, or scattered. SIX might find THREE to be inconsiderate and ill-humored, while SEVEN could perceive THREE as superficial. EIGHT might find THREE to be pessimistic while NINE could see it as childish. When THREE is out of balance it can move to one of two poles; it can be loud and belligerent, or quiet and withdrawn. This is a time for THREE to give itself a big hug and then to trust and express what is within. Remember that THREE requires the patience and the long leash that you reserve for young children. A large part of its job is to lighten up the situation.

If THREE is a major VIBRATION in your CHART, you came here to inspire others. Never hide your light under the proverbial bushel basket, but instead overcome your fears and doubts and express what you have within you. Welcome the spaces that life presents to you and have fun with them. It is not your job to do the work; it is your work to show others what their job could be, to show them their divinity, to raise the bar. For the rest of you, enjoy that creative space whenever it comes. Have a ball!

A VIBRATION on the EMOTIONAL PLANE

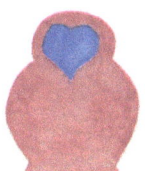

In timing, ONE was about taking a new direction; TWO was about reestablishing balance; THREE was about visualizing where you really want to go; and now FOUR is about beginning to build that dream.

FOUR is practical, hardworking, determined, trustworthy, and reliable. When FOUR tells you that it will be done, it will be done. FOUR may be slow to get started, but that is because it wants to do the job right. FOUR understands that anything worth doing is worth doing right, and FOUR is not going to waste its time and energy. FOUR is the square (four-sided)—solid, foundational. Without that solid foundation you are building on shifting sands. On top of that strong underlying base, anything can be built. Notice how long it takes for the foundation of a house to be built. Then, suddenly there are walls and a roof.

Take a look at the symbol. It is nothing but straight feminine and masculine lines, with two angles showing a focus on change looking both backwards to what has existed and upwards toward spiritual truth. There is nothing subtle or subconscious. It is all on the surface. What you see is what you get.

If you want somebody to be honest with you, to really tell you the truth--then ask FOUR. FOUR is loyal. But don't lie to FOUR; once you lose a FOUR's trust, you will have a hard time earning it back. FOUR believes in earning things. FOUR gets great satisfaction from working hard toward a goal. THREE may be just as happy getting something for nothing, but for FOUR there is satisfaction in struggling and in overcoming odds to reach the goal. Let's face it, FOUR just isn't happy without something to do, something to be working toward. FOUR tends to be practical and pragmatic, but that doesn't mean the goal is mundane. The FOUR approach is organized, methodical, systematic, regimented, and efficient. FOUR is the most serious, sound, and prudent of VIBRATIONs. FOUR is down to earth and doesn't care much for the bells and whistles. FOUR is direct--not creative, playful, or expressive. FOUR is predictable. FOUR tends to be conservative because it trusts what is tried and true. But FOUR is realistic, so if the old ways are not working it will try to build new standards. In general, FOUR is slow to jump on the bandwagon, but once the FOUR decides to get on board--stay out of the way. FOUR is enduring, persistent, and disciplined. FOUR will get there.

FOUR has the potential to operate on a higher plane and can build on the international stage, bringing deep spiritual truth to its activity. As the master builder, FOUR constructs on an enduring, practical, yet idealistic level. If out of balance, the energy can be overly ambitious and ruthless. If imbalance is realized, focus on self-respect, composure, and letting go of blame.

Judgments of FOUR energy usually come from a VIBRATION that is out of balance. ONE might find FOUR to be pig-headed, while TWO could see it as jealous. THREE might react to FOUR as vengeful or stubborn, whereas FIVE might see FOUR as slow and plodding. SIX may think FOUR is greedy, while SEVEN finds it crude. EIGHT could perceive FOUR as rigid, while NINE sees it as sadomasochistic. When FOUR is out of balance it might express in one of two extremes. It might become firmly dug-in and unmovable, or it might become demanding and cruel toward self and others. In such times FOUR is served by learning to love itself.

If FOUR is a major VIBRATION in your CHART, you happily take on the work that others avoid. You hold the mirror of truth up to the rest of us. You develop the systems that make things work. Without FOUR the world is in danger of sliding into chaos. You are the holder of divine truth and you help it take form. For the rest of you, when you have those times in life when the best choice is to just do it, put your nose to the grindstone, get down to basics, and accomplish the task at hand – It feels good afterwards. Welcome to the world of FOUR. It likes it that way.

A VIBRATION on the PHYSICAL PLANE

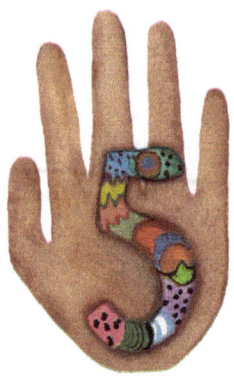

In timing, the foundation has been built by the FOUR. Now it is time to dance on it. We've reached the halfway point in the journey from ONE to NINE. FIVE is right in the middle between beginning and ending, between birth and death. FIVE is the most earthbound, the most physical of the NUMBERS. It represents the FIVE senses; it is experiential. You have FIVE fingers to grasp and manipulate the world. FIVE is a VIBRATION of opportunism. FIVE wants to make the most out of life. It wants to pick up the pace, to find the fastest and most efficacious way to its goals. FIVE wants to find the new, improved way of doing things. Leave repetition to the FOUR; FIVE wants every day to be different. FIVE wants to travel, to have adventures, to try everything once. FIVES are incurably curious, particularly about anything new. It is no accident that there are five senses; FIVE wishes to experience them all fully.

Just by looking at the shape of the 5 you can get a feel for all the movement involved. The feminine horizontal line in the spiritual world represents its natural intuitive ability. That information is then brought down for application to the mental/emotional worlds through a masculine vertical line, and then manifested in the physical world through the semi-circle which represents the unconscious or creative energy.

The Roman symbol for FIVE is "V", which shows energy coming down at an angle (change) from the spiritual down to the physical (in midstream) and then returning at a sharp angle to the spiritual. The physical world is clearly the center for the FIVE. It has a zest for life and more passion for the physical world than any other VIBRATION. FIVE loves life.

FIVE is the natural salesperson, with the ability to persuade others to its point of view or course of action. FIVE is innovative, resourceful, and adaptable. Not only is FIVE good at business, it is also good at sports because of its competitive and physical nature. FIVE loves freedom and can be a difficult child to raise because it is going to try everything and do its best to manipulate authority. If you were to pick one word to represent FIVE, it might be change. FIVE is the agent for change and progress in the world. It is not the true originator like the ONE, but FIVE has an instinct for finding the better way. This is partly due to FIVE's desire to minimize work in order to maximize pleasure.

When there is judgment of FIVE it might say more about the source than the target. ONE might find FIVE to be a rolling stone, while TWO might find it tactless, irritable, and indiscreet. THREE can see FIVE as a bullshit artist, while FOUR can think that FIVE is moving too fast, is boastful, a gambler, and acts irresponsibly. SIX can feel FIVE is too selfish, takes advantage of others, and is not respectful of group values, while SEVEN can find FIVE to be over-indulgent on every level. EIGHT might find FIVE to be an underminer and overly competitive, while NINE might wish that FIVE would expand its horizons. But these judgments are more a case of challenges for the other VIBRATIONs to let go of than innate difficulties of FIVE. Out of balance FIVE can, on one extreme, be afraid of change, or, on the other extreme, be so changeable that it can't succeed at anything. FIVE does best when it remembers to trust it's instincts and is willing to take chances.

If FIVE is a major VIBRATION in your CHART, you are vitally alive. The world might be a pretty boring place, a place that isn't firing on all cylinders, without you. You are willing to take chances and have an uncanny ability to land on your feet. You are the spiritual WD-40[1] for planet Earth. If things are stuck, you will get them moving and have fun doing it! FIVE is divinity come to earth to marvel in its own creation. For the rest of you, there is always a time for adventure and stepping out of the daily routine. Take a walk on the wild side.

A VIBRATION on the PHYSICAL PLANE

---

1) WD-40 is a spray lubricant found in most American homes that is used to free up objects that have become stuck due to rust or other causes, but has thousands of other uses.

In timing, we have a movement that began with the thrust of ONE, followed by the balancing and sensitivity of TWO, the vision and expression of THREE, the building and structure of FOUR, and the change and expansion of FIVE. Now it is time for the social, serving SIX, which brings to completion what are known as the lower level VIBRATIONs. Lower level is not to be taken as a judgment but as an acknowledgment that these VIBRATIONs are focused on the Earth plane of existence. SIX is the family, the group, the tribe, the school, the business. SIX is the social glue that holds us all together. SIX is the caring, helping, service that supports life. Notice that the social insects have SIX legs, that the honeycomb has SIX sides. According to Bucky Fuller, the hexagon is the strongest of shapes. Above all, SIX is the vibration of love. It loves and loves to be loved.

With SIX it is one for all and all for one. It is the village it takes to raise a child. Those who are strong in SIX are group oriented. SIX want to belong. SIX doesn't enjoy being alone as much as being part of a collection of people. Whether it is the child, the adolescent, the young adult, the provider, or the elder, SIX enjoys playing its role in the giving and receiving that makes up group life. It is not surprising to find SIX in the helping professions: teachers, health care workers, social workers, preachers, and counselors. SIX is friendly, idealistic, protective, and responsible. SIX loves beauty and romance. SIX is almost suspicious of and at least concerned for the loner. SIX wants everyone to feel as if they belong.

SIX can also operate at a higher spiritual level as the master teacher, the cosmic parent, or the possessor of great wisdom. When out of balance, this SIX can experience mental imbalance, perhaps neurotic or even psychotic energy can be manifested. If imbalance is realized, focus on self-acceptance, tranquility, and mercy.

The Numbers – SIX

Look at the shape of 6. It is all curves, all subjective feeling. It has a subconscious connection to the spiritual world from the mental/emotional worlds, but then brings it down in the form of a circle (wholeness, heaven on earth) to the physical world.

The judgments of SIX are likely to come from imbalances within the beholder. ONE might accuse SIX of being interfering, while TWO might judge SIX as gossipy. THREE might use the term self-righteous, while FOUR might find SIX to be too possessive. The wild and adventurous FIVE can feel hemmed in by the overly-conventional SIX. SIX has been accused of appealing to the lowest common denominator because it wants activities and energies that all can take part in. Because of this, SEVEN, which appreciates what is unique about each individual and which enjoys alone time, can have trouble with SIX. EIGHT might see SIX as a domestic tyrant, while NINE could think that SIX is too provincial. Remembering always that judgment says much more about the judger than the judged, SIX out of balance can be all of these things. At one extreme SIX can be controlling and judgmental. At the other extreme SIX can avoid its responsibilities and the group out of fear of being dominated. It is always good for SIX to remember that it is welcomed and that its services are valuable.

If SIX is a major VIBRATION in your CHART, you came here to serve and to love. Without you the world would be a colder and lonelier place. No wonder corporate advertising uses your images to sell products. You are represented as the world's welcome mat, its master of ceremonies, and its home cooked meal. You make sure that everyone is cared for. You leave the light on for us. In an increasingly corporate, competitive, isolated world, you hold out the promise of community, of a place where everybody knows your name. Sometimes we want you to go away, but never too far away. You are the divine parental love that accepts us no matter what. For the rest of you, there is always a time for family, for community, for service, and for caring. SIX models how to do it.

A VIBRATION on the EMOTIONAL PLANE

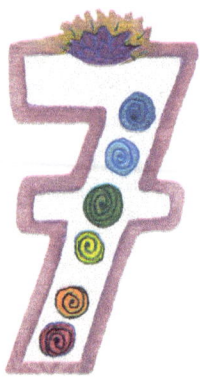

In timing, SEVEN is the Sabbath, the day that is set aside, the rarified time. I won't repeat the litany of timing that was given in SIX, showing the progression of the lower VIBRATIONs, but let's just say that SIX is very busy taking care of people. And on the SEVENth day he rested. SEVEN begins the higher VIBRATIONs. SEVEN, EIGHT, and NINE deal with the spiritual world, perhaps to a higher degree than with the physical world. SEVEN has earned a rest. It is time to ask the question "why"? It is time to ask what this is all about. SEVEN is analytical and searching. SEVEN wants answers and is not easily satisfied by the glib responses society has provided.

SEVEN is the VIBRATION of faith and of trust. SEVEN believes in the perfection of what is happening. SEVEN trusts that there is a plan, that there is a method in this madness of life. SEVEN seeks understanding. SEVEN is analytical, technical, and scientific, but does not see a schism between the scientific and the spiritual. It does not take religion on faith, yet will infer more into the facts than meets the eye. SEVEN is professional, the specialist rather than the generalist, and is selective. SEVEN seeks out what is unique in others. SEVEN is silent, ascetic, the loner. A party given by SEVEN would be an event full of people who might have little in common but would each be unique in some way. The host might have a wonderful time talking with each guest, while taking little care to make sure everyone is having a good time. You may be starting to see why SEVEN and SIX are not a natural mix. Perhaps you have heard the expression "at SIXES and SEVENS", meaning at odds with each other or with yourself.

SEVEN is discerning and subtle. SEVEN is mysterious, esoteric, and reserved. It is not easy to get to know SEVEN. But SEVEN carries an aura of wisdom, inner peace, and profundity. It is the job of SEVEN to look at the things that the rest of us don't have time for, either because we are too busy, not paying attention, or simply don't care. Because SEVEN lives in a rarified air, it is there to support others when the time for introspection and soul searching comes. SEVEN is always searching. Sometimes the things that are found are published, sometimes they are taught in the halls of higher education, sometimes they are shared from the pulpit. SEVEN can also be an artist, one who has finesse and a high level of craftsmanship.

As you have probably guessed, SEVEN can be perceived as out of balance by those who may themselves be out of balance. ONE might think SEVEN is a fake or a quack, while TWO could see SEVEN as uncommunicative. THREE might feel SEVEN to be repressed, while FOUR might find SEVEN to be shrewd and deceitful. FIVE might say SEVEN is inhibited, while SIX could think that SEVEN is withdrawn and an eccentric misfit. EIGHT could see SEVEN as faithless and cynical, while NINE might think SEVEN is misunderstood. Again be warned that much of this may be in the eye of the beholder, but when SEVEN is out of balance, it is usually a question of faith. Without a strong faith, SEVEN is powerless. A false faith, one that is rote and not deeply understood, is of little use, but the other extreme of agnosticism, atheism, or a belief in a random, meaningless universe also leaves the SEVEN unable to function in the most positive way. SEVEN will benefit from meditation and other spiritual practices. Reminding itself that there is a good reason for everything is important.

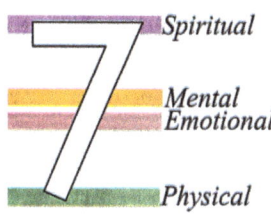

In many ways 7 is like 1. It stands alone with the masculine energy of the vertical stroke, making it impervious to the influence of others. Yet that stroke is also at an angle, focusing on the past, but bringing change. There is a horizontal vertical line on the spiritual world showing how it hangs out there, drawing its sustenance, which it then brings back to the physical world. For all of us.

If SEVEN is a major VIBRATION in your CHART, you came here to spread faith and understanding. Without you the path to ASCENSION might become overgrown and hard to find. It is your energy that questions and is never satisfied with anything short of the truth. To choose to realize ASCENSION is to choose to have moments of absolute aloneness, of terrifying fear. You are leading the way. For the rest of you, there are always times for introspection, for aloneness, and for facing fears and doubts. SEVENS make those times a little easier for you.

A VIBRATION on the SPIRITUAL PLANE

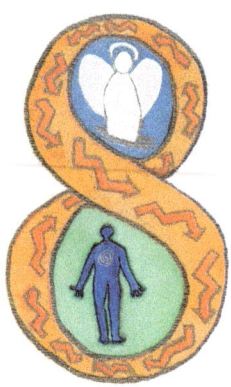

In timing, following the sabbatical that is SEVEN, it is time to come back down to Earth in full power. EIGHT is the VIBRATION of power and manifestation. EIGHT is leadership; a leadership that is not focused in an ego-need to be in charge. Unlike ONE, it is not blessed with an idea that people are compelled to follow or by an aura that draws followers. EIGHT is the leadership that comes from spiritual awareness, farsightedness (seeing the big picture), and a strong, balanced sense of justice. EIGHT is administrative because it sees the true potential of others and helps to lead them to their personal power. Eight is able to delegate; its job is to direct those best able to carry out the job, rather than doing the work itself.

Symbolically EIGHT is "as above, so below" — the circle above, the circle below. The circle represents the super-consciousness. The top circle between the mental/emotional worlds and the spiritual world shows the plan being visualized in spirit. This could also be read as a channeling of what already exists in the spiritual world, the blueprint for heaven on earth. This vision then becomes manifested in the physical through right use of mind and emotion of the EIGHT, that is, the heart being filled with unconditional love and the mind focused on the desired outcome—which is of benefit to all. Tipped on its side, EIGHT represents infinity.

EIGHT in its full power realizes that there are no limits, except those set by humans. This is the potential of EIGHT. Obviously, this is a tremendous challenge which all EIGHTS are not necessarily ready to handle.

EIGHT is strong, ethical, and tough. It is able to set aside emotional concerns to make the "hard choices" that will pay off in the future, even if they may prove difficult to handle in the present. EIGHT is uncompromising, expansive, and dignified. EIGHT is the most ambitious of all VIBRATIONs, but to be successful, the ambition would be for the group, for the whole, not for the self.

When EIGHT is out of balance and not up to the task, ONE might find it to be indecisive, while TWO might experience EIGHT as unsentimental. THREE could find EIGHT to be pompous and self-glorifying, while FOUR could see it as unscrupulous and ruthless. FIVE might think EIGHT is mercenary, while SIX could be more concerned with its greed and heartlessness. SEVEN may find EIGHT to be pretentious, while NINE might see EIGHT as intolerant. Again, remember that one's judgment of an EIGHT out of balance can reflect one's own tendencies in that direction. EIGHT out of balance fears, misunderstands, and mistrusts power. At one extreme it uses its power to control and dominate, making sure that it gets more than its fair share, fearful of its ability to manifest in any other way. At the other extreme it denies itself so that others can have something, fearful that there is not enough to go around. EIGHT is to remind itself constantly to return to a state of unconditional love and then focus on its infinite creative powers to manifest what is desired. There is no such thing as scarcity, unless one is operating in a state of fear.

If EIGHT is a major VIBRATION in your CHART, you came here to make the world a better place for everyone. You have unlocked some of the secrets of the universe and are here to share that wealth, thereby empowering others. You are one with the divine creativity that formed this physical world. They say it is lonely at the top. You are not easy to befriend, because you aren't attracted by many of the carrots that others chase after. The benefits of personal relationships don't offer as strong a draw to you because you seek a larger success. You see no limits to the human potential. You visualize things in a big way. For the rest of you, there are times when you are required to deal with power, whether with big corporations, government, institutions, or simply your fears about survival. If all positions of political or economic power were filled with a balanced EIGHT, we might have heaven on Earth. In the meantime EIGHTs are here to show you how things could be better.

A VIBRATION on the MENTAL PLANE

In timing, NINE is the end of the line. It is now time to surrender and to prepare to move to the next level. "Let go and let God" are the watchwords for NINE. NINE is universal; it is the VIBRATION of unconditional love. While SIX loves as an integral member of the group, NINE loves without attachment, loving all equally, selflessly, without prejudice. NINE is a VIBRATION of compassion, of tolerance, and philanthropy. The cycle of SEVEN (1-7) is called the cycle of man (the week, the moon cycles), but the cycle of NINE (1-9) is the divine cycle.

The circle of the symbol 9 is between the spiritual world and the mental and emotional worlds, then curving down (or sometimes straight down) to the physical world. Whereas EIGHT tries to bring heaven to Earth, NINE wishes to live more in the fantasy of heaven; only reluctantly coming down to earth to share the vision

In its purest form, NINE is the Bodhisattva, the evolved being who stays behind to serve others. All NINES are not that evolved, but all NINES have a flair for the dramatic, are visionary, and artistic. NINES are metaphysical crusaders that all people feel drawn to. NINE brings the message to accept all of humanity without regard to race, religion, national origin, gender, age, sexual preference, wealth, or political beliefs. NINE has a particular quality. If you add NINE to any other VIBRATION you end up with that other VIBRATION after simplification (see page 278) — try it!. As a result, all other VIBRATIONs see themselves reflected in the NINE. They all feel connected.

NINE is the VIBRATION of the old soul who has done this many times before. This is not the easiest VIBRATION for childhood, which is normally a time of beginnings, but NINE comes in already old. More than any other VIBRATION, NINE is interested in completing with the Earth world. NINE is not a VIBRATION full of goals or desires to amass material, social, or career successes. Efforts in that direction don't tend to end well, because the only goal of NINE is to let go. It is a dreamer and is drawn to many different things, finding it difficult to focus on just one thing or in just one area. NINE is the least practical of all VIBRATIONs.

How do others perceive the NINE? Without a cause or a sense of doing something worthwhile with its life, NINE can feel out of balance. At one extreme NINE can have delusions of grandeur and invincibility and at the other extreme be deluged by feelings of hopelessness and worthlessness. ONE might see NINE as being aimless, while TWO might find NINE to be overemotional. THREE can think NINE is alternately morose or a drama queen, while FOUR could be more concerned with it being impractical or dissipated. FIVE might think NINE is sarcastic, while SIX could experience it as hateful or nomadic. SEVEN may might find NINE to be either overly-passionate or paranoid, while EIGHT might experience NINE as either sentimental or subversive. Though these criticisms may always say more about the judge than the judged, NINE is to remember that it is innocent and unconditionally loved, that none of this is real, to let go, that there is a reason for everything, and to know that it is always protected. Everyone is served by knowing these truths, but for NINE it is paramount.

If NINE is a major VIBRATION in your CHART, you came here to be of service to the masses. The day to day work on the planet is taken care of by ONE through SIX, but it is SEVEN through NINE that provide the reason for it all. You represent the unconditional love and acceptance of the divine. You constantly remind yourself that understanding, compassion, and letting go are what is being asked of you. And that is probably a tall enough order. Remember that you chose your NUMBERS. Your higher self would not have plotted a course that you were not fully capable of traversing. NINE, you are loved and you are love. For the rest of you, there are always times when you are asked to let go, to have forgiveness and compassion, and to be understanding. NINEs are there lighting the way for you.

A VIBRATION on the SPIRITUAL PLANE

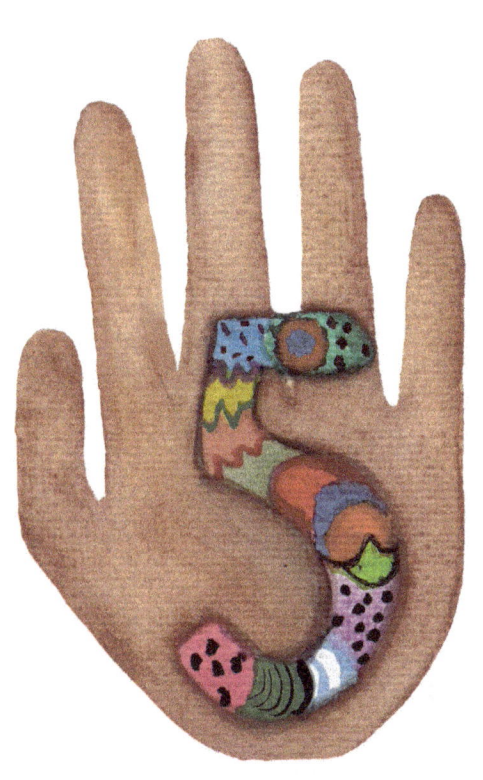

MOTIVATION

YOUR HOTLINE TO YOUR HIGHER SELF

Your MOTIVATION POSITION represents the primary way that you view the world. It is through the MOTIVATION that your higher self speaks to you. It represents what you most want, how you deeply wish to be, and what types of people or situations you are drawn to. Your MOTIVATION is your primary guide to spiritual growth. It is through following the passions of this POSITION's VIBRATION that your direction can be established and your accomplishments can be realized. Your passions are your hot-line to your higher self. Your MOTIVATION represents how you wish to be and how you direct your life, but not necessarily how you actually act in the world. If you are not listening to and following your MOTIVATION, you cannot realize your ASCENSION. If this VIBRATION is KARMIC, you have created a particular challenge for yourself in knowing how to get what you want. There is one sentence included in your MOTIVATION description to give you an idea of the KARMIC effect, but read more about your KARMIC NUMBER for a deeper understanding. Please keep in mind that this is only one MAJOR POSITION of twelve, standing by itself. You share this VIBRATION with approximately 11% of the planet. This is just a piece of you; there are many other aspects to follow which help to make up the unique you. *It is through listening to your MOTIVATION that you find your direction in life.*

ONE wants to be independent. You are strong minded. You don't really care what others think; you want to choose and act for yourself. You don't like to be told what to do. You are courageous and willing to be a pioneer. You have a singleness of focus and will not easily be deterred. You want what you want right away. You have a fire inside of you. You like to start new things, though you are less motivated to carry them through to completion. You have more integrity than most people and your first reference is always with yourself. It is not an issue of narcissism; it is simply that only you know which way to go. If KARMIC, you have a deep fear about going it alone and doubt your ability to stand on your own. *You find your divinity through your courageous willingness to explore the unknown.*

TWO wants peace and cooperation. You would rather work with another than alone. You do not choose the limelight, but prefer to be the behind the scenes support. You are sensitive to the details more than to the big picture. You are sensitive to timing and emotions and dislike conflict and dissidence. You want to be in a partnership but would sooner be alone than in constant disharmony. You seek peace and are good at compromising because you are able to see both sides of the situation and you can take many approaches. You try to be tactful, gentle, and adaptable. You tend to stay focused in the moment. You want to bring everything into balance. If KARMIC, it is difficult to be sensitive to others because you tend to take everything personally. *You find your divinity in the faces of others.*

THREE wants to communicate and to be heard. You are creative and playful. You never want to grow up. You are in the moment. Your work is imagining. You hope to entertain and inspire others. You can see the big picture. While you are usually buoyant, like a child you can be swept by the thunderstorms of emotional tantrums. They usually don't last long. You are not particularly concerned with others except as playmates or as an audience. You feel hampered by routines and attempts to make you more disciplined. You dream big and want life to be a fun game. If KARMIC, you doubt your own creativity and may be afraid to express it. *You find your divinity through your own creative expression.*

FOUR wants to build and wants to know the truth. You take a while to get started because you are in it for the long run. You want the facts before investing your energy. You like to work hard toward a goal and are determined and tenacious once your course is set. You are not sidetracked by small emotional setbacks. You want things to be fair and you try to be honest. You also expect honesty from others. You tend to be scheduled and busy in the present. The future is mapped out with plans and goals. You are slow to accept the new, having respect for what has stood the test of time. You are not happy without a project. If KARMIC, you have a hard time seeing the truth about yourself and others, as well as difficulty with self-discipline. *You find your divinity through your persistent search for truth.*

FIVE wants to experience things. You are curious and want freedom to explore every aspect of life. You want to try everything at least once. You want to use all your senses and to manipulate the physical world to make it to your liking. You want change and progress. You are quick to act. You always want to try what is new. Speed and efficiency are important. Routine and repetition are anathema to you. You like to convince others to follow your plan, which you are still forming and evolving as you move forward. You want to change everything you see so that things work better and faster. This gives you more time to do the things you want to do. If KARMIC, you fear change and have difficulties controlling your impulses. *You find your divinity in the adventure of the physical journey.*

SIX wants to take care of others. You want to feel that you are a part of a group and you take your responsibilities seriously. How you perceive your role in the group will change as you mature, but you always want to be a player. You want to be a teacher or a healer or a counselor or a social worker or a socially involved religious worker. You want a family. You want to love and to be loved. You want to nurture others and to be a solace for those who feel left out. You look for the similarities in people rather than their differences. You relate to the personal more than the universal. If KARMIC, you have trouble feeling that you belong in any group and have difficulty working with others. *You find your divinity through loving service.*

SEVEN wants to investigate things at a deep level. You want to have time alone in order to pursue your interests. You are a perfectionist and your thoughts will likely draw you into spiritual and/or scientific directions. You question everything. Matters of faith are important to you. You want to be the professional, the specialist. You appreciate what is special and unique about other people and will likely have an interesting mix of friends. You are not attracted to the everyday life, but choose a more rarified air in which to operate. If KARMIC, you have deep fears and confusions that can paralyze you and you may be consumed by the need to prove everything. *You find your divinity through faith and trust.*

EIGHT wants to be powerful. You want the big house and an important job. Manifestation is of great importance. You want to have an effect on the world. You always think big. You can be a crusader, wanting to right all the wrongs in the world. You have a low tolerance for the abuse of power by other people, institutions, or governments. You are interested in politics. You want to be a leader and to empower others. You don't enjoy taking orders or working at lower levels. You want to act with authority. You think more about the good of society than of your personal self. If KARMIC, you have a fear of power in yourself and in others that blocks you from asserting yourself fully. *You find your divinity through your power of manifestation.*

NINE loves without borders. You appreciate the drama of life. Coming in with the VIBRATION of endings, you are not motivated in any particular direction. You want all people to be treated fairly and lovingly. You are an idealist and can be happy living in a fantasy world. You want to make the world a better place, but are probably more aware than any other VIBRATION of your desire to complete with the cycle of reincarnation. Your focus is more on endings than beginnings, which can make childhood — a time of beginnings — somewhat problematic. Adolescence and early adulthood can be challenging too, because it is difficult to focus energy in one direction to create a career, or indeed any long term goals. You love without limit and will eventually find a focus for that energy. If KARMIC, you have a great fear of letting go and tend to visualize the worst possible outcomes for yourself and the world. *You find your divinity through unconditional love and letting go.*

This is the first MAJOR POSITION in your CHART (there are twelve in all) and also the first of the trilogy of NAME NUMBERs. The MOTIVATION can also be called the Soul Urge, the Soul Number, the Heart's Desire or simply the INNER VIBRATION. It is derived from the vowels in your name (see "COMPUTATIONS" on page 280).

The vowel sounds are all created in the heart chakra. When you sing, you are mostly expressing vowel sounds. This is the feeling that is expressed from your heart. Meaning comes when consonants are clipped on to the vowel sounds, but the heart and feeling of the song is expressed in the vowels. Likewise, the vowels in your name express the heart of you.

In ancient times the sacred truths were written without vowels. In this way the uninitiated could neither fully understand them nor chant the special words to invoke divine energy. It took the guidance of one from the inner circle to whisper to the initiate the vowel sounds in order to open up the spiritual abilities. But, now divine guidance is open to all. You need no special initiation, only your intention.

Your MOTIVATION shows a reservoir of your focus from previous incarnations. It represents your dreams and ideals and what you enjoy doing the best. Your MOTIVATION is obvious to you, but not as easily seen by others. Only you receive the message clearly. People who know you well or who are intuitive will be aware of it, but not as deeply as you are. Young children show this VIBRATION more strongly to the world as do those in old age. Other ages are perceived by others more for their VIBRATION in the PERSONALITY POSITION.

If you don't connect with your MOTIVATION VIBRATION, the first question you can ask yourself is how you would feel if this NUMBER truly represented the INNER you. If that feels good, allow yourself to move more and more into that direction until you fully accept yourself. On the other hand, if you have judgment about the NUMBER in your MOTIVATION, it will be valuable for you to do forgiveness work around this VIBRATION. You are likely finding yourself feeling quite blocked in your life experiences. There may be an intense self- judgment. This is a good place to seek the support of others.

If you have a KARMIC VIBRATION on your MOTIVATION POSITION, you didn't come in knowing how to do what you most want to do. A KARMIC NUMBER always brings confusion and discomfort. When it falls on your MOTIVATION, the clumsiness becomes particularly acute. Even if your MOTIVATION number is not missing in the letters in your name, it still might operate like a KARMIC VIBRATION when you are judging yourself. Remember that you chose this challenge to stimulate a deeply desired spiritual growth. Karma is not forever.

Above, I have modeled how to read a specific VIBRATION in this POSITION. Keep in mind that this is only the first word on this NUMBER in this POSITION. I am being general, not specific. I would have more to say if I were reading your CHART directly to you. As you continue to meditate upon the nature of your NUMBER and of the POSITION of the MOTIVATION, you will gain more insights. Also, please keep in mind that this is only one POSITION of twelve, standing by itself.

Through your MOTIVATION your higher self is guiding you toward the realization of your ASCENSION.

KARMIC NUMBER

YOUR ACHILLES HEEL

KARMIC NUMBERs represent liabilities from former lifetimes. They show a place of vulnerability. You were not born with a natural ability to deal with this VIBRATION. Situations that call for the expression of your KARMIC NUMBER can be uncomfortable for you and may be poorly handled. There is an imbalance that results in an over expression or an under expression of the KARMIC VIBRATION. If you have a KARMIC NUMBER that falls on a MAJOR POSITION, you have a particular challenge. You may have anywhere from none to several KARMIC NUMBERs. You will develop the required skills as time goes by. This drives you to grow spiritually toward the realization of your divinity. *You will eventually be stronger in your KARMIC VIBRATION than most people who are not KARMIC there.*

HAVING NONE does not imply that you have no karma. It is only a sign that you do not have any particular VIBRATION that is strongly out of balance. This is neither a good nor a bad thing, but it does carry significance. Because you have no particular vulnerability in any of the VIBRATIONs, life can be easier or less of a challenge for you than for somebody who has confusion about how to deal with a certain VIBRATION. There is less holding you back from developing quickly and going far. On the other hand, a karmic liability acts as a spur to force you into spiritual growth. You have nothing driving you to heal your karma. If you are lacking a KARMIC NUMBER, be careful to avoid the trap of complacency of thinking that you've got it all handled. Also be cautious of developing spiritual arrogance, feeling superior to those who wrestle with their karmic liabilities. *A mantra for NO KARMIC NUMBERs is "I see the divinity in everyone".*

A KARMIC ONE (which is rarely found) presents a challenge to integrity and courage. It is hard for you to stand up for yourself and be assertive. You don't really know how to be true to yourself. You can vacillate between being overly bullish and spineless. You can be terrified of acting on your own. You may be overly influenced by others. You may even assertively act out their ideas. In past lives you were probably a bit of a bully, forcing your will upon others. You are terrified of being that way again. As with all KARMIC NUMBERs, the lesson is gradually learned. The swings become less dramatic. Courage and independence develop. *A mantra for the KARMIC ONE is "be true to yourself".*

The KARMIC TWO presents a challenge to sensitivity and timing. You seem to vacillate between hypersensitivity and insensitivity. Your feelings are hurt very easily. You take everything personally. Then, because you are so focused on your own feelings, you don't notice how others are feeling. This makes you timid when it comes to being in a one-to-one relationship. Life, of course, brings you continual opportunities to learn how to balance the sensitivities. You gradually learn that the emotion you are feeling may have been picked up from the person you are with. The KARMIC TWO also is challenged when it comes to timing. Here your focus may be so inward that you have difficulty flowing with life. Musical training can be helpful. There may also be a challenge with patience. Over time you can become a master of sensitivity and patience. *A mantra for the KARMIC TWO is "don't take it personally".*

The KARMIC THREE presents a challenge to creativity and self-expression. You have difficulty expressing yourself and don't believe yourself to be creative. In childhood this may be reflected in a speech defect. As with all KARMIC NUMBERs, there is some pull to situations that require the competent expression of the VIBRATION. The KARMIC THREE can swing back and forth between inappropriate expression—a blurting out—and holding back from any expression. Any training in the creative arts will be helpful. Opportunities to be playful are also supportive, as you have a tendency to be too serious. Over time, you become more and more comfortable with your creativity and your ability to express clearly and powerfully. *A mantra for the KARMIC THREE is "if I can dream it, I can do it".*

The KARMIC FOUR presents a challenge in seeing the truth and having self-discipline. You have difficulties seeing others for who they are, and you also likely misjudge yourself. This can cause painful experiences in relationships, both working and intimate. Karmically, you are afraid of what you might see. You can vacillate between being too hard on yourself and others and on being too lax. In work habits you can go from being undisciplined and never finishing things, to being overly rigid and stuck in the mire. There seems to be a fear of total commitment. The KARMIC FOUR gets plenty of opportunities to do things over until they get it right. You gradually learn to be disciplined and structured. You learn how to read others and yourself accurately. *A mantra for the KARMIC FOUR is "it is safe for me to see the truth".*

The KARMIC FIVE (which is the rarest of all KARMIC NUMBERs) does not have a natural ability to be flexible and adapt to change. You may be afraid to try something new, preferring to follow familiar ways. You can find yourself either taking reckless chances or refusing to take any chance whatsoever. It is the opposite challenge to the KARMIC FOUR. Where the KARMIC FOUR wants to seek change rather than following through with a plan, the KARMIC FIVE is afraid to make any change. Of course changes continually come into your life and you learn how to adjust. As with all KARMIC NUMBERs, you may find yourself growing stronger around FIVE than those who were never KARMIC. *A mantra for the KARMIC FIVE when confronted with change is "I am flexible and adaptable and can handle anything".*

The KARMIC SIX presents a challenge in working with groups and in serving others. You often feel like you don't belong. You feel awkward and uncomfortable in group settings (families, schools, workplaces, clubs, organizations, etc.) and do not naturally serve others. You have the fear that you will lose your independence to the group. Therefore, you tend to run away from the group if things aren't going your way, or else you may try to be the leader of the group so you can control its direction. The challenge is to learn to trust the group and to learn to be of service to others without expecting something in return. You will eventually become strong at this and will one day feel at home in all groups. *A mantra for the KARMIC SIX is "I am loved and supported by this group".*

The KARMIC SEVEN presents a challenge in trusting that there is any meaning to the universe. You live in fear rather than in faith. You do not have a belief that everything is perfect, that things happen for a reason, or that everything will eventually work out. On one extreme, you may rigidly believe in some faith or dogma, but when a crisis happens the belief is not strong enough; it doesn't work for you. This can throw you into a state of atheism or at least agnosticism where you don't trust anything. That also doesn't work, so you swing back to a new belief and the cycle continues. Gradually your faith becomes stronger and can carry you through a crisis. Your faith becomes more dependable than those who have not been so tested. Before that time, a lot of testing will occur. *A mantra for the KARMIC SEVEN is "everything is perfect".*

The KARMIC EIGHT presents a challenge in dealing with power and authority. This is the most common of all KARMIC NUMBERs. You don't trust power, especially male power. Karmically, you have abused power and now fear it in yourself as well as in others. You don't understand how manifestation works. You believe in scarcity. Revisit the description for the NUMBER EIGHT and learn how power really works. Your KARMIC EIGHT vacillates between avoiding all contact with power, and trying to seize control. Neither works until you learn how to let power work through you. Power is about taking full responsibility for what is and choosing to create your own reality. It is not about amassing wealth or position, but is about having what is required to do what you wish to do. You get stronger with this over time. *A mantra for the KARMIC EIGHT is "I am the power in my life".*

The KARMIC NINE (which is rarely found) has a challenge with idealism, acceptance of differences, and letting go. On the one had you may be overly dramatic, out of touch with reality, and reckless; at the other extreme you may be fearful and unforgiving of any differences in other people. You are going to learn how to let go, both emotionally and materially. You will be given opportunities to do just that. You will also learn to love unconditionally, both yourself and others. Travel can be helpful, especially to places where you will be exposed to other cultures. Over time you will learn to be more accepting of others, more understanding, generous, and forgiving. *A mantra for the KARMIC NINE is "let go and let God".*

MORE ABOUT

Everyone has karma to work out, that is, you have the task to bring balance and harmony into your life. But, please don't accept this as a punishment or a life sentence. Karma forces you onto the next phase of spiritual growth. Yes, you did things in past lives that you are ashamed of. You name it, you've done it. The good news is that nobody is judging you for any of this other than you. The divine does not judge. The divine loves unconditionally. You are free to do anything you wish on this planet of free will. It happens to work out that what makes you feel the best is to treat others and yourself with love. You have karma because you are still judging yourself. As soon as you stop beating yourself up, the karma is gone. The easiest way to see if you still have past life karma is to see where you are judging others. That is where you are still judging yourself. Forgiveness is the key to releasing karma. Forgive, forgive, forgive. You will create an abundance of situations to support you to work out the karma. In fact, there is often a direct relationship between the volume of challenging situations that come into your life and the strength of your commitment to spiritual growth.

If a NUMBER is not represented by the VIBRATION values for the letters in your name, it is a KARMIC NUMBER for you (see "COMPUTATIONS" on page 286). If a VIBRATION is KARMIC for you, it functions as a blind spot. You don't have a natural feel for working with its energy. It can be a stumbling block, and it draws situations that force you to use that VIBRATION so that you get better at it. You will get stronger and more balanced with the VIBRATION as time goes on. However, you will always be sensitive to where it remains out of balance. Even as you become better at working with your KARMIC NUMBER than most other people demonstrate, you are aware of what is lacking. In this way, your VIBRATION continues to drive your movement toward realizing your ASCENSION. If you are not KARMIC in a certain VIBRATION, you have at least a capability of handling situations calling for that energy, even if you don't particularly enjoy yourself or excel there. Even if a number is not missing in your name, it still might operate like a KARMIC VIBRATION when you are judging yourself.

The readings suggested above for KARMIC NUMBERs can be considered as guidelines for your understanding. As you continue to meditate on the qualities of your particular KARMIC VIBRATION, you will gain more insights as to how it is getting in your way and quicker ways to bring the VIBRATION into balance for you. As always, this is just the first word. *I'm not going to say that your task is easy, but it is achievable, and the process will be one that brings you a growing sense of accomplishment.*

IN MAJOR POSITIONS

When you have a KARMIC NUMBER in a MAJOR POSITION in your CHART, you will be called to use that VIBRATION often, but you aren't playing with a full deck. Remember that great challenges are a sign of the potential for great spiritual growth. This is one way you might have set yourself up for such growth. Not only does the KARMIC NUMBER draw experiences for its own development, but the focus of a MAJOR POSITION increases the opportunities for growth exponentially.

The first place to look for the possible effect of a KARMIC NUMBER is in the MOTIVATION. This is a particular challenge because the way that you most want to be, you don't really know how to be. Let's say that your MOTIVATION is FOUR and what you want most is to see the truth and to work hard toward your goals. However, it is difficult for you to recognize the truth, even when it right before you, and you have difficulty staying disciplined and completing your goals. Obviously, there is strong impetus for you to strengthen your ability with the FOUR. Until you do there will be a good deal of frustration and dissatisfaction with your life.

Similar challenges arise wherever karma intersects with any other

MAJOR POSITION. We will deal with the effect of karma on those POSITIONs as we reach them.

The most important things to remember about KARMIC NUMBERs are:
1. *You chose them to encourage your spiritual growth.*
2. *You will get better at that KARMIC NUMBER over time.*
3. *Consciousness of your KARMIC NUMBER accelerates the balancing process.*
4. *Eventually you will be stronger in your KARMIC NUMBER than many people are who were born without the VIBRATION being KARMIC.*
5. *There is great satisfaction in healing a KARMIC NUMBER.*
6. *Forgive, forgive, forgive.*
7. *With ASCENSION all karma is dissolved.*

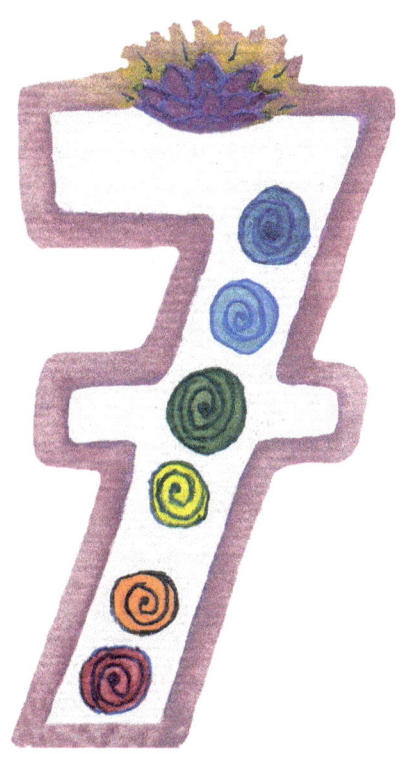

PERSONALITY

HOW YOU DO WHAT YOU DO

Your PERSONALITY POSITION represents how you automatically act and respond to the world, without conscious intention. This is the OUTER shell of you that others see and react to. You see yourself more from the perspective of your MOTIVATION, but you operate and are perceived more from the perspective of your PERSONALITY. Your PERSONALITY is directed by your MOTIVATION. They are equally valuable aspects, but you may have a tendency to see your MOTIVATION as a more accurate description. In order to express the fullness of who you are and to realize your ASCENSION, it is necessary to allow your PERSONALITY to fully express itself. If your PERSONALITY is a KARMIC NUMBER for you, this can actually be more of a challenge for others than for you, as you only discover from others' reactions how you are actually acting. There is one sentence included in your PERSONALITY description to give you an idea of the KARMIC effect, but read more deeply about your KARMIC NUMBER for a deeper understanding. *It is primarily through your PERSONALITY that others see the divinity in you. Accept this part of your divine nature as a full partner.*

ONE demonstrates courage and integrity. You are seen as independent, doing things in your own way. You may not seem to be a good listener because you are so focused on the direction you are headed. You are singled-tracked in your focus. Others always knows where you stand on a question. You may appear to be impatient, and forceful about having your way. You don't back down easily. You are seen as a leader rather than a follower. You are good at initiating activities, though others may be of help in bringing them to completion. You are courageous. You don't seem to be afraid to stand out from the crowd, and you appear to have a great deal of integrity. You are not influenced much by the actions and opinions of others, instead following your own compass. If KARMIC, you may at times be seen by others as alternately over- or under-assertive. *ONE is seen as strong willed and independent.*

TWO demonstrates thoughtfulness and patience. You make others feel important and listened to. People feel that you are on their side. It may be hard to get an opinion or a decision out of you. You do not seem to have a strong preference or direction and can wait for others to set the course. You are comfortable being in a supportive position. You often seem to act in such a way as to avoid conflict. You are sensitive to the little things and work in a cooperative way with others, especially on a one-to-one basis. You bring peace and calm to situations, having the natural ability to see both sides and to appear neutral, though supportive. You have a natural sense of timing. If KARMIC, you may at times appear to be either hypersensitive in your reactions or insensitive to others. *TWO is seen as sensitive and attentive.*

THREE demonstrates creativity and expression. You are the eternal child and bring joy to every event. You are not to be counted on to be responsible or dependable. You avoid self-discipline and the control of others, acting more as a free spirit and in the moment. You can be counted on to be creative and to help others to feel happier. You demonstrate great artistic talent and have a way with words. You are free and spontaneous with expressing your thoughts and feelings. Though, usually buoyant, you do not hold back your tears or anger from others. You inspire people with your expression, encouraging them to be more fully themselves and to follow their dreams. If KARMIC, you may at times withhold your expression or release it inappropriately. *THREE is seen as fun and playful.*

Personality

FOUR demonstrates a reliable and truthful nature. You are a person whose word can be trusted. You work hard, do a good job, and get the job done. You tend to do things for yourself, rather than relying on others. You are inclined to be conservative and can be stubborn. You are both slow to try new things and a slow starter, but there is no stopping you once you get up a head of steam. You are able to overcome any adversity and have great endurance. You don't seem to let your emotions stop you from completing the task. You are loyal to people and to your promises. You treat people fairly, but may be a little hard on them. If KARMIC, you may at times appear to be harder on others and seem to have a difficult time seeing things and people as they actually are. *FOUR is seen as hardworking and determined.*

FIVE demonstrates flexibility and a zest for life. You are always trying something new and might seem to be a bit on the wild side. You bring a spirit of adventure into the lives of others. There isn't a dull moment when you're around. You mix well with others and are naturally persuasive. This makes you a natural salesperson, especially for whatever things or ideas you have excitement for. You don't tend to follow the rules or directions well. You are more likely to charge off in any direction than you are to follow routines. You learn by doing and work quickly. You are good at landing on your feet. This makes you a good problem solver. If KARMIC, you may at times alternate between appearing to be out of control and being clamped down. *FIVE is seen as lively and adventurous.*

SIX demonstrates a caring and supportive nature. You are always doing things for others and are rarely found alone. You work and play in groups and make others feel welcome. You get involved in others' lives, drawing them into your circle of endeavors. You let your opinions be known, but welcome those of others. People see you as responsible, nurturing, and caring. You are tireless in your support of them. If you are not a parent, you will still likely find a way to spend time with children. Your work is usually in the service professions. You tend to go wide rather than deep, attempting to pull all outliers into the group. If KARMIC, you may at times not appear to cooperate well and may seem to use others. *SIX is seen as helpful and loving.*

SEVEN demonstrates wisdom and skill. You appear hard to get to know well, but it is worth the effort. You are highly skilled at whatever you do, a real professional. You go deeply into things. There is always a spiritual aura about you; perhaps this appears as you possessing a sense of the mysterious. You don't seem to live in the everyday world. Not a party person, you are, nonetheless, always interesting to talk with. You appear to be wise beyond your years and people are drawn to you for your counsel. You are there for people when they are having a moment of inner crisis. If KARMIC, you may sometimes appear to be a downer for others and there may seem to be holes in your reasoning. *SEVEN is seen as deep and talented.*

EIGHT demonstrates capability and leadership. You effortlessly take over in most situations or perhaps people tend to put you in charge. Not necessarily a "people" person, you appear much more concerned about getting things done. You act to achieve the highest good for the group, rather than for your personal gratification. However, you often show the trappings of success, because you are naturally talented at manifesting in the physical world. You are good at managing others and at delegating authority. You act to right wrongs. You may become politically active. If KARMIC, you may at times seem to abuse your power by either an over- or an under-expression of it. *EIGHT is seen as powerful and as an authority.*

NINE demonstrates selflessness and acceptance. You can be all things to all people; that is, everyone finds something of themselves in your personality. You are selfless in your actions and broad in your perspectives. You act in a non-discriminatory fashion, working comfortably with all types of people. You are often found working with the underdogs. You seem to be at home in any environment. You are not materially focused, and bring a spiritual subtext to all endeavors. You can be charismatic, acting in a dramatic fashion. Sometimes you may appear to be rudderless, but you work to make the world a better, more loving place. If KARMIC, you may at times appear be less selfless — seeming to use your charisma to control others, or you can appear to just give up. *NINE is seen as dramatic and caring.*

Personality

The second MAJOR POSITION in your CHART and the second of the NAME NUMBERs is also known as the OUTER VIBRATION. The PERSONALITY is derived from the consonants in your birth name (see "COMPUTATIONS" on page 280); so let's look further at them.

Consonants are formed in the mouth and throat. They give meaning to words, where vowels give them feeling. Consonants represent the outer vibrations in life or the form, that which can be directly noticed by the senses. The consonants represent the physicality of you — your anchor to Mother Earth and your body. While it is the most obvious point of reference for others, you are more likely to relate to your MOTIVATION than to your PERSONALITY.

This does not mean that your PERSONALITY is a lesser POSITION; it only means that it is naturally of a lesser focus to you. However, your PERSONALITY is the actor. Your MOTIVATION has little power to act in the world, particularly after childhood. Your MOTIVATION indicates how you want to be, but your PERSONALITY shows how you actually do things. There is no hypocrisy or loss of integrity in this. Both VIBRATIONs are part of you. This is how you set things up. It is important that these two parts of you work together in a cooperative fashion (see "STRESS NUMBER BETWEEN MOTIVATION AND PERSONALITY" on page 104).

I have modeled for you how to read your specific VIBRATION in the PERSONALITY POSITION. Keep in mind that this is only the first word on this NUMBER in this POSITION. As you continue to meditate upon the nature of your NUMBER and of the POSITION of the PERSONALITY you will gain more insights. Think also about how your PERSONALITY might relate to your MOTIVATION. *Keep in mind that you are only looking at two of the twelve MAJOR POSITIONS, and that you share these VIBRATIONs with slightly over 1% of the planet. You are only beginning to touch on the uniqueness that is you.*

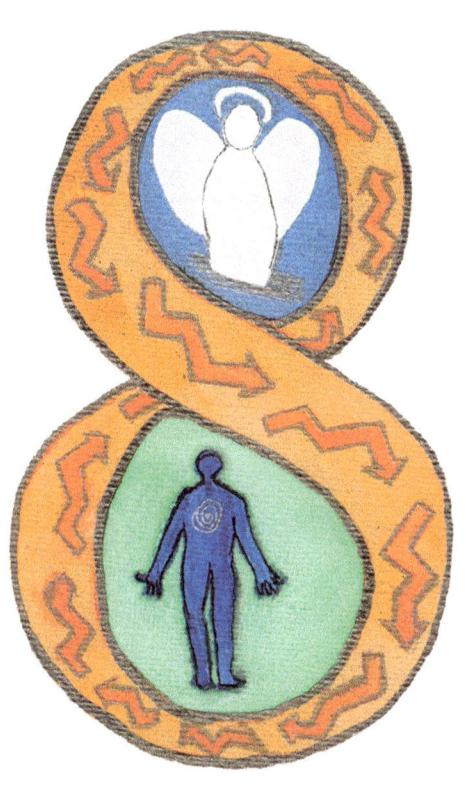

STRESS NUMBER
BETWEEN **MOTIVATION** AND **PERSONALITY**

YOUR PROBLEM TRULY IS YOUR OPPORTUNITY

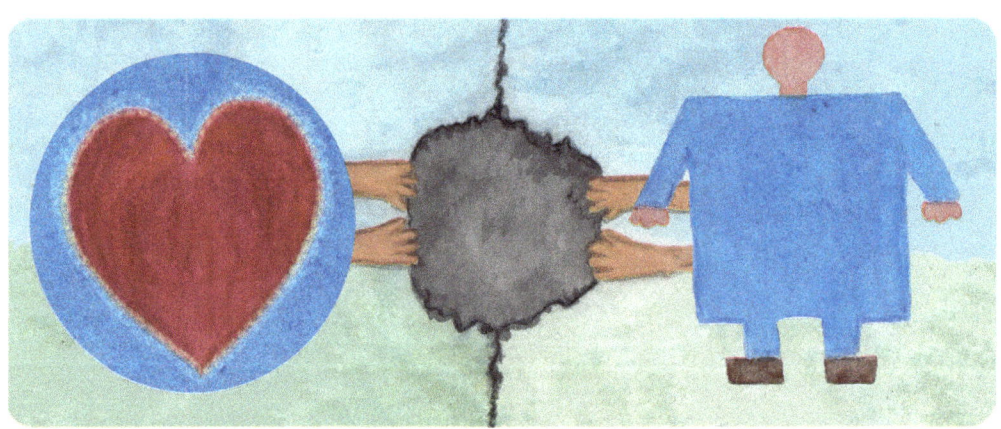

When you have two different VIBRATIONs in separate MAJOR POSITIONs in your CHART, the interaction between them is represented through the STRESS NUMBER. We are going to look at the stress between your MOTIVATION and your PERSONALITY. If your MOTIVATION and your PERSONALITY NUMBERs are different, they won't necessarily work together in a cooperative manner. For each STRESS NUMBER there is a brief description, followed by all possible MOTIVATION/PERSONALITY combinations for that STRESS NUMBER. If your STRESS NUMBER is KARMIC, the importance of bringing balance is magnified. Read more deeply about your KARMIC NUMBER. In the readings that follow, the pronouns "you" and "your" are asked to perform extraordinary duties. Because there are two equal aspects of you, an INNER and an OUTER self, I am using the schizophrenic sounding "you" to represent each part. The wording may sound confusing, so read it over until you feel the two distinct parts of yourself. You will have a tendency to favor your INNER self over your OUTER self. You want to use your INNER nature as a tool to fully love and accept your OUTER nature as a full partner. Your OUTER nature just acts. You can't "use" it; you can only allow it to act, unfettered. *The STRESS NUMBER shows both the nature of the potential conflict between the two VIBRATIONs and also the possible path of resolution. It is there to lead you higher by helping you to fully accept your OUTER way of doing things and to fully integrate and find the harmony between your two sides. Use the divine aspects of the STRESS NUMBER to align your INNER drive with your OUTER way of acting.*

Ascension Numerology

If your MOTIVATION and your PERSONALITY are the same, your STRESS NUMBER is the CIPHER. That's right, you have no stress between what you want to do and the way in which you act. What you see is what you get. You are the same inside and outside. The good news is that there is nothing to balance internally. You can pursue your heart's desire without interference from your OUTER nature. The bad news is that means you are driving with no brakes. There is nothing to stop you from being extreme when pursuing your goals. However you might experience a different polarity of your VIBRATION in your INNER and OUTER VIBRATIONs. For example, your MOTIVATION might under-express the VIBRATION while your PERSONALITY over-expresses it. Anyway, that is how you set things up. If the VIBRATION is KARMIC, the challenge is bigger. I am not going to bother with specific readings for the different double NUMBERs, just reread the NUMBER description and its interpretation for your MOTIVATION and your PERSONALITY. Then, think "no holds barred". *Find the divinity in your VIBRATION and always strive to express it.*

Stress number between motivation and personality — ONE

Your STRESS NUMBER ONE shows that there is a basic misalignment between your INNER and OUTER self. One of them is even and the other is odd, because they are contiguous VIBRATIONs. Contiguous VIBRATIONs do not get along with each other easily. The odd NUMBERs are more inwardly focused, the even NUMBERs more outwardly directed. Each one tries to take control. Therefore, you are likely to lose focus. What is instrumental is for your two parts to have a single, common goal. That goal will be set by your MOTIVATION, but it is one that can be carried out by your PERSONALITY. This is not so much a marriage as it is a business partnership between two very different people with different personalities and talents, pursuing a common goal. *Focus on a single goal.*

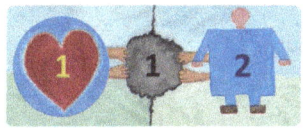

Your INNER ONE is focused and assertive. Your OUTER TWO is diffused and cooperative. Something has to give. Your INNER ONE is frustrated because your OUTER TWO goes along with everyone else and doesn't push an agenda. Meanwhile, while seeming to be sensitive to others, there appears to be a hidden agenda. Your INNER ONE tries to find a way to get what that part of you wants while acting in a TWO manner. *You are able to realize your goal as you find a path that can be achieved in your gentle, subtle manner.*

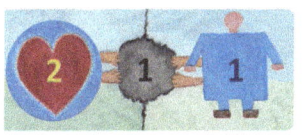

Your INNER TWO just wants to get along with others, but finds your OUTER ONE being aggressive and a bit pushy. Others respond to your OUTER ONE strongly and that can hurt your INNER TWO's feelings. Your INNER TWO wants to create peace in life to be happy, so you learn to focus your OUTER ONE energy toward that goal. *Be single minded toward bringing more harmony to every situation, even if that requires you to be outspoken. Peace at all costs.*

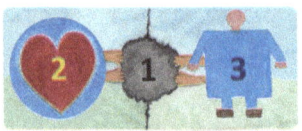
There is a frustration because your INNER TWO wants to create close sensitive relationships and your OUTER THREE is a little too outspoken, self-centered, and irresponsible to be the most sensitive friend. The challenge for your INNER TWO is to focus energy in a directed way so that the creativity of your OUTER THREE expresses your INNER TWO's desire for peace and sensitivity. *You will always be on stage. Let the show promote peace and sensitivity.*

Your INNER THREE wants to play and express, but your OUTER TWO is cautious about standing out and is more concerned with making others comfortable. In order for this combination to work, your expression will be of a nature that makes others feel comfortable. Things also are to be designed so that there is a demand from others for the creative expression your OUTER TWO feels comfortable in carrying out. Writing, music, or visual arts might help to bridge this gap with greater ease. *Decide what you most want to communicate and express it. You will do it in a sensitive manner.*

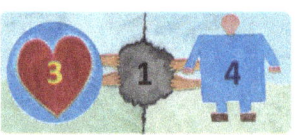
Your INNER THREE wants to express, and your OUTER FOUR is not really the expressive type. But your OUTER FOUR is always believable and trustworthy, so if your INNER THREE can create a format through which your OUTER FOUR can deliver your message (after a great deal of rehearsing) much can be accomplished. As always with your STRESS NUMBER ONE, a singleness of focus is helpful. *Push through your reluctance to express what is within you. It may not look exactly like what is in your heart, but people will understand the message.*

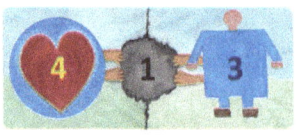
Your INNER FOUR is frustrated with your OUTER THREE. Your INNER FOUR is deadly serious, but who can take your clowning OUTER THREE seriously? What works for your INNER FOUR is to build a discipline for your OUTER THREE to follow that will be fun and creative, but will also lead to the realization of your INNER FOUR's goals. *Your potential for creative development is great when there is singleness of focus accompanied by discipline.*

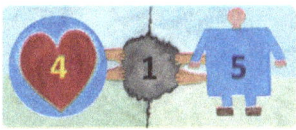
Your INNER FOUR and your OUTER FIVE are both results oriented. However, your OUTER FIVE is always running out ahead of where your INNER FOUR is comfortable being. This might be experienced as impulsiveness and a failure to follow through on your plan. Your INNER FOUR will want to have a goal that will keep your OUTER FIVE both involved and excited, particularly one involving multiple tasks. *Things may always move a little too fast for your comfort, but the results can exceed your expectations.*

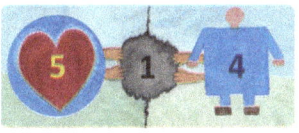
Your INNER FIVE and your OUTER FOUR are both results oriented. However, your OUTER FOUR seems to be too slow and cautious in acting. Your INNER FIVE wants to be on to the next thing, but your OUTER FOUR completes the task at hand and does a thorough job. Your INNER FIVE can take this into consideration when making plans, both by being very clear about your goal and by giving your OUTER FOUR smaller tasks that can be completed more quickly. *Once you get past your frustration of the pace, you might find that more ends up being accomplished.*

Your INNER FIVE wants freedom, adventure, and progress while your OUTER SIX is busy taking care of the problems of others and giving your energy for the good of the group. Your INNER FIVE could revise your goals to align with the good of the group, looking at how to optimize the group's progress and the way its members are supported in freeing themselves up from restrictive energy. The group can also be working to improve something for society. *Narrow your focus and welcome others into your plans.*

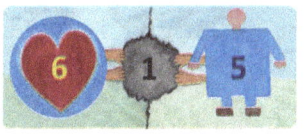
Your INNER SIX cares most about people and service and working together, whereas your OUTER FIVE is more about movement, experience, and progress. Your heart wants to be helping others, but your OUTER FIVE acts in a more opportunistic fashion. Your INNER SIX can set a goal where your OUTER FIVE can sell others on an idea that benefits other people while helping them to activate that change in their own lives. *It is okay to help yourself and others at the same time.*

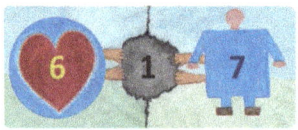
Your INNER SIX wants to be with people, while your OUTER SEVEN is more aloof. This combination works best if your INNER SIX lets your OUTER SEVEN develop an expertise in some area that can directly help others and then finds a group or groups where the ability can be shared. Your INNER SIX is not likely to get all the warmth and brotherhood you desire, but a great service can be performed. *Focus on service first and let your sense of belonging find its way to you.*

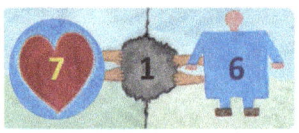
You have a people pleasing personality with no INNER attachment to being liked. Your INNER SEVEN would prefer to be alone, yet your OUTER SIX is a people magnet that is helpful to others. Your INNER nature requires more space in order to follow and perfect your passions, while also taking care to find venues to share your developments with others in a mode that still allows you some sort of escape hatch. Your passion learns to express yourself in a way that supports people. *Accept your social nature, but don't allow it to dilute your message.*

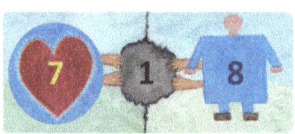
Neither your INNER SEVEN nor your OUTER EIGHT tend to seek personal gain. Your INNER SEVEN learns to give up some privacy to your more public OUTER EIGHT. What unites this pair is having a spiritually or scientifically focused goal for your OUTER EIGHT to execute. It is important to maintain a space where your expertise can continue to develop. Because your OUTER EIGHT maintains a certain distance from others, your INNER SEVEN can keep your comfort zone. *Accept your power and use it to manifest your INNER desire for perfection.*

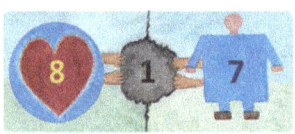
The power that your INNER EIGHT wants to manifest is left in the hands of your more reclusive OUTER SEVEN, so you may feel some frustration at not being recognized as the leader you are. This will come in time as your OUTER SEVEN is recognized for your own depth of expertise. Your leadership will fit into an area of narrower scope where your OUTER SEVEN lets you finesse your way into power. *You want the world, but take it one chunk at a time.*

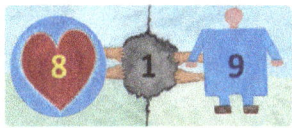 Your OUTER NINE has the ability to provide dramatic leadership for the desires of your INNER EIGHT, but first you are going to be reined in. Your OUTER NINE can be all things to all people and can be all over the map with your varied activities. Your INNER EIGHT finds a platform broad enough and humanitarian enough to utilize the energy of your OUTER NINE. This can be a very powerful coupling for leadership. *You can share your INNER power with the world, but you decide where to start.*

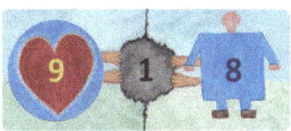 It takes a while to find an expression for the idealism of your INNER NINE. You have many different interests and little desire for power. Meanwhile your OUTER EIGHT has a tendency to take control of whatever situation you are in. This can be a very powerful situation if your INNER NINE can decide on an area in which to focus your energy so that your OUTER EIGHT can do what you do best. There is great potential for accomplishment along humanitarian lines. *You can share your unconditional love with the world, if you are willing to let the power move through you.*

With your TWO, the stress is always around sensitivity. You are dealing with either two odd NUMBERs or two even ones. Your fight is not so much one for control, as with the ONE STRESS NUMBER, but one of a balancing of more similar energies. Your main challenge with all TWO STRESS NUMBERs is a tendency toward criticism, whether it is inner or outer directed. There is also the challenge of letting the little things get in your way. The RELATIONSHIP between your two sides is more like that of a marriage, where your parts are relatively compatible, but it is important to remain sensitive to each other's desires and natures. *Always be supportive of yourself.*

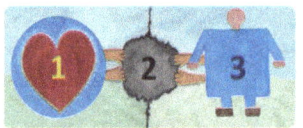

Your INNER ONE is focused and driven, but your OUTER THREE is light hearted, playful, and unfocused. The danger is one of being too self-critical about not moving forward in a more serious and directed manner. This might also manifest in critical attacks upon others. Your INNER ONE becomes more sensitive to the ways of your OUTER THREE, realizing that your nature is to be creative and expressive, and chooses goals that can be realized in such a way. The sensitivity is also to your acceptance that your OUTER THREE will never move in a straight line, but if given its wings your OUTER THREE might make some amazing and unexpected leaps. *Focus on loving all of your expressions and creations.*

Your INNER TWO wants to get along with others, to let them take the lead. Meanwhile, your OUTER FOUR is a bit harder on others and less warm than your INNER TWO would prefer. Your OUTER FOUR seems to be more concerned about getting the job done than in worrying about other's feelings. Your OUTER FOUR is also too willing to honestly let others know how you feel about their words and actions. There is the danger of a great deal of self-criticism and nitpicking. Your INNER TWO can work on picking partners, playmates, and workmates who can take the honesty and directness of your OUTER FOUR. *Take it easy on yourself. It is okay to be honest with others.*

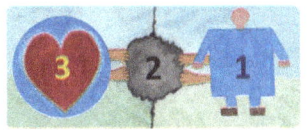
Your INNER THREE wants to have fun and to be creative and expressive. Meanwhile your OUTER ONE is a bulldog, acting often in a forceful and independent manner. This chases away some of your INNER THREE's playmates and, perhaps commits your INNER THREE into directions and commitments you might not have chosen to make. Your INNER THREE gradually realizes that your OUTER ONE is going to act in a focused and independent manner and to choose creative ways for your OUTER ONE to direct your energy. *Have courage and don't second guess your choice.*

Your OUTER FIVE keeps your INNER THREE busier than you would like to be, but it tends to be interesting stuff. Still your INNER THREE may periodically go into a pout and want your OUTER FIVE to give you a break. Things work best if your INNER THREE chooses a direction for your OUTER FIVE where there are lots of possibilities for expression, creativity, and playfulness. Otherwise there will be fiery inner battles or outer skirmishes with others. *You are not meant to fit any molds, so don't hold yourself back.*

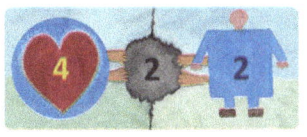
Your INNER FOUR drive is for honesty and for getting things done. Your OUTER TWO softens the directness of your comments and helps your INNER FOUR work more cooperatively with others. While your INNER FOUR still might feel that your OUTER TWO is wasting too much time with vacillating and being overly concerned with other's feelings, the job still gets done, though there is a danger of overworking. Your INNER FOUR will do best by choosing goals that include working with and/or helping others. *Take it easy on yourself. It is okay to be diplomatic with others.*

Your INNER FOUR is a little frustrated by your OUTER SIX's penchant for serving others and making sure that others are comfortable and participating. Your INNER FOUR wants to get to the truth of the matter and to reach your goal. It helps to be sensitive to the fact that your OUTER SIX is always going to be focused on others and act in ways that are group and service oriented. Your INNER FOUR also learns to be careful not to push your OUTER SIX or others too hard. You can be very driven to achieve your goals and become too demanding. *Be sensitive toward yourself and others. Everyone is doing a fine job.*

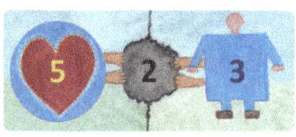
Your INNER FIVE wants to go five different ways at once, but your OUTER THREE has found a sixth way to go that is not necessarily supporting your plan and is not in any rush to get back on schedule, not that your INNER FIVE is a master of sticking to plans to begin with. So, we have a volatile combination that is capable of some amazing things, but can also crash and burn. Fortunately, your INNER FIVE is good at landing on your feet and your OUTER THREE can't be held down for long. It helps if your INNER FIVE remembers who is doing the heavy lifting, and makes sure that the load isn't all that heavy. *You are not meant to fit any molds, so go where your fancy takes you.*

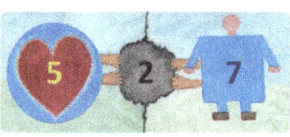
Your INNER FIVE wants to manipulate, change, and improve everything. Your OUTER SEVEN acts in a subtle way that leaves others unaware of what you are up to. However, your OUTER SEVEN's technical ability and aura of spirituality garner the respect of others. The only hitch is that your INNER FIVE wants a little more action than your OUTER SEVEN is offering. This combination is particularly effective when the changes your INNER FIVE wishes to implement are spiritually based. *Be patient with yourself. Your methods will pay off.*

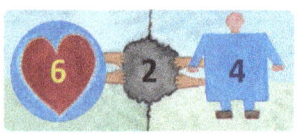
Your INNER SIX wants a warm group feeling and to put people first, while your OUTER FOUR acts in a more pragmatic, efficient, and terse fashion. Your INNER SIX begins to realize that your OUTER FOUR is not going to change, so it works best to find your place of service where your OUTER FOUR's tenacity and honesty are vital to the success of the group.

Stress number between motivation and personality — TWO

Your OUTER FOUR is not cold and indifferent. You are loyal and dedicated, but just not the people pleaser that your INNER SIX may feel motivated to be. *Love and support your efficient way of dealing with people and situations.*

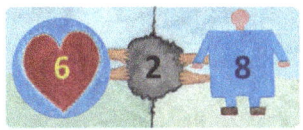

Your INNER SIX has a struggle with your OUTER EIGHT who puts business first and seems to take over every situation. Your INNER SIX wants teamwork and cooperation, but your OUTER EIGHT is seen by others as a natural leader, and with good reason. Your INNER SIX wants warmth from the group, but people rarely offer that kind of companionship to those perceived as leaders. Your INNER SIX comes to accept the situation. You may find it better to work in more philanthropic fields where people are more "touchy-feely" and the goal is to serve. *Let yourself be powerful and the sense of belonging will come.*

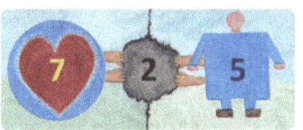

Your INNER SEVEN wants your space and wants to have the time to go deeply into things. Your OUTER FIVE, meanwhile, is jumping from one thing to the next and is a little worldly and advantage seeking for your more purely focused INNER SEVEN. It helps if your INNER SEVEN finds an area to develop that uses the versatility and the salesmanship of your OUTER FIVE. Otherwise you will have a feeling of selling out and losing touch with your soul. *It's okay to jump into things before you think you are ready. Just pay attention to the universe's reaction.*

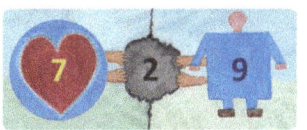

With your INNER SEVEN there is a desire for solitude and the space to develop things on a deep level. Your OUTER NINE is very much out there in the drama of the world. However, because your OUTER NINE can be all things to all people—that is, each person sees her own reflection in your NINE, there is something impersonal in your PERSONALITY that helps to shield your INNER SEVEN. Still your INNER SEVEN might be critical of your OUTER NINE for being too far out there, for tipping your hand too soon, or for attracting too much attention. *You are engaged in the ancient argument over whether faith or good works is the key. Give it up. There is a time for each.*

Your INNER EIGHT is ambitious and thinks big, while your OUTER SIX is more socially focused and less driven for success. There is always a challenge for your INNER EIGHT with a lower level PERSONALITY NUMBER because your goals are so big you can get frustrated having to express through what feels like a smaller vehicle. Remember that there are no accidents and no bad CHARTs. When I say that a combination is more challenging, that implies an opening for spiritual growth. The desire of your INNER EIGHT for power is to be blended with your OUTER SIX's talent for serving others. Your power is to be used in the support of others. *Don't criticize yourself or others for not achieving more. Your time will come.*

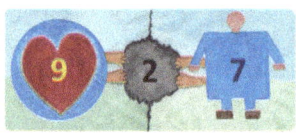
Your INNER NINE is idealistic, loving, and humanitarian. You are also not highly motivated to get out into the world and do something. Your OUTER SEVEN makes it easy to stay hidden away while maintaining a spiritual focus in the world. It may take a while for your true talents to blossom. In the meantime it helps if your INNER NINE finds a rarified place where your OUTER SEVEN can develop its specialized service. There is the danger of being self-critical about lack of achievement. *You are engaged in the ancient argument over whether faith or good works is the key. Give it up. There is a time for each.*

Stress number between motivation and personality – THREE

When THREE is your STRESS NUMBER there is a friction between an even and an odd NUMBER. Since these NUMBERs are not adjacent, your conflict is not as severe. However, there is still the conflict between an introverted and an extroverted nature. The conflict can lead to childish outbursts and unreasonableness. There can also be blocks on self-expression. The balancing energy will be connected to self-expression and freeing yourself up from whatever feels restrictive. *Express what you are feeling.*

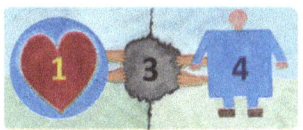

Your INNER ONE is inspired and wishes to charge off in a direction. Your OUTER FOUR works diligently at what is before you. Your INNER ONE wants to do it in a new way. Your OUTER FOUR operates more comfortably by working in more established manners. Eventually there will be an explosion. Communication will always help. Your INNER ONE expands to see a bigger picture of where you are heading, so that your OUTER FOUR can work systematically toward your goal. It will also help to be more communicative with people you are working with. Your INNER ONE might exchange a little of your independence for the possibility of better results. *Lighten up! A little play can unblock any situation.*

Your INNER TWO wants to be sensitive, to have peace, and to stay in the background. Your OUTER FIVE is a bit of a loose cannon, likely to say or do anything and potentially creating one uncomfortable scene after another for your more reticent INNER TWO. To facilitate more ease in this "marriage", your INNER TWO can learn to approach this as a game where your challenge is to balance every action of your OUTER FIVE, without thwarting your efforts. Your INNER TWO is in for a wild ride but can realize your goal of bringing more peace and harmony to the world. *Don't hide your light from the world.*

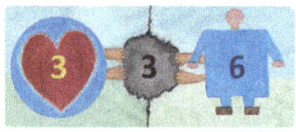
Your INNER THREE wants to play and have fun, but your OUTER SIX acts in a way that shows concern for others and support for the group. This means that some of the expression of your INNER THREE gets suppressed. Your INNER THREE wants to be free from responsibility, but your OUTER SIX always takes it on. On the other hand, your OUTER SIX always attracts an audience for your INNER THREE's performance. Your INNER THREE learns to surrender to your OUTER SIX way of doing things, and finds that it will always be a more fun group with your presence. *Know your means of expression through groups rather than by yourself.*

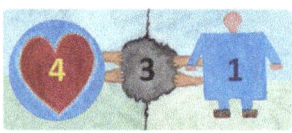
Your INNER FOUR plans carefully toward reaching a goal and then your OUTER ONE chooses your direction, refusing to follow your plan. Your INNER FOUR feels like you can never stick to anything and achieve your goals. You come to learn how to set your goal and then turn your OUTER ONE loose to find the best way there. Big surprises are in store with this combination. Serendipity is an appropriate word to toss about. *Lighten up! A little play can unblock any situation.*

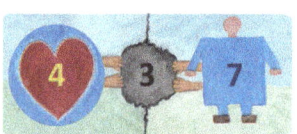
Your INNER FOUR has little attachment as to whether your goals are met alone or in concert with others, as long as they are met. So you have no difficulty with your OUTER SEVEN's lack of sociability but can enjoy the perfection with which you work. There is also a harmony between your INNER FOUR's search for the truth and your OUTER SEVEN's spiritual nature. You may be perceived as a wise person. The only warning is that your combination might become too narrowly focused and work bound. *Be sure to express to others what you have planned, and remember that a little play will keep things freshened up.*

Your INNER FIVE is chomping at the bit for action and adventure while your OUTER TWO is slow to initiate any movement, waiting more on the cues of others before taking action. Your INNER FIVE can find a little faster crowd to hang out with than your OUTER TWO naturally attracts. In some ways your FIVE now has carte blanche, because no matter how wild your plans might be, your OUTER TWO will always provide a safety

net by being sensitive to how things are actually being done. Your INNER FIVE is likely to always be a bit frustrated until you find more creative ways to reach your desires. *Lighten up! A little play can unblock any situation.*

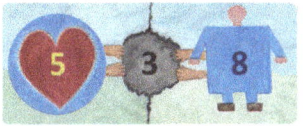

Your INNER FIVE wants movement, change, and experiences while your OUTER EIGHT takes control of the situation. A lot is going to happen. Communication is essential or others may feel manipulated by your energy. You INNER FIVE may feel tied down by the responsibilities your OUTER EIGHT takes on and may not follow through on everything. It is important for your INNER FIVE to choose a direction for your OUTER EIGHT's actions that requires flexibility while letting your OUTER EIGHT lead. Less might be accomplished, but in the long run it will be of greater practical effect. *The best way for you to create the movement you desire is to unleash your creativity.*

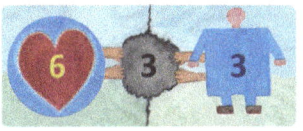

This is a deceptive combination because your OUTER THREE presents a childlike, devil may care way of doing things while your INNER SIX is very serious and caring and wishes to be responsible for others. Your INNER SIX will learn how not to be a scolding parent to yourself and to allow for your OUTER THREE's fun nature to be both a magnet to others and a playful way to dispense the advice that your INNER SIX wants to give to them. Be sure that what is most important gets communicated. *Your service is going to look a lot like having fun. Don't be afraid to let it all out.*

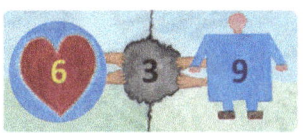

Your combination of the SIX and the NINE is quite interesting, because they both are VIBRATIONs of love. Your INNER SIX represents a more emotionally involved, familiar love while your OUTER NINE is a more universal, unattached love. Either way, there is a challenge. For your INNER SIX there is a desire for belonging, for marriage, for being part of a group. Meanwhile your OUTER NINE is a magnetic personality, but at the same time doesn't tend to form the more intimate bonds that INNER SIX wants. *Communicate, communicate, communicate. Express, express, express.*

There is some concern that your INNER SEVEN wishes that your OUTER FOUR would be more meticulous in what you do. Your OUTER FOUR can work directly with others, without violating the privacy your INNER SEVEN desires. Your true motives may always be hard for others to know, so more self-expression and playfulness will stimulate a fuller realization of your potential. You are seen more as an everyman, but with an INNER wisdom. Your tendency is to be terse. *Be sure to express to others what you have planned, and remember that a little play will keep things freshened up.*

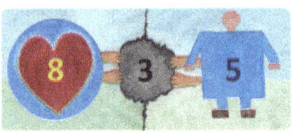
Your INNER EIGHT may be a little frustrated as your OUTER FIVE fails to carry out all your grandiose plans. Your INNER EIGHT could be a little more creative in thinking because your OUTER FIVE is not going to follow any prescribed course. It is valuable to keep in mind that the changes your OUTER FIVE initiates may improve the overall plan. It is also likely to take longer to get there because, even though your OUTER FIVE does tend to find the fastest route, you are also constantly changing directions. *Being more expressive helps you bring about the big changes you want.*

Your combination of the SIX and the NINE is quite interesting, because they both are VIBRATIONs of love. While your INNER NINE is always looking at life in a more universal way than your OUTER SIX expresses, the challenge may be harder for others who want to get closer to your OUTER SIX but find your INNER NINE more distant. Service to others is a central focus. There is always a desire while rendering service to raise the consciousness of others to a higher level. Communication is the key to success. *Share your vision with others constantly.*

With your FOUR STRESS NUMBER your difficulties center on either a lack of discipline and follow through or a stifling rigidity. The answer is either in becoming more organized and finishing what is started, or in loosening up a little while realizing that the purpose of self-disciple is to help you in realizing a goal, not as an end in itself. There is also the danger of your being too hard on yourself and perhaps on others, also. Be sure that you are seeing the truth of what is there. Your stress is between either two odd NUMBERs or two even NUMBERs, in either case enhancing your introversion or extroversion. *Be fair with yourself and others.*

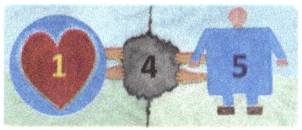

Your combination is screaming out for a little discipline. Your INNER ONE has a singleness of focus that wishes to go off in a new direction, while your OUTER FIVE is going in five directions at once. Your INNER ONE can be frustrated by all of the tangents your OUTER FIVE takes off your original plan. Eventually your INNER ONE learns to accept this nature in your OUTER FIVE and realizes that all that tinkering will improve your original plan. *A little structure will actually bring you more independence.*

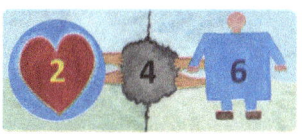

With your INNER TWO calling the shots there is a desire for peace at any cost and a great value placed upon your one-to-one relationships. Meanwhile your OUTER SIX will do whatever is necessary to support the interests of the group as a whole and is more group than individually focused. You can be very hard on yourself and on others when they cross the line. Your INNER TWO could toughen up a little and accept that the struggle for peace is not going to be fought one battle at a time, but with whole groups working it out together. Much more is possible, but it will take a lot of work. *Be sensitive for when "tough love" is appropriate.*

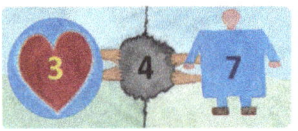
Your INNER THREE wants to have fun, to be in the moment, and to be creative. Your OUTER SEVEN appears to be more serious, reserved, and deep. This makes it harder for your INNER THREE to find playmates. Meanwhile your OUTER SEVEN takes your INNER THREE's ideas and delves into them deeply, taking them more seriously than your INNER THREE had planned. Of course your INNER THREE doesn't plan. Your INNER THREE gradually surrenders to this discipline and enjoys seeing your ideas take form. *Develop a plan for unleashing your creativity. You could add in a little self-discipline.*

With your INNER FOUR there is the drive for truth, hard work, and the setting and reaching of goals. With your OUTER EIGHT, you are less likely to do the work yourself than you are to delegate it to others. This is a challenge for your INNER FOUR because you derive great pleasure from doing it yourself. There is likely to be some guilt until your INNER FOUR recognizes that your goals can be larger and the work you are to do will be more managerial. *Be careful not to be overly structured. Take some time off.*

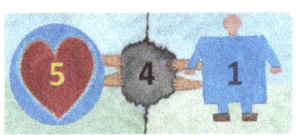
Your OUTER ONE tends to take just one of your INNER FIVE's many ideas and put all of its energy into it. Your INNER FIVE is disappointed because this part of you wants to do so much more. It will help to understand that your OUTER ONE has the tenacity and courage to push that one idea through to completion. Your INNER FIVE just selects the idea you most want your OUTER ONE to grab on to. The discipline will happen if your INNER FIVE can stay a little bit out of the way. *A little structure will bring you more freedom.*

Your combination is explosive and screaming out for a little self-control. Your INNER FIVE wants to try anything and everything and is striving for freedom and opportunities. Your OUTER NINE is open to all possibilities with a willingness to help all people by any suitable means. There is no direction and focus and you are likely to be all over the map until your INNER FIVE chooses a more specific direction to bring change to and allows some sort of self-discipline to take effect toward real-

izing that goal. Still, yours will be an exciting and unpredictable energy. *It is not possible for you to become too structured; allowing a little structure in will help you to move faster.*

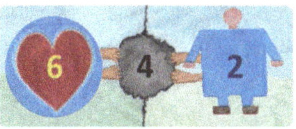

Your INNER SIX places the good of the group and service above all else. You feel as if your OUTER TWO is operating in a much too subtle way. Your INNER SIX wants to be more out there in influencing the dynamics of the group, but your OUTER TWO works so as not to hurt anybody's feelings and so as not to rock the boat. Your INNER SIX learns to develop patience and realizes that your OUTER TWO will eventually get your work done, though in a kindlier, gentler way. *Find a way to speak the truth.*

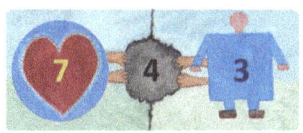

Your INNER SEVEN enjoys solitude and looks on the world in a serious and analytical manner. Your OUTER THREE is the perennial child, fun to be with and very outgoing. Your INNER SEVEN finds your space invaded and your concerns not taken seriously. This is likely to result in your being very hard on yourself until your INNER SEVEN realizes that your OUTER THREE isn't going to change stripes, and you devise ways for your OUTER THREE to express and share with the world your INNER SEVEN's inner workings. *Don't be so hard on yourself. Enjoy!*

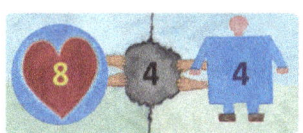

Your INNER EIGHT has large goals and wants everything to be big in your life. Your OUTER FOUR works more slowly and insists upon carrying most of the load, so that less can be accomplished. There is a constant sense of under-achievement until your INNER EIGHT surrenders to your OUTER FOUR's honest pursuit of what is true and what is right. Your INNER EIGHT's big goals can be realized, but the form and the timetable will change as your OUTER FOUR does the work in your dependable manner. Still, your eyes are likely to remain bigger than your stomach. *Working harder will not get you there faster. Give yourself some breathing space.*

Your INNER NINE is humanitarian in outlook, but is less motivated to follow any course of action. You are more likely to perceive an idealistic outcome than to have any idea of how to reach it. Your OUTER FIVE is meanwhile following whatever interest and excitement presents itself. Yours is a well-intentioned but philandering energy until some sort of plan and discipline evolves. Your INNER NINE is always concerned that your OUTER FIVE's heart is not big enough, but your OUTER FIVE does have the ability to effect improvements in the world that your INNER NINE deeply desires. Meanwhile, little is going to happen until a plan is devised and is methodically carried out, or at least as methodically as your OUTER FIVE can be. *It is not possible for you to become too structured; allowing a little structure in will help you to realize some of your dreams.*

Your STRESS NUMBER FIVE is a challenge in flexibility. It may be a case of being blocked by routine and a fixed way of doing things, or it may be that there is too great a tendency to go with every whim or influence. There also may be a pattern of running away from situations rather than dealing with them. The balance comes by recognizing when change is necessary and when flexibility is important. The stress is between an even NUMBER and an odd NUMBER, with the even NUMBER pushing more toward rigidity and the odd more toward freedom. The importance of which of them falls on your MOTIVATION can show in which direction you might be inclined to lean. It may help to promote your ideas. *Be flexible and willing to take chances.*

Your INNER ONE knows what you want and does not want to be deterred. Your OUTER SIX is a people pleaser and goes along with the group. How frustrating for your INNER ONE! You're never going to be happy if you don't get your way. Your OUTER SIX is always going to work for what is best for the group. The obvious solution for your INNER ONE is eventually to run away. As a long range solution, that just doesn't work out. Your INNER ONE learns how to choose the right groups to be with and then uses your personable ways to manipulate others into supporting your goals. Sounds cold and heartless unless your INNER ONE makes sure that others' desires are being met by your solution. *Allowing yourself a little more flexibility each day can prevent you from feeling that you have to run away.*

Ascension Numerology

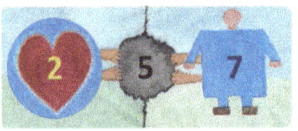
Your INNER TWO cares more about partnership than anything else. Your OUTER SEVEN is more of a loner and is hard to get close to. Your INNER TWO has little personal agenda, being more concerned with supporting others with their goals. Your OUTER SEVEN is focused on perfecting your own skills and wants help only when asked for, and then only for a specific question. The word manipulation keeps coming up with the STRESS NUMBER FIVE. Your INNER TWO can find subtle ways to support those drawn to your OUTER SEVEN. It can be easier if your INNER TWO develops your intuitive side and use it to support the spiritual nature in others. *You want to let others take the lead, but it is time you learn how to take some chances.*

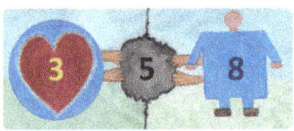
Your INNER THREE wants to express and your OUTER EIGHT provides an audience, as that part of you commands respect. However, your OUTER EIGHT is much more serious and responsible than your INNER THREE wishes to be. Eventually, your INNER THREE wants to run away from the demands that are placed upon your OUTER EIGHT. It is important for your INNER THREE to choose a stage where your OUTER EIGHT can be powerful, but in a playful way. *Make sure that you do a good job with delegating so you have more flexible time available.*

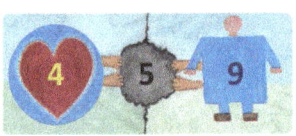
Your INNER FOUR wants to set goals and work toward their successful completion, but your OUTER NINE is more likely to respond to the challenges and wishes of everyone else and does not easily stay on task. The upside is that this has a constantly uplifting effect on the consciousness of your INNER FOUR, but your INNER FOUR will do some work to perceive things that way. Open yourself up to the inevitable changes that your OUTER NINE will bring to you. *Don't let your desire for structure hem you in. Leave room for flexibility and for giant steps.*

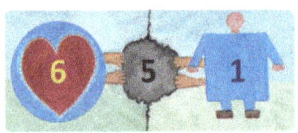
Your INNER SIX wants to belong, to be accepted, and to serve others; while your OUTER ONE acts in your own interest, doesn't seem to care what others think, and is fine going it alone. Your INNER SIX is never going to be happy if you aren't knee deep in a group. It helps if your INNER SIX is willing to manipulate your way into being in charge or at least

not being controlled by the group. It will help if the group is made up of free thinking individualists. Your INNER SIX can provide the glue to hold such a group together. *The key word for you is "stay"; stay put and stay flexible.*

Your INNER SEVEN wants to be left alone to follow your deep interests. Your OUTER TWO is sensitive to everybody else's imbalances and has a hard time saying no. It is important to your INNER SEVEN to follow your interests wherever they lead, so it helps to nurture friends with like interests. It may be that your OUTER TWO will let others seem to take the lead and perhaps get the credit. Your INNER SEVEN will handle this best if you aim to develop your spiritual nature. This spiritual focus can then be used in the support of others. *Be more opportunistic in letting others know all that you have to offer.*

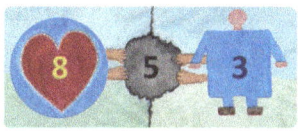

Your INNER EIGHT has large aspirations, while your OUTER THREE is a playful child. Others are not taking your OUTER THREE very seriously, which makes it difficult for your INNER EIGHT to exercise your power. Your INNER EIGHT realizes that your best path to influencing others is through the expressions of your OUTER THREE. This is leadership through inspiration. *Give yourself the freedom to be spontaneous.*

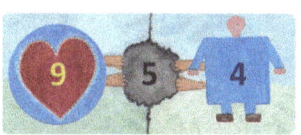

Your INNER NINE is idealistic and unfocused. Your OUTER FOUR is reliable, trustworthy, and hardworking. While your NINE has no difficulties with that, your goals are loftier. It's not enough to do well without a positive outcome for the larger world. Your INNER NINE constantly find ways to expand your OUTER FOUR's horizons. Your INNER NINE is also being forced by your OUTER FOUR to get off your dreamy couch and to do something. Change is in the air. This can help your INNER NINE feel a larger sense of contribution to humanity. *Movement is called for. Guide it toward changes you would like to see happen.*

Ascension Numerology

Your stress is related to the pressures of the group. With STRESS NUMBER SIX, your conflict centers on the extremes of letting yourself be controlled by peer pressure or contrarily to avoid working with others altogether out of the fear of giving up autonomy. At any rate, your struggle is about working with others and a sense of belonging. Your stress is between likes, that is, between two odd NUMBERs or two even NUMBERs. There are only splits between the lower and higher VIBRATIONs, with the challenges being greater when your higher VIBRATION is the MOTIVATION. *Put the group first without forgetting that you are a part of it.*

Your INNER ONE is strongly led only by your divine guidance, while with your OUTER SEVEN you work better on your own to develop and refine your skills. Your INNER ONE pushes your OUTER SEVEN more out into the world, because that is where your goals lie. All of this forces a working together with others because nobody can accomplish anything alone. Your challenge is to maintain integrity while also maintaining a working relationship with others. People respect your OUTER SEVEN, but are a little surprised at the intractability of your INNER ONE. *To realize your goal, involve other people.*

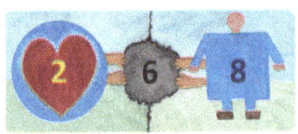

Your INNER TWO wants companionship, to be sensitive, and to be in a supportive position with others. Your OUTER EIGHT acts powerfully, is not particularly warm, and tends to take charge of situations. This makes it difficult for your INNER TWO to have the intimacy you desire. You learn to achieve that end surreptitiously, by sensing the subtle aspirations of those being worked with and by supporting each member of the team to reach their potential. Few people will suspect the softie that lingers within. *Let yourself be powerful. Be of service.*

Stress number between motivation and personality – SIX

Your INNER THREE wants to be the eternal child, to play and be creative. Your OUTER NINE appears to have a certain wisdom and you seem to be generous and selfless with your time and energy. This is all a little too much for your INNER THREE, for you are likely to walk, if not run, away from responsibilities. The group is crucial. Your INNER THREE wants playmates and everyone sees a little of themselves in your OUTER NINE. Your INNER THREE finds the group you are willing to stay with and allows your OUTER NINE to act out the role you wish to play. *You have a great flair for the dramatic. Express it in some form of service.*

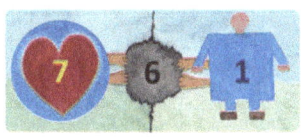
With your INNER SEVEN, your drive is not so strong, but there is a deep desire for perfection and spiritual growth. Your OUTER ONE is more abrasive and independent. You are going to be in charge, not only because of your skills, but because there will be no taking a back seat. Your challenge is in working with others. Your INNER SEVEN knows that your way is the best and your OUTER ONE will not be stopped. As your OUTER ONE develops the skill of people management, there are no limits. *In order for you to develop things to the depth you desire, bring in other people.*

You want to exert power in your environment, but your OUTER TWO is gentle, sensitive, and not at all aggressive. People enjoy being with your OUTER TWO but hardly perceive you as a powerful authority to be respected. The upside for your INNER EIGHT is that your OUTER TWO attracts people. Your power, however, is to be exerted in subtle ways. Both VIBRATIONs find their meeting place in the milieu of group activity. Your INNER EIGHT wants to control the group, but your OUTER TWO makes sure that everybody is comfortable. The fun begins. *Put service to others above your personal ambitions.*

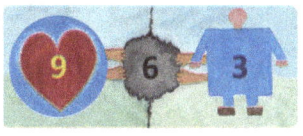
Your INNER NINE wants to make the world a better place, but does not know how to go about doing it. You are a bit impatient with your OUTER THREE to whom everything can seem to be a joke. Your INNER NINE is going to change the world through inspiration and THREE is just the one to express your NINE's dreams to others. On the road there, your INNER NINE seeks to find the right support group, because your OUTER THREE is always going to be a little of a prima donna. There is no danger of anything ever being either dull or overly practical. *You will only realize your dreams when you bring them down to earth in the form of service.*

Ascension Numerology

This STRESS NUMBER is involved with questions of faith and issues of perfectionism. The pairings match a higher VIBRATION with a lower. Your challenge involves going more deeply within yourself and moving through fear. There may be issues of over-rationalizing things and being too much in your mind. Your path to wholeness will come through an increase of faith — in self, in the unprovable, in intuition. *Trust that things are happening perfectly.*

Your INNER ONE knows what you want and wishes to move unquestioningly in that direction. Your OUTER EIGHT easily assumes leadership to carry out the vision of your INNER ONE. There is some friction as your INNER ONE is not concerned with the administration and completion of your idea, but wants to go start something new. *Outer success can come easily to you; it will only be fulfilling when you are able to find a larger reason.*

Your INNER TWO wants peace and cooperation. You want partnership and to stay comfortably in the background. Your OUTER NINE is a dramatic character, drawing all types to your field of energy. Your INNER TWO can be overwhelmed by the exposure and wish to hide away. Spiritual development is essential to your success. You can become powerful in helping to bring peace to others, as your OUTER NINE has the ability to reach many. *Learn to replace fear and doubt with love and trust.*

Your INNER EIGHT wishes to use your power in order to create a just and fair world. Your OUTER ONE tends to act in a more self-centered fashion. Though your combination is likely to reach success in your endeavors, your INNER EIGHT may be frustrated by not having a greater impact. A crisis in faith is likely to follow. Your INNER EIGHT eventually finds a more spiritually directed cause that your OUTER ONE can grab by the horns and run with. *Outer success can come easily to you, but it will only be fulfilling when you are able to find a larger reason.*

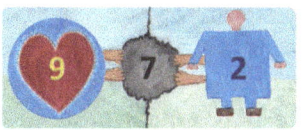
Your INNER NINE has big dreams, but your OUTER TWO does not assert itself in the world strongly enough to make things happen. In a way, the dreamy side of your INNER NINE can be okay with that, but still there is a sense of leading a worthless life. Your answer is through spiritual development. Along with the increase of self-love that growth brings, will come more self-confidence for your OUTER TWO. Your OUTER TWO can become an enormously attractive energy then, drawing others to you as the moth to the light, while your INNER NINE sees your large humanitarian goals realized. Your main stress comes from a tendency to hide feelings in order to make others comfortable. *Spiritual growth is essential to your success. Learn to replace fear and doubt with love and trust.*

Ascension Numerology

Your STRESS NUMBER EIGHT brings challenges centered in the very use of power. Is it for good or evil, or is that even the highest question to ask? Understanding the true nature of power is central to unleashing the tremendous potential of these combinations. Mastery of the NUMBER EIGHT and an understanding of how manifestation truly takes place are important for you. *Remember that love is the power that manifests everything.*

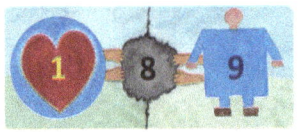

With your pairing you have the alpha and the omega. Your INNER ONE is the beginning. You are guided to new creations, answering only to your own vision. Your OUTER NINE is the VIBRATION of endings and completion. You act with no personal agenda and are all things to all people. Your self-centered INNER ONE can be very frustrated by the magnanimity of your OUTER NINE. Your path to integration involves looking at what the intervening time between beginnings and endings is all about. What is with all of this physical-ness? Your INNER ONE learns to be okay with letting go of everything it creates. *You will always manifest whatever is required in order to pursue your goal.*

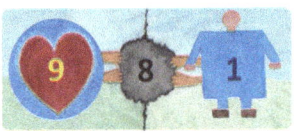

Your INNER NINE is, always, the idealistic dreamer, coming in with no agenda and a good deal of wisdom. Your OUTER ONE acts in a very independent way, with no apparent concern for others. Your selfless INNER NINE seems to turn into a selfish OUTER ONE. It is important to understand the laws of manifestation. Your OUTER ONE can then move from being a model for selfishness to being a model for independence and self-reliance. Your INNER NINE can show the world how it is done, so that others can learn to be equally strong. *Be willing to be powerful to manifest your dreams.*

MORE ABOUT

STRESS NUMBERs can be calculated between any two POSITIONs in your CHART (see "COMPUTATIONS" on page 281). You can also look at the STRESS NUMBER between the VIBRATION in a particular POSITION in your CHART and the VIBRATION in the same POSITION in another's CHART (say between both of your MOTIVATIONs). This is valuable when doing a relationship reading. For the present I have only looked at the stress between your INNER and OUTER natures. Later we will deal with the STRESS NUMBERs between the MOTIVATION and the LIFE PATH.

I will continue to talk about your MOTIVATION and your PERSONALITY as separate entities, because that is what the language allows. The ultimate goal, however, is to see yourself as a unified whole. Having a different NUMBER for your heart VIBRATION than you have for your OUTER way of doing things causes a certain amount of confusion. You see yourself one way and the world sees you in another. You want to approach the world in a certain manner and yet you find yourself acting in a different way. There is a residual tension between these two VIBRATIONs. Bring that into balance, so that you can operate efficiently and experience joy in your life.

Since the PERSONALITY truly begins to express itself around puberty, this added to the confusion about adolescence. "Who am I?" you asked yourself." "Why am I acting differently when I'm around my peers?" you wondered. It wasn't just hormones. Your PERSONALITY was kicking in and you were first beginning to experience the stress between it and your MOTIVATION.

I have given you a sample of how each STRESS NUMBER might be read, followed by suggestions for each combination. I cannot overly "stress" that the examples I have given to you are just starting points. They are the first word, but never the last. Use your intuition and your knowledge of the NUMBERs, of the POSITIONs, and of yourself to go deeper. Go back and review the NUMBERs or the POSITIONs as often as is helpful. You can read how you would be different if your INNER and OUTER VIBRATIONs were flipped. This will help you in grasping your own pattern. Though you may be interested only in reading your particular combination; if you choose to peruse others you may pick up an increased understanding of all nine VIBRATIONs. There are also tidbits of general information sprinkled throughout, so a quick scan might be helpful in surprising ways.

One final reminder: if you have a KARMIC NUMBER for one or both of these VIBRATIONs there is a major effect. It always throws a monkey wrench into the situation. If it is in the MOTIVATION, it makes it much more difficult for you to get along with yourself and to feel satisfied, and if it occurs in the PERSONALITY, it makes it harder for others to get along with you and for you to work effectively with them.

The end goal is to have your INNER and OUTER natures working in perfect harmony, where you listen to your MOTIVATION without blocking it and you allow your PERSONALITY to fully express itself.

INTEGRATED SELF

GETTING IT ALL TOGETHER

The INTEGRATED SELF POSITION represents you when you have it all together. It shows your highest potential, your real talent that you can share with the world. It does not tend to operate in a negative way; it either operates strongly, less strongly, or hardly at all. The strength with which it acts depends upon how well you have resolved the tension between your MOTIVATION and your PERSONALITY. Your success at activating the balancing aspects of your STRESS NUMBER determines how fully your INTEGRATED SELF is actuated. This is a significant POSITION to look at in terms of your vocation or calling. A general reading for each NUMBER is given, as well as additional information for each possible MOTIVATION-PERSONALITY pairing that could lead to that INTEGRATED SELF. If your INTEGRATED SELF VIBRATION is KARMIC, the development of your talent will be slowed as you balance your karma. Read more deeply about your KARMIC NUMBER. In the readings that follow, the pronouns "you" and "your "are asked to perform extraordinary duties. Because there are two equal aspects of you, an INNER and an OUTER self, I am using the schizophrenic sounding "you" to represent each part. The wording may sound confusing, so read it over until you feel the two distinct parts of yourself. *It is through the INTEGRATED SELF that divinity shares your unique talent with others.*

You came here to blaze new trails. You demonstrate courage and integrity. Though your purpose is to follow the inner direction that you have been given, you also provide inspiration for others. You model how to be true to yourself as you follow your own inner light. *You know how to stand up for yourself and how to keep your focus on reaching your goal.*

Though there is singleness to your focus, there is universality to your mission. Many are drawn to follow you. Be a leader without being influenced by your followers. Teach them how to fish so that you are not weighed down by their demands.

Your gentle INNER TWO moves fully into your ONE INTEGRATED SELF's strength and independence. It's a long road to get there. You will still be bringing peace to the world, but it is a peace that comes through inner strength. Your power could come through intuitive sensitivity. Though you will be working with others, follow your own guidance.

This is interesting as the playfulness of your INNER THREE becomes focused and sharpened through your OUTER SEVEN, resulting in a truly unique application. Your trio of odd NUMBERs is a true original, unaffected by nearly all outside influences — as odd NUMBERs are more introspective and therefore less likely to be affected by the desires of others.

Your combination is slow to find your unique path. However, once you build up momentum, nothing will be able to stop your movement. Your INNER FOUR is pleased to have a clear direction which will involve your OUTER SIX's service to others, but on your own terms.

Integrated self – ONE

Yours is a "double". Because there is nothing but FIVE, inside and out, you will have a tendency to be extreme, to be the rolling stone that gathers no moss. It will take some time before you stop jumping from thing to thing and find your purpose in life. Then, even though your focus will be singular, your options, approaches, and flexibility will be impressive.

Your INNER SIX wants so much to be part of a team that it is hard to find your individual direction and to go it alone. Your OUTER FOUR will slowly build up a body of achievement that leads your INNER SIX to realize that you can only serve others as you wish by going it alone.

Your INNER SEVEN is finally drawn out into the world by your OUTER THREE and the result is the application of your deep thinking and perfectionism in a totally new direction. While your OUTER THREE is able to keep everyone's attention, your INNER SEVEN sneaks right past them to show them something unexpected.

Your INNER EIGHT's learned patience finally pays off. Your OUTER TWO's sensitivity to others and your balancing energy has led your INNER EIGHT to an unanticipated place of an independent expression of power. The power is thrust upon you because of your deservedness; rather than being grabbed — as your INNER EIGHT would be more naturally inclined to do.

Yours is an integration that will be slow coming into maturity. Your INNER NINE cannot choose a direction, but you are displeased with whatever direction your OUTER ONE takes off in. Your OUTER ONE has no patience and doesn't want to wait for instructions. Eventually you find a direction your OUTER ONE and INNER NINE agree on and the world will be a better place for it.

You are a peacemaker. You can see both sides of any situation as well as feel where both sides are coming from. You are a healer who can sense what another is holding on to and reflect it to them in such a way that it can be received and then released. Your sensitivity is intuitive or psychic as well as emotional. *Your only agenda is peace.*

With ONE as both your INNER and OUTER natures, this is the farthest away you could start on your journey to your TWO INTEGRATED SELF. You want to follow only your inner voice and that is just what you end up doing. Because you have a double (both an INNER and an OUTER ONE), you have nothing to balance. Nobody can stop you from doing exactly as you please. Eventually, you hear the divinity within so well that you realize there is only love, that nothing else matters. You shine this unconditional love on everyone you meet and the rest is history.

You have a relatively easy transition to your TWO INTEGRATED SELF. You have simply raised the energy to a higher level. Your OUTER NINE has opened you up to a bigger world. Your TWOs may be elevated to a higher level of intuitive sensitivity. Many are drawn to you. They can see themselves reflected in you. You handle them gently and with great love and attention.

The balancing act that your INNER THREE has done to adjust to your OUTER EIGHT now gives you the ability to bring anything into balance. People respect your tough OUTER EIGHT exterior, but feel your INNER THREE warmth and joy beneath the surface. You are inspired to say the right words at the right time, and people are able to receive what is offered.

People feel your OUTER SEVEN wisdom. They sense that INNER FOUR honesty and truth lies beneath it. You are not the most verbal of people, but your words are golden. Your presence calms and stabilizes any situation. Though you can work on a one-to-one basis, you also can bring peace to larger situations through finely developed communications.

Integrated self – TWO

Once your INNER FIVE has learned to cooperate with your OUTER SIX, everything else is easy. Your INNER FIVE enjoys bringing change to others. You like helping them find the same peace you have found. Your OUTER role may seem to be one of being a particular type of caregiver. You do that well, but the real work is taking place on a more subtle, intuitive level.

You are a smooth salesperson with a heart of gold. Your OUTER FIVE can sell others on following their best interests. The tendency of your INNER SIX to want to control gives way to a knack for helping others listen to themselves. They may be surprised at how well you read them and the deep sense of caring that you have.

People trust your OUTER FOUR's honesty, your hard working nature, and your dedication. You seem to have a cornucopia of common sense. Though few detect your INNER SEVEN's deep inner wisdom, they turn to you in times of trouble and find peace in your presence.

You are so much fun to be with that you disarm people. Though they may not sense your INNER EIGHT power, your OUTER THREE guides them to find their own peace and to sense themselves more fully. You are particularly effective in working with highly stressed individuals.

Your OUTER TWO has a way of making everyone comfortable. You make them feel that you are on their side and they are your favorite person. You help to bring out the best in them and to increase their estimation of what is possible for them. Your INNER NINE changes the world one person at a time.

Ascension Numerology

You are here to inspire others through your expression. This might be through words, pictures, sounds, or any other medium. You show others the potential of what they can accomplish. You maintain an eternally youthful spirit and are particularly effective at communicating with younger generations. *You live in the moment and demonstrate to others that life is meant to be enjoyed.*

You are what could be called the perfect triangle. Your INNER masculine energy marries your OUTER feminine energy producing your eternal child. Your INNER ONE propels you into the playful expression of your THREE, but your TWO softens the impact and removes any hard edges. Your ONE creates having your way through expression rather than through action.

You are what could be called the perfect triangle. Your INNER feminine marries your OUTER masculine to produce your THREE child. Your INNER TWO finds that the way to achieve the peace you desire is through the power of expression. Your OUTER ONE is going to follow your own drummer, but your message will be one of cooperation.

Your INNER THREE wants to be playful and expressive and not take things too seriously. Your OUTER NINE takes things to a whole other level so that your expression becomes a universal message that offers light to all. Your INNER THREE is the eternal child, all grown up but as playful as ever.

The road to your THREE INTEGRATED SELF is likely to be long. Your INNER FOUR is all work and no play. Your OUTER EIGHT often takes upon itself large responsibilities. It is not until your INNER FOUR allows for more changes to enter the scene and permits your OUTER EIGHT to lighten its load by becoming more administrative that the space for creativity opens. Your THREE INTEGRATED SELF now broadcasts your INNER FOUR's truth with your OUTER EIGHT's powerful voice.

Integrated self — THREE

The expression of your THREE INTEGRATED SELF carries the refinement and the spirituality of your OUTER SEVEN, while being driven by your INNER FIVE's desire to bring change and improvement. People may not realize what hit them, but they like it. There is a purity in your message that is so inspiring, but it is also carefully crafted to reach the heart of its target.

Your double (both INNER and OUTER SIX) presents an extremity of group focus. A KARMIC NUMBER in the "double" VIBRATION would be particularly challenging to deal with, affecting both self and others. You are all about serving others, loving others, and putting the group first. Somehow your SIXness morphs into your THREEness. The transition will be slow and gradual, but the result is a lightening up, a letting go of controlling things and a loving expression that supports, and is supported by, the entire group.

This is quite a journey, traveling from the solitude and seriousness of your INNER SEVEN all the way to the playfulness and expression of your THREE INTEGRATED SELF. Your INNER SEVEN's acceptance of your OUTER FIVE's way of dealing with the world is what allows this to happen. There is nothing subtle as your OUTER FIVE brazenly sells your INNER SEVEN's deeply thought out reality through the most efficient means possible — mass communication.

Your INNER EIGHT gradually realizes that your OUTER FOUR will always work in a steady methodical manner and the only way to have the powerful effect you seek is through creativity and expression. Your message is trusted by others because of your OUTER FOUR's honesty and reliability, but the impact is magnified by the enormity of scope of your INNER EIGHT. Mountains can be moved.

Your INNER NINE comes down to earth a little and find its service on a smaller scale where your OUTER THREE can play at the same time. As your OUTER THREE finds your true voice, the scope can expand without limits. Wherever NINE is involved, things end up moving to the next level. Never has unselfish service to humanity looked like so much fun.

You are the world's reality check. You were born mature, but your body and age have now caught up. You are honest; you are dependable. Your word is golden. You cannot be bought. With you on board the task will be completed on time and done as well as required. And you love it that way. *You carry with you the blueprints for building things that work.*

The world can have little influence over you. Your INNER ONE follows your own lead while your OUTER THREE fools people with your youth and playfulness. When maturity finally hits there is an enormous creative energy for implementing your INNER ONE's directions from the divine. The integrity of your INNER ONE doesn't waiver as your OUTER THREE broadcasts it to the world. You can take the information to the bank.

Your double (both INNER and OUTER TWO) leads first to extreme energy and then to unexpected results. You have a great sensitivity and a strong desire to stay in the background, while supporting others to be all they can be. Your skills are developed to such a level that you have an intuitive knowing of how to support everyone in every situation. The result is a mirror of truth in which all can see themselves.

Your INNER THREE never wants to grow up, but your OUTER ONE acts independently and takes care of yourself. So, your INNER THREE is forced to grow up, but you still want the world to be a playground for everyone. Your resulting FOUR INTEGRATED SELF both inspires people and forces them to take stock of themselves and see if they are being true to their heart's mission.

Your INNER FOUR was born mature but with a more limited set of goals and possibilities. Your OUTER NINE takes it to another level. What started out as personal truth becomes cosmic truth. The building is for the good of humanity. The foundations are deep and broad. There is enough support for everyone.

Integrated self – FOUR

When your INNER FIVE spirit of change acts through the executive power of your OUTER EIGHT an interesting thing happens. Organizations don't change direction easily and the instilling of new habits can help make the change permanent. This requires systems and discipline. Your INNER FIVE realizes that if it becomes more of a FOUR it can bring about the institutional changes it desires. There will be great flexibility in the forms.

Your OUTER SEVEN acts in a way that makes it hard for your INNER SIX to feel the group inclusion you so much desire. The result is that your INNER SIX steers your OUTER SEVEN's abilities in a direction where they are useful to others. The abstractness of your OUTER SEVEN becomes of great FOUR practicality to people. It may also raise their spiritual sense, which is always of immense practical value. The truth sets you free.

People are drawn to your OUTER SIX and you serve them well, but you would rather be left alone to hone your INNER SEVEN skills and to follow your spiritual path. The people don't go away and you can't stop yourself from being of service, so you are forced to share the deepest part of you. The spiritual and esoteric become every day, practical, and useful. It may take a while for all of this to percolate, but the tangible results are worth waiting for.

With your INNER EIGHT you have a desire for power and to work in large ways. Your OUTER FIVE is more of a salesperson than a manager, and you have difficulty staying in the same place for long. Your INNER EIGHT settles for allowing your power to be used to create the kind of change that supports others in finding their own personal power. This leads to the taking of practical steps and the development of new habits. Good intentions are not enough, so your OUTER FIVE manipulates people into doing what is good for them.

Your INNER NINE is by nature as impractical as your OUTER FOUR is by nature practical. Your INNER NINE has no choice but to guide your OUTER FOUR's work ethic in the direction of universal service. So, your FOUR INTEGRATED SELF is as hard working, reliable, and determined as your OUTER FOUR, but you are guided by the idealism of your INNER NINE. Slow to reach full maturity, but your potential is infinite.

Without you everything would become stagnant. Necessary improvements would not take place. You are the pragmatist. It must work and it must work better, or you are not interested. There is no fancy philosophizing. What is there is a flexibility that accepts nothing at face value. The eternal question is "How can it be made better?" Then you sell it to the world and the world cannot resist your charm or your idea. *You are the agent for change in the world.*

Your INNER ONE wants to build a whole new world. Your OUTER FOUR works to keep things as they are. Your INNER ONE lowers your sights a hair and lets your OUTER FOUR operate more in your comfort zone. Instead of a whole new invention, you pick a part of what is and set your OUTER FOUR to work building an innovation. This is changing the world one small solid step at a time. The steps will grow bigger over time.

The changes you bring about will come more in the area of human relations. Your INNER TWO wants change only in ways that lead to more harmony and peace between people. Your OUTER THREE acts in often irresponsible ways but is fun and inspiring to be around. Your INNER TWO is able to steer things in such a way as to help your OUTER THREE's sense of timing and sensitivity. Your message can be received and behavior changes occur. It will take a while to get this dance down.

Your INNER THREE isn't particularly concerned with changing others but you are a channel for positive ideas. Your OUTER TWO holds back your expression until you feel the time is right. Because of the perfection of your timing, your message can be received. You can become an excellent counselor, helping others make changes they desire.

Your INNER FOUR wants to work hard with what is in front of you, building slowly towards your goals. Your OUTER ONE is a spontaneous and strong willed actor, often leaving tasks unfinished to move off in a new direction. Your INNER FOUR learns to choose a goal that allows your OUTER ONE to have more independence and more singleness of focus. The result is change that is rooted in a carefully formed foundation, but is thrust firmly out to the world.

Integrated self – FIVE

Your INNER FIVE wants nothing more than to have changes happen. Your OUTER NINE acts for change on a more idealistic basis, but lacks follow through. Your INNER FIVE narrows your focus to more humanitarian actions. Something is found that draws your INNER FIVE's abiding interest but carries with it wide, limitless, opportunity for the world to become a better place. Big changes can happen.

Your INNER SIX wants to be part of a group and serve others in and through that bond. Your OUTER EIGHT naturally assumes leadership of the group, but loses some of the close bonding your INNER SIX desires. Your INNER SIX realizes it is better to sacrifice some of your emotional desires in order to allow your OUTER EIGHT to serve others in the highest way. Then your OUTER EIGHT empowers others to change in ways that promote their personal power and increase their service to others.

Your double (both INNER and OUTER SEVEN) produces an unexpected conclusion. The natural desire of your SEVENs to be reclusive and to delve deeply into the perfection of thoughts, ideas, and skills is amplified. There is nothing to draw you out into the real world. Yet, what you develop in that laboratory becomes a great catalyst for change in the world. You travel the entire distance from esoteric to highly functional.

Your INNER EIGHT's frustration with your OUTER SIX's scope of vision is bridged by your willingness to use your OUTER SIX's ability to work with others to foment positive change in the world. Your INNER EIGHT wants to see power used effectively. Your OUTER SIX is able to help others to do just that. Your work is best carried out within organizations.

Your INNER NINE is an idealistic dreamer wanting to make the world a better place, but having no idea where to begin. Your OUTER FIVE is constantly active with one thing and then another. The key is linking your OUTER FIVE's motion to your INNER NINE's dreams. It will be worth waiting for that to develop. Your OUTER FIVE's boundless energy and flexibility will lead to large changes that will benefit all, with your OUTER FIVE also being a tireless promoter of the new.

You are the world's doctor, nurse, healer, social worker, therapist, teacher, chef, champion, and friend in need. You work to strengthen the ties of communities, workplaces, and families. You labor tirelessly to lighten the load of others. People (and then animals) come first. Though you care about all people, your primary concern is with your own backyard. There is plenty there to keep you busy. *You are here to serve others and to make the world a more caring and loving place.*

Your INNER ONE marches to your own drummer, uninfluenced by others. Your OUTER FIVE is impulsive, following every new thing and trying to experience it all. You are good at getting your way. Somewhere you gain some self-discipline and some focus of working toward a goal. That goal ends up being tied to the serving of others. You will do so in a unique way. It may look manipulative to some, but it works and people are greatly benefited.

You are ideally suited for service to others. Your INNER TWO is sensitive to the wants and challenges of others. Your OUTER FOUR is a tireless and dependable worker in the service of others. There is a no nonsense approach where your FOUR lets others know where they can pitch in to their own and others' betterment, but this is easily forgiven because of the 100% effort that you give.

You have a double dose of THREE (INNER and OUTER). Your THREEs want to have fun and to be creative and expressive. There is nothing practical or responsible. You are the eternal child who others cannot help but to like and to enjoy being around. So what happens? One of those miracles of maturity finds your THREE's creativity and talent used for the inspiration and general lifting of the spirit of all who come to play. You become the funnest teacher in town. Play on!

You are ideally suited for service to others. Your OUTER TWO is soft and likable while the underlying drive of your INNER FOUR pushes relentlessly. You are the salt of the earth; your whole life is built around service to others. You don't really know how to play and need to be careful not to overwork. You are a good person to know.

Integrated self – SIX

Your INNER FIVE is more interested in your own experience than in focusing on others. Your OUTER ONE acts independently rather than going along with the group. You begin to develop some discipline. Your INNER FIVE narrows your scope so that your OUTER ONE can act in your single-focused way. Somehow, after some time, you become an engine for change who provides direct service to people. What a dynamo!

The service that comes from your combination raises your efforts to a broader geographic and ethnic group. Your OUTER NINE brings an all-encompassing feel for humanity, bridging all gaps. Your INNER SIX desires family, but humanity becomes family; your personal family may find itself taking the back seat (if it gets a seat at all). Great humanitarian service is offered. Your life is dedicated to others.

Your INNER SEVEN is less focused on service to others and group activity than any other VIBRATION. However, your OUTER EIGHT moves to a place of power within the group, which necessitates involvement with others. Your INNER SEVEN's focus becomes one of how to become the best administrator as well as how to bring a spiritual energy to the work. Your administrative job is to maximize the potential of the group and each of its members. In this way your focus becomes one of SIXness.

Your INNER EIGHT wants power. Your OUTER SEVEN works in a more isolated fashion. In order for your INNER EIGHT to realize your dreams, you will find yourself working with others. Though your OUTER SEVEN is somewhat aloof, you become both good at working with others and focused on dealing in a powerful way with their spiritual development. Though you always maintain some distance from the group, the group benefits greatly.

It may take you a while to find your place of service. Your INNER NINE is a dreamer, but impractical and you are a little hesitant to get your hands dirty. However, your OUTER SIX is always helping others. Eventually the right place is found where the vastness of your INNER NINE's vision can be played out. Though you work well with others and are a true team player, there is always some sense of being on a different page. Still, a great humanitarian service unfolds.

Through your influence, people are encouraged to look more deeply within themselves and to question what is really important. Even if the focus is not overtly spiritual you are a specialist and a perfectionist in the highest sense of the word. You go deep rather than wide and show others how to fully appreciate the specialness that is before them. You both model and teach trust in the perfection of what is happening in life. *You are a catalyst for greater faith.*

As your INNER ONE learns that you can only get your way if your way includes serving others, an interesting transformation takes place. Though your OUTER SIX is always going to automatically come to the aid of those around you, your INNER ONE still wants to follow your own voice. Increasingly your voice is a spiritually oriented one. Your INNER ONE is never lacking in courage, but it is a big step to trust that the places that life and others lead you to, are perfect. Now it is your turn to touch others as deeply.

Your INNER TWO wants a calm peaceful ride, but your OUTER FIVE offers everything but that. There is no constancy so your INNER TWO finds solace in bringing peace to each moment on your ride. This requires the development of faith that there is a method in the myriad changes. As your faith grows, your FIVE convince others to come on board — while your INNER TWO luxuriates in the joy of sharing the peace with others and watching them find balance in their own lives.

The singleness of focus that is necessary for you with your STRESS NUMBER ONE is that of faith and spirituality. Your INNER THREE wants to express and this is your message. Coming through your OUTER FOUR, your message is trustworthy and down to earth. Your OUTER FOUR walks the walk before it talks the talk. Once you find your rhythm (which might take quite a while) your focus of spirituality becomes a natural fit.

Your OUTER THREE does not easily inspire faith and trust. Your INNER FOUR sees your best laid plans poorly executed. Ultimately, you find the message that your OUTER THREE can deliver. The message is one of faith and trust. Your INNER FOUR will take its time getting there. Your OUTER THREE will resist growing up. All will happen in good time. All will benefit from it.

Integrated self – SEVEN

Your OUTER TWO's constant thwarting of your INNER FIVE's wild desires provides a long and difficult challenge. Your INNER FIVE is finally left little choice but to make its changes internal ones instead of external. Others are drawn to the great peace that your OUTER TWO now projects. As your OUTER TWO senses the openings in each individual you meet, your INNER FIVE's agenda of inner spiritual change is communicated. This could lead to a larger effect through the use of writing or some other media.

Your INNER SIX wants to be deeply involved in the everyday lives of others. You have little innate draw to questions of faith or to delving deeply into things or to perfecting yourself and your skills. Your OUTER ONE acts independently without stopping to see what others might desire or lack. The spiritual focus is the only place where your VIBRATIONs can find a common ground. Your INNER SIX is into it as a way to serve others. Your OUTER ONE's integrity can align with the purity of your SEVEN faith. Others are inspired by your model and have a desire to follow.

Your INNER SEVEN wants nothing more than to be fulfilled with a lifetime of spiritual focus. The actual expression of that will come as somewhat of a surprise as your OUTER NINE ups the ante by outing your INNER SEVEN's energy to the wider world. It is part of your INNER SEVEN's learning of trust to operate in this more public way. Your spiritual growth is available to be shared with even more people.

Your double (both INNER and OUTER EIGHT) wants power and acts in a powerful way. It doesn't seem like anything can stand in your way. So what do you do with such a power? Power for power's sake is a dead end. Ultimately, your EIGHTs find a higher purpose. When you throw all of your weight behind spiritual development, powerful change is going to happen. Many will be shown how to use spiritual power.

Your INNER NINE dreams big and your OUTER SEVEN develops that dream as you slowly perfect yourself and your product. The world senses the wisdom and depth of your OUTER SEVEN as the immense scale of your INNER NINE slowly unfolds. Your OUTER SEVEN humbly goes about your tasks of transforming the faith of others.

Ascension Numerology

You understand the truth of manifestation and understand that each individual incarnated with unique skills which will benefit all others when expressed. Your job is to help them discover their talents and then to have the courage to stop doing other things with their lives and to start doing what they came to do. Of course you do this for yourself first. *You came to teach others how to use their own power.*

Your INNER ONE wants to be independent and to follow your INNER voice. Your OUTER SEVEN acts in an individualistic manner, honing your skills while staying somewhat aloof. Your OUTER SEVEN moves progressively into a spiritual direction as your INNER ONE's emphasis is increasingly on merging with the creative force. Empowering others becomes your singular focus. Others are impressed with your dignity and courage as you move into your place of true power.

You came here to serve others. Your INNER TWO wants to cooperate with others and is happy to stay out of the limelight, while acting as the support person. Your OUTER SIX, however, is right in the midst of things as a server, helper, and opinion dispenser. Your EIGHT INTEGRATED SELF is slow to develop. Over time the combined sensitivity of your INNER TWO and the loving support of your OUTER SIX lead to superior ability to support others in becoming stronger. You are a leader with great heart.

Your INNER THREE wants to express and inspire. Your OUTER FIVE acts in such a way as to bring about change. Though your INNER/OUTER VIBRATIONs don't come from a place of leadership, you end up there. Your OUTER FIVE sells your INNER THREE's inspired message to others. The message includes the idea that you are here to have fun and to make the most out of your experience.

Not only do you have the "double" FOUR, but FOUR and EIGHT aren't all that far apart. It is largely a question of scale. Your FOURs are happy doing everything yourself. You build slowly and surely, wanting to prove things for yourself first. Eventually you claim your full power, step things up several notches, and become a true leader. You then become a powerful teacher of truth, a truth with tangible results.

Integrated self – EIGHT

While your INNER FIVE is adventurous and always seeking something new, your OUTER THREE has little follow through and is no hurry to grow up. So we wait and wait to see what develops. The wait is worthwhile. Your OUTER THREE inspires people to get out of their ruts and take some chances. You let them know that life is too short to be bogged down in "shoulds" and being "responsible". "Take your power. I have and look how much fun I'm having!" is your message to the world.

Your INNER SIX wants to help everybody and for the world to be in one big happy family. Your OUTER TWO makes everybody comfortable and cared for. The case is that you are the last one to realize you are management material. You slowly rise through the ranks, not by grabbing power, but by attracting it. As a leader you are sensitive to the desires and challenges of others and always act in their highest interest.

Your INNER SEVEN enjoys delving within and working alone, but your OUTER ONE will launch your projects out into the universe in a forceful manner. You are not so concerned with the reactions of others, but they are drawn to what you are creating and you find yourself as a leader with followers. You maintain your independence by successfully empowering them.

You have a true power combination and came here to lead. Your INNER EIGHT wants power. Your OUTER NINE acts selflessly and magnanimously. The only delay is in finding the singularity of your purpose. You are a popular figure, exercising power for the good of all. Big things will happen for many people.

With your INNER NINE, it might take a while to find your way. Your desire is to look out for all others, but your OUTER EIGHT appears to be more power driven. People, however, respect your authority. Eventually your INNER NINE will realize where to focus your energy. Big things will happen for many people.

Ascension Numerology

You have the ability to let go of judgment and limitation. It is a constant process for you and an inspiration for those who are involved with you. You aspire to spiritual completion and yet you are very much a part of the world. You immerse yourself in the very drama of life while being aware that it is only a movie. The pairings all require a resolution between seemingly opposite VIBRATIONs. *You are here to teach and to demonstrate unconditional love and total acceptance of all differences.*

Yours is one of the most powerful combinations for creating earthly success. Your INNER ONE knows just what you want and your OUTER EIGHT is able to coordinate the efforts of others to create your vision happening. Your INNER ONE becomes frustrated with being tied down by your OUTER EIGHT's executive responsibilities and will want to give away what has been built in order to start a new project. Your projects continually move into the area of humanitarian care.

Your resolution is between your INNER TWO's desire for partnership and for giving sensitive support to others and your OUTER SEVEN's aloofness and inward focus on spirituality and perfection. Your INNER TWO gives up the personal and settles for supporting others without a direct and connected involvement. Your OUTER SEVEN demonstrates a wisdom and serenity that is healing for others to be around, and the writing and performance skills may project this to a wider audience.

Your INNER THREE wants a life free of responsibilities in order to play, express, and create. Your OUTER SIX can't help serving, loving and taking care of others. Your INNER THREE will not be happy until the service becomes a fun game. Your message is that life is meant to be enjoyed and not taken too seriously. All that is important is loving and taking care of each other. Your service moves from a personal to a more universal level.

Your resolution is between your INNER FOUR's desire for truth and for working hard toward goals and your OUTER FIVE's quick actions and manipulative ways with others. Truth and dedication will win, but this will be realized in an innovative, efficient manner. Yours is the most grounded and materially focused of all combinations; your results are reproducible systems that work. All people will benefit from your inner struggle.

Integrated self — NINE

Your resolution is between your INNER FIVE's desire for speed and experience and your OUTER FOUR's patient, step-by-step approach. You appear to be much more conservative than your INNER FIVE feels. With the pushing of your INNER FIVE, your OUTER FOUR takes larger and larger steps. Eventually they are enormous, and you find yourself to be a selfless server.

Your INNER SIX cares most about being with and helping people. Your OUTER THREE is a lot of fun to be with, but not naturally responsible for others. The best way for your INNER SIX to accomplish your service is through the creative expression of your OUTER THREE. Through a chosen medium, your service is offered to the world. Many are inspired by the message.

Your INNER SEVEN develops a deep spiritual nature. This is largely hidden from the world by your modest OUTER TWO, which makes others feel comfortable. Your OUTER TWO's willingness to stay in the background allows a space for your INNER SEVEN to flourish. With impeccable timing, you provide spiritual support for others. This is likely to take place on a one-to-one basis. Your service is so powerful that it is likely to become known to a larger audience.

Yours is a powerful combination for creating earthly success. Your INNER EIGHT wants power and thinks very big. Your OUTER ONE cannot be stopped, working aggressively to follow the goal that has been set. To find your spiritual peace, a higher purpose will be found for your expenditure of energy and your manifestations. Your purpose is the betterment of mankind. Your INNER EIGHT then takes it to the level that will touch the most people.

You have the only triple NUMBER combination. You have nothing but idealism and universal love. You have no urge to succeed, no follow through, and no discipline. You are an enormously likable person with many talents, many plans, and a great vision. It may take some time for maturity and focus to happen. Anything less than a full involvement in the transformation of the planet is unacceptable. That will come with the support of a divergent community. Great things will happen.

Ascension Numerology

MORE ABOUT

The third and final NAME NUMBER is called the INTEGRATED SELF and may also be known as the character or the self-expression. It is computed by totaling both the vowels and the consonants, so it represents the whole you (see "COMPUTATIONS" on page 281). This begins to develop in your early twenties. Obviously, your focus in life is going to be aligned with your MOTIVATION or you will have no juice for it. It will be a work that your PERSONALITY can carry out. But, in the final analysis it is the INTEGRATED SELF that shows the fullness of the direction and the impact your existence will have on others.

I have given a brief idea of what the INTEGRATED SELF might mean for each of the 81 possible combinations. I cannot repeat too many times that this is the first word and hardly the last. Go back to the general description for your NUMBER in CHAPTER 4 and then reread your INTEGRATED SELF above for a fuller understanding. Listen to your own intuitive voice. It can be helpful to revisit what has been said about your MOTIVATION and your PERSONALITY. Also, reread what has been said in the previous chapter on STRESS NUMBERs for your particular combination, while you think about how your NUMBERs integrate. *If you don't feel that you are realizing the potential of your reading, remember that the power with which your INTEGRATED SELF service is expressed continues to grow continuously through your life. Hold this as a an inspirational goal for the unfolding of your true nature.*

LIFE PATH

WHY IT ALWAYS HAPPENS TO YOU

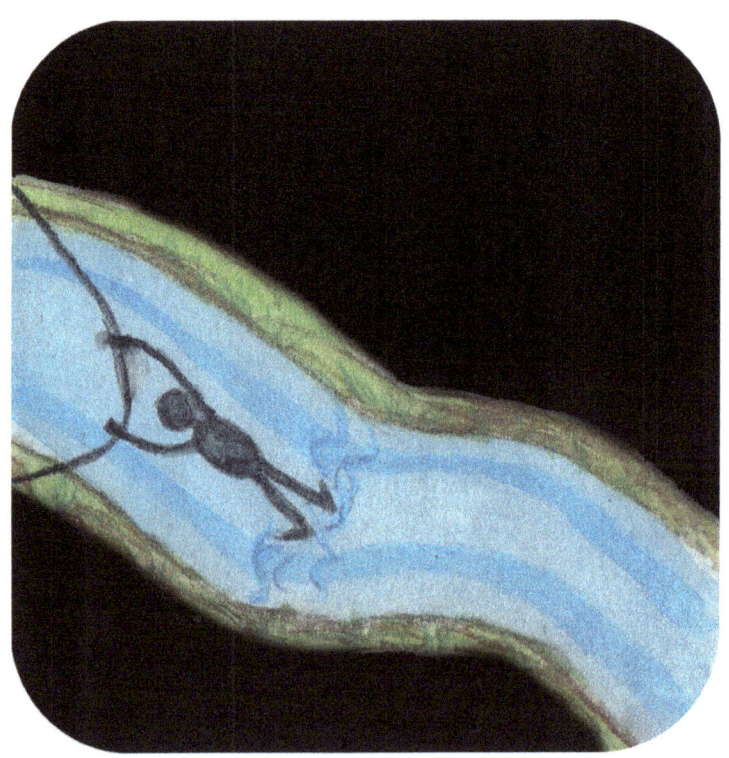

The LIFE PATH POSITION represents the major way that life seems to act upon you. It often feels to you as if this is an outside force that is neither part of you nor controllable by you. The truth is that you and your higher self planned these experiences and this energy before your birth in order to encourage a certain type of soul development. You can fight it or you can flow with it, but you will not be able to change it, at least not before you surrender to it. When you are resisting your LIFE PATH, you are drawn to your ANTI-NUMBER VIBRATION, which will be discussed later in the chapter. You may experience a deep empathy towards and from those who share your LIFE PATH. You are fighting the same battle. Your challenge is to make peace with your LIFE PATH and to embrace it. If your LIFE PATH is KARMIC, you will have a more difficult time surrendering to it. You will still get there, but it will take a little longer. *This is your major life lesson. This is the path that leads to the realization of your ASCENSION.*

Ascension Numerology

Life is encouraging your independence. It wants you to stand on your own. In childhood you might either find yourself abandoned on some level, or the opposite situation could occur; you might have an overbearing parent that drives you to go off on your own. Life wants you to develop courage. It wants you to learn to trust your own inner voice. You are being encouraged to follow the road less traveled, to go where others have not gone. It might feel safer for you to work within an existing larger structure, but that will tend not to work out for you. Life wants you to start something new. You are to be absolutely true to yourself, to have a deep level of integrity. You are to be a pioneer. If KARMIC, there is greater challenge for you to find the courage to act with integrity and to follow your inner voice. *Your path is to choose to be one with God.*

The major life lesson for you is one of timing. You are to learn patience and to respond to what is presented to you rather than initiating actions on your own. Your greatest spiritual growth and progress are likely to happen within relationships. You may be asked to take the back seat there. You might be tempted to try to live without a relationship. That choice is not likely to work well for you. Life is training you to be a great listener and to become sensitive to others. Your time will come and the call that propels you into your full power will come from the outside rather than the inside. Your job is to flow with whatever comes your way. You are to open your heart and really feel for others, to learn how to be compassionate rather than reactive. If KARMIC, you have a greater challenge being sensitive to others and to life. *Your path is to find unity with each person you meet.*

Life wants you to be creative and expressive. To most of the world, your path looks like a piece of cake. You are being asked to enjoy life. You are given more than your share of leisure time and fewer responsibilities. To you, this is terrifying. This space is given in order for you to develop your creativity and expression so that you can share it with the world. Your fear is that you are not really creative. You also worry that you won't be able to support yourself without finding some reliable form of work, or that you need to do something more valuable with your life. Your fear may lead you to follow a life of service, but this will not be fulfilling. Your job is to be a creative force, and creativity utilizes a lot of space in order to develop. Life wants you to be a playful child. Life wants you to inspire others and to show them what is truly possible through your expression. If KARMIC, you have a harder time believing in your creativity and letting yourself play. *Your path is to be a voice for light and love at every opportunity.*

Life wants you to be more disciplined and hard-working. Life wants you to do it over and over and over again. Life wants you to face the truth without flinching. Everybody resists their LIFE PATH and there is no exception with you. Everybody wants to go in the opposite direction when fear arises. For you this might mean running away or it could be you want to try something new, hoping for more adventure and excitement. When the dust clears, nothing has changed. You are back facing the same challenges. Nothing is any easier. You are becoming stronger. You are a source of reliability for others. You can be counted on for an honest evaluation. You can achieve anything you set out to do. You are the rock upon which anything can be built. You are the embodiment of truth. If KARMIC, you have an added challenge with self-discipline and being able to see the truth in yourself and others. *Your path is to find the truth.*

Life is going to teach you about change and flexibility. The hands you are dealt are never the same. The only thing constant is change. While this might sound like an exciting life, you are more likely to meet it with resistance. You seek to slow things down and to bring some constancy into your life. No matter what choices you make, you can't get off the roller-coaster. Life is teaching you how to land on your feet and how to think quickly. You are learning flexibility and how to be opportunistic. You are to become the world's WD 40[1], unsticking whatever is stuck, becoming an agent for change for others. You welcome change and thrive with it. You know, and help others see, that all problems are really opportunities. If KARMIC, you have increased difficulty dealing with change and taking chances. *Your path is to recognize that what is most important can never change.*

---

1) WD-40 is a spray product found in most American homes that is used to free up objects that have become stuck due to rust or other causes, and which has numerous additional household and work-site uses.

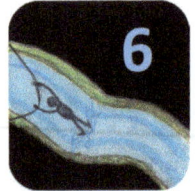
Life is teaching you how to serve. It is teaching you how to let go of your personal desires and replace them with whatever is best for the group. You probably don't want to do this. You would probably rather take your ball and go home. But, when you get home you will probably be asked to mow the lawn and clean your room. Life wants you to learn to love to be of service. You are to be a teacher, a parent, a healthcare giver, a counselor, joiner of groups, and a lover of companionship. You belong. You feel loved and accepted. Everyone feels welcomed by you and knows that you are always there on their side. Every day you make a difference in at least one person's life. If KARMIC, you have more trouble working with and trusting groups. *Your path is to find divinity through relating to and serving others.*

Life wants you to develop a deep sense of faith and trust. It wants you to look inside of yourself, for there is no other place to go. While you may be drawn to religion, that can only be a starting point. When you face a crisis—and your life will be full of them—there will be no person or organization present and able to help you. You may seek a partner or a friend when you feel you need help, but somehow they are never there for you. You will be drawn to learn and develop different spiritual techniques. You will become very skilled at a profession. Your faith will become so strong that others turn to you in their time of need. You are not meant to live in the everyday world, but in a rarified space. When others can use that kind of space they will seek you out. The divine always is speaking to you. If KARMIC, it is even harder for you to trust when things happen that are hard for you and to find a higher purpose in everything. *Your path is to trust the perfection of everything in your life.*

Life is going to teach you about power. You are surrounded by powerful people and energies. You are particularly sensitive to power out of balance. You are to confront this imbalance. You would probably rather not deal with all of this. You would rather just go off and work with your own power on your own. Life doesn't allow this to work out well for you. You are to overcome your mistrust of power and to learn how power actually

Life path

manifests results (read about EIGHT). You are to go right into the belly of the beast and show all what power really is and how they can use it in their lives. "There are no victims" are your watchwords. Power to the people. If KARMIC, you have more difficulty trusting and working with power in yourself and with organizations. *Your path is to give up your fear of God and to let divine power work through you.*

Life is teaching you how to let go. Whatever you are attached to, life will try to wrest it from your grasp. You are to learn that you only "need" whatever it is that allows you to perform today's service in the highest way. Life wants you to give up all judgments. If you don't, you will find yourself becoming the one you judge. You are being taught to love unconditionally. Like the FIVE, you will experience many changes, but when life changes for you, there is no road back. You can only move forward toward completion. You are being asked to move to a selfless spiritual level where your joy comes from following the guidance that life provides. You are to recognize the drama of life for the "drama" it is and to help others to rise above it. NINE's ANTI-NUMBER is itself. You are drawn to go in any other direction but that of letting go. None of them work for you. You are always thrown back to the NINE. If KARMIC, it is more difficult for you to let go of people, things, ideas, and prejudices. *Your path is to give everything to God.*

MORE ABOUT

While the NAME NUMBERs deal with VIBRATIONs that describe your desires, talents, and ways of acting, the BIRTH NUMBERs (derived from your birthday) represent the energies that seem to be acting upon you from the outside, from your environment. These are elements of time and timing. They neither feel to be an intrinsic part of you nor do they seem to be your own choices. This is, of course, an illusion. You are simply out of conscious touch with that part of you that chose these paths and these lessons. These are the opportunities and challenges that you (and your higher self) designed in order to encourage the spiritual growth you desire to accomplish in this incarnation.

The first and most important of these VIBRATIONs is your LIFE PATH (see "COMPUTATIONS" on page 282). This POSITION is also known by the terms destiny, fate, life number, and birth force. Just as your MOTIVATION is what it is for this lifetime, so is your LIFE PATH. The free will that you have is to resist or to surrender to it. If you resist, your life will be a constant struggle and you will not realize your ASCENSION. It is that simple. Flowing with your LIFE PATH is not easy, but ultimately it is easier than fighting. Imagine your life as a river. Fighting your destiny is like swimming upstream. It is exhausting, and if you don't change your plan, you will eventually drown. Going with your birth force is like floating down stream. Of course, you still want to pay attention, but you have a lot more energy available to deal with whatever might surface.

The LIFE PATH energy is subtle. It explains why things happen to you and not to others. This is where your NUMEROLOGY CHART is truly a gift from your higher self. Of course, you are presented with the energy of all nine VIBRATIONs in your life, but your LIFE PATH VIBRATION is the one that impacts you the most strongly. By knowing what your LIFE PATH is and by having an understanding of what it is asking of you, it is easier to know how to flow with it. Because the energies are subtle, you can pick them out of a crowd and consciously choose to flow with them. You can recognize and welcome events instead of fearing and rejecting them. The challenge is to reach the point where you welcome your LIFE PATH VIBRATION in the same way that your MOTIVATION seeks out certain types of events. The goal is to cultivate a passion for your LIFE PATH similar to the one you were born with for your MOTIVATION.

You may be thinking that you get a free pass if your MOTIVATION is the same VIBRATION as your LIFE PATH. While this certainly eases things to a degree, it is not as simple as all of that. Just because you have desire for something, it doesn't mean you want it at every moment. You wish to have some control over how it unfolds. What you thought you wanted might be taking you in a direction that you don't wish to take. Is it beginning to get clearer? There is no such thing as a free pass for your LIFE PATH. It will always feel like a challenge, like something you aren't choosing. It is always a spiritual demand, a call for growth.

If your life path is a KARMIC NUMBER, you have chosen a great challenge for yourself. You don't really know how to surrender to this VIBRATION. The learning of the karmic lesson becomes more uncomfortable, stimulating a, hopefully, shorter learning curve. Go back and study the qualities of your KARMIC NUMBER and learn all you can about that VIBRATION in general. You never bite off more than you can chew when you design an incarnation. However, it is time to roll up your sleeves and get to work.

The preceding descriptions of the LIFE PATH VIBRATIONs are, as always, only a beginning. As you look at the events of your life, both past and present, and think about your particular VIBRATION, you will continue to gain more insights.

The wonderful news is that your greatest opportunities are presented under the guise of a challenge from your fate VIBRATION. Herein lies your best hope for happiness, success, and the realization of your purpose and your ASCENSION. Eventually you will realize this. You will be able to look back and to see the value of the roadblocks that befell you. The challenge is to realize now that a gift has been presented to you, even if you don't recognize just what the gift is or why it is a gift. Your challenge is to love everything that life presents to you.

ANTI-NUMBER

Every LIFE PATH VIBRATION has an ANTI-NUMBER.

When you are resisting your LIFE PATH, your tendency is to attempt to move in the direction of the ANTI-NUMBER VIBRATION (see "COMPUTATIONS" on page 283). However, things don't seem to work out and you are nudged by life back in the direction of your LIFE PATH.

All of this has the benign purpose of helping you to fully surrender to your LIFE PATH, the only place where you can find true peace and full sense of purpose. This is the lesson you chose to come and learn. Anything less than a full acceptance of your path will bring about a failure to accomplish what you came to do. This is of course okay. You will survive anything. But, it leaves a sense of dissatisfaction with yourself and your life. The LIFE PATH points out the best direction for success and satisfaction. If your ANTI-NUMBER is KARMIC, it might actually be easier for you not to be drawn to it, but more difficult for you when you are. Individual readings for the ANTI-NUMBER are not provided. If you would like a better feel for that vibration, you can either read the LIFE PATH for the number or go back to Chapter 4 and read about the vibration there.

MORE 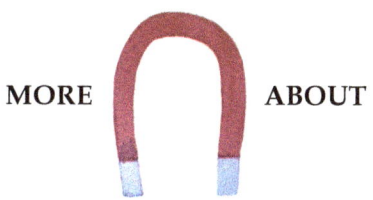 ABOUT

Wherever the ANTI-NUMBER appears in your CHART it causes some confusion and disorder. This is particularly challenging if the ANTI-NUMBER is one of your NAME NUMBERs. Here are a few examples:

- If your MOTIVATION is the same as your ANTI-NUMBER, you are drawn to make choices that run away from the direction your LIFE PATH is leading you in. You have created a challenge for yourself. Awareness of its nature can help guide your choices.
- If your PERSONALITY is the same as your ANTI-NUMBER you automatically act in ways that resist your LIFE PATH. Knowing that you have this tendency can help you deal with it.
- Having your INTEGRATED SELF match your ANTI-NUMBER means that your talent is in some ways opposite to what life is asking you to do. In this case you have a NINE ASCENSION NUMBER. The balancing of these opposite VIBRATIONs will assist you in learning to accept everything in your life.
- Your ANTI-NUMBER on a PLANE OF EXPRESSION indicates some vulnerability on that PLANE.

Your ANTI-NUMBER is the complementary or opposite VIBRATION to your LIFE PATH. The two of them will always total NINE. It is "the grass that looks greener on the other side of the fence" when you are not enjoying your path. Ultimately you will find that only your LIFE PATH leads to your ASCENSION.

STRESS NUMBER
BETWEEN MOTIVATION AND LIFE PATH

SAYING YES TO WHAT YOU CAN'T UNCHOOSE

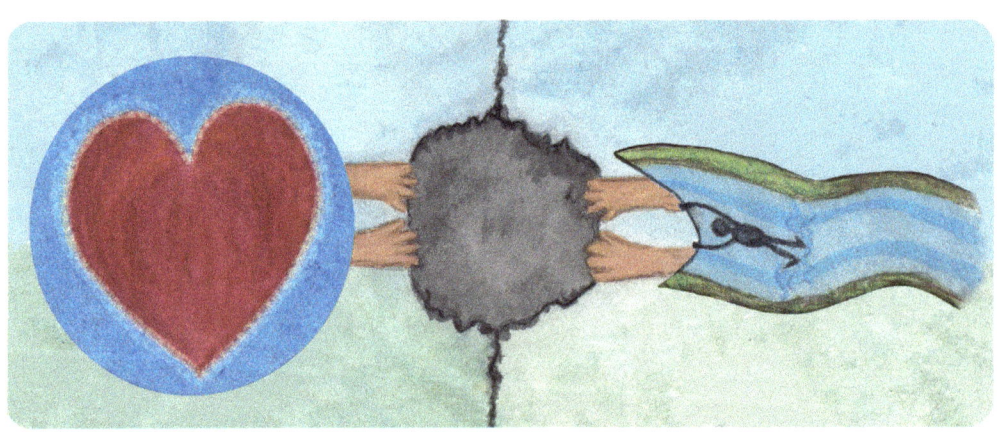

When you have two different VIBRATIONs in separate MAJOR POSITIONs in your CHART, the interaction between them is represented through the STRESS NUMBER. We are going to look below at the stress between your MOTIVATION and your LIFE PATH. Everyone resists their LIFE PATH. Your MOTIVATION shows what you want out of life, while your LIFE PATH VIBRATION shows what life is delivering to you. This difference is a frustration for you. The STRESS NUMBER shows both the nature of the potential conflict between the two VIBRATIONs and also the possible path of resolution. Anything less will likely bring pain and suffering. If your STRESS NUMBER is KARMIC, the importance of bringing balance to it is magnified. Read more deeply about your KARMIC NUMBER. *The bottom line is that your MOTIVATION's desire will eventually learn to surrender to your LIFE PATH energy with as much strength as it has to pursue your own conscious agenda.*

If your MOTIVATION and your LIFE PATH are the same, your STRESS NUMBER is 0. That's right, you have no stress between what you want to do and what life is presenting to you. This is not the free pass that you might visualize it to be. Your MOTIVATION always has the element of choice. Your LIFE PATH energy comes whether you want it then or not. It is as if you love chocolate, but not, perhaps, when you first wake up, or to the exclusion of all other foods, or having it forced down your throat. *The challenge is to welcome this VIBRATION whether you would have chosen it now or not, or else you will suffer.*

Stress number between motivation and life path — ONE

A STRESS NUMBER ONE shows that there is a basic misalignment between your MOTIVATION and your LIFE PATH. One of them is even and the other is odd, because they are contiguous VIBRATIONs. Contiguous VIBRATIONs do not get along with each other easily. The odd NUMBERs are more inwardly focused, the even NUMBER more outwardly directed. What is necessary is for your two parts to have a common goal. The goal will be set by the requirements of your LIFE PATH, because it is not going to budge. *The challenge is for your MOTIVATION to do whatever it can to accept and flow with the LIFE PATH, without sacrificing itself in the process.*

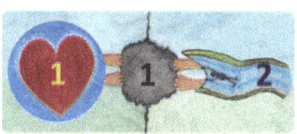

Your INNER ONE is focused and assertive. Your TWO LIFE PATH is asking you to be sensitive and to flow with what is happening. Something has to give. You are frustrated because life wants you to go along with everyone else and not push an agenda. *The challenge is to make it a primary goal to learn how to become a TWO. It is time for a crash course in listening, patience, cooperation, and nurturance. You are asked to learn to reach your goals through this path. Otherwise, you will likely fail, and it will hurt.*

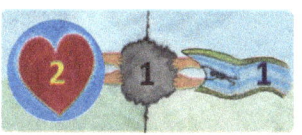

Your INNER TWO wants to work in a supporting role with others but your ONE LIFE PATH is demanding that you learn how to stand on your own feet and become independent. You want to be gentle but life is teaching you to be tough. *The challenge is to accept that the final decisions are yours to make. You can work in a sensitive way with others as long as you learn to be a single parent to your life, taking on both masculine and feminine roles.*

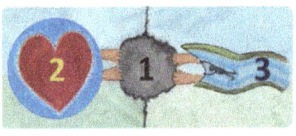
Your INNER TWO wants to create close sensitive relationships but your THREE LIFE PATH is not encouraging a focus on partnership. Life is keeping you free from entanglements so that your playful creative energies can be developed. Find others to play with, but the relationships will become strained if you allow them to control how your creativity is to be expressed. *The challenge is to fully express your creativity, no matter what the criticisms of others about you or your own self-criticism might be.*

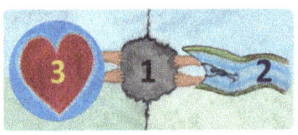
Your INNER THREE wants to be the playful, expressive child, but your TWO LIFE PATH demands that you be sensitive to others. You are to put their desires above yours, but just the thought of that makes you want to throw a tantrum. You are to find that your creativity will be best expressed through cooperative work with others, where the other calls the shots. *The challenge is to learn to support the desires of those close to you. Only after mastering that will you find the space for your own expression.*

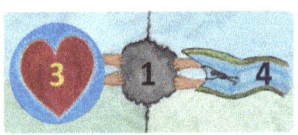
Your INNER THREE wants to play and express, but your FOUR LIFE PATH wants you to become more disciplined and hard working. You want to kick and scream, but that will change nothing about what you are facing. *The challenge is to surrender to the work and discipline. It will make a superior artist out of you. There is always a fun and creative way to do every job.*

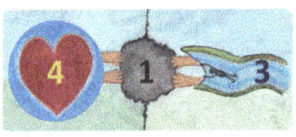
Your INNER FOUR is frustrated. All you ask for is to have a goal that you can work industriously toward, and your THREE LIFE PATH sets you up so that you can take it easy. However you try to do something practical, life tries to turn it into a game. *The challenge is to accept your creativity and agree to play with it. Then you can work as hard as you want at playing and creating.*

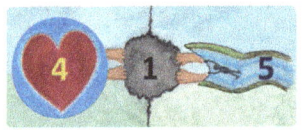
Your INNER FOUR has quite a challenge with your FIVE LIFE PATH. You want to set a goal and to work toward it, but life keeps moving the target. You just want the rules to stay the same, but life keeps shuffling the deck. *The challenge is for your INNER FOUR to learn to take the changes in stride. When the alteration comes, just draw up a new plan. Do it daily if necessary. Life's plan is better than yours. Stick with it, however it may wiggle and morph.*

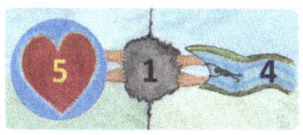
Your INNER FIVE wants change, variety, excitement and freedom. Your FOUR LIFE PATH brings stability, and repetition, requiring an aptitude for discipline and hard work. Your INNER FIVE wants nothing more than to escape from such a destiny. It's not going to happen. *The challenge is to surrender to the demands of your life and to know that the change you desire will come, but it will come slowly. You may work hard for it, but when the movement comes it will bring permanent positive improvement.*

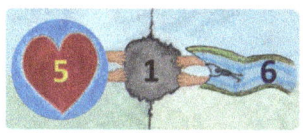
Your INNER FIVE struggles with your SIX LIFE PATH. You want freedom, adventure, and movement while your SIX LIFE PATH wants you to be responsible, taking care of the problems of others and giving your energy for the good of the group. The power of the flow of your LIFE PATH is greater than any resistance that can be provided by your MOTIVATION. You are smart and quick, but cannot outwit life. *The challenge is to surrender to the requirements of the group. Your desired changes and movement will be realized through it.*

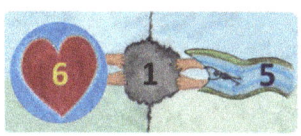
Your INNER SIX wants to be part of the group and to be there to help others. The group won't sit still. Everything keeps changing with your FIVE LIFE PATH, so you find yourself giving more attention to dealing with the changes than to being of service. You want to slow everything down, but you can't. *The challenge is to deal with the changes – first for yourself, but then helping others to cope also. You will find the way to be with your group (or more likely – groups), but not until you decide to roll with the punches.*

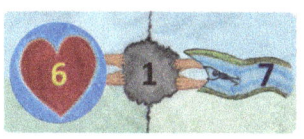
Your INNER SIX wants to be with people, while your SEVEN LIFE PATH leads you to separation. You want to deal with your challenges, as they arise, in a social way, but life wants you to solve them alone. You want to find your answers in and through others; life wants you to find them within yourself and with the divine. *The challenge is to surrender to this path of faith. You will then be able to help lead others to drink from the spiritual waters when their trials come. That will be worth waiting for.*

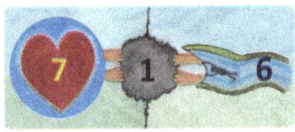
Nothing gives you greater pleasure than your own company and the pursuit of your rarified interests. You don't suffer fools easily. But, life is asking you to do just that. Your SIX LIFE PATH constantly throws you into social situations where you are called on to serve every kind of person. You just want to be left alone. It "ain't" going to happen. That is a word that probably drives you crazy, but one you will likely hear from those you are involved with. *The challenge is to perfect your talents for working with others. You will eventually find the spiritual gems you desire through your involvements in the unlikeliest places.*

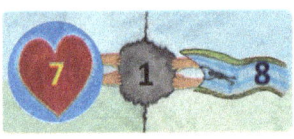
Your INNER SEVEN wants solitude in order to develop your specific interests and talents. Your EIGHT LIFE PATH pulls you fully out into the world to deal with power structures. Though you would prefer not to dirty your hands in that way, you are fully capable of meeting the demands of your life. *The challenge is – though you prefer not to deal with power at all, or, if necessary, to deal with it alone – that you likely find yourself working with power within structures. You will get it down and enjoy the loneliness at the top.*

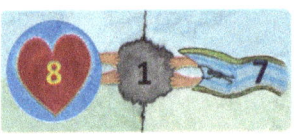
Your INNER EIGHT wants power and position. Your SEVEN LIFE PATH keeps pulling you out of the center of things. Instead of building your dreams, you find yourself dealing with one dark night of the soul after another. Life wants you to develop a deep and unbending faith. *The challenge is for you to realize that nobody else is the cause of or the solution to your problems, which you alone end up dealing with. Then you will find an enormous strength in your ability to help others find their true power.*

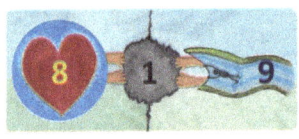
Your INNER EIGHT has big dreams and wants to accomplish much. Your NINE LIFE PATH asks you to be willing to let go of everything. Life always demands a lot, but you have the most to lose because you want so much. *The challenge is to realize that your power is to be used to support a humanitarian agenda and that everything that is not part of what you came to create will be swept aside, so that you can keep your eye on the real goal. That goal will far exceed your original dreams.*

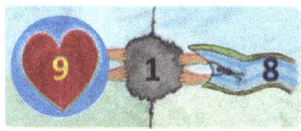 Your INNER NINE is an idealistic dreamer. You have few personal goals and have little desire to get involved in the day to day battles of life. Your EIGHT LIFE PATH asks you to get involved. You find yourself dealing with power structures and are made all too aware of where things are out of balance. *The challenge is to learn how to participate in a powerful way. You don't want to do this, yet life is relentless in its demands. You finally take on your power because in the end it serves everyone.*

With the TWO the stress is always one involving sensitivity. You are dealing with either two odd NUMBERs or two even ones. The fight is not so much one for control, as with the ONE, but one of a balancing of more similar energies. The main challenge with all TWO STRESS NUMBERs is a tendency toward criticism, whether it is inner or outer directed. There is also the challenge of letting the little things get in the way. *The challenge is for your MOTIVATION to be sensitive to the demands of your LIFE PATH while developing patience.*

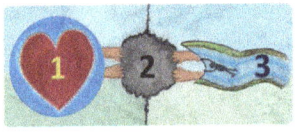

Your INNER ONE is focused and driven, wanting to rush off and make your mark on the world. Your THREE LIFE PATH lets you know that there is no hurry. Space is being provided to develop your creative talents. You have doubts about your creativity and try to push out in other directions. You try to fill your time with involvements and commitments. *The challenge is to surrender to your creative side. It will allow you to move into the uncharted territory that draws you.*

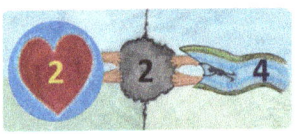

Your INNER TWO wants to get along with others, to let others take the lead. Your FOUR LIFE PATH demands that you be the one to set goals. You want a gentle, peaceful, cooperative existence, but FOUR forces you to face facts and to toughen up. You may have no difficulty with the hard work and the repetition that FOUR calls for, but can balk at the naked honesty that is required. *The challenge is to learn that honesty delivered with your sensitive approach is the best way to support others.*

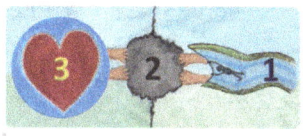
Your INNER THREE wants to have fun and to be creative and expressive. You want to remain the child. Meanwhile your ONE LIFE PATH demands that you grow up quickly and learn how to stand on your own two feet. You want to be pampered. The realization slowly descends that it is your independence that allows you to remain a creative child. With nobody to tell you what to do, you are free to express in whatever way you choose. *The challenge is to get tough, take charge, and do it your way.*

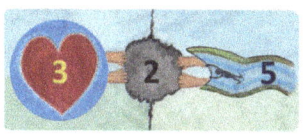
Your INNER THREE wants to play and to be free of responsibility. Your FIVE LIFE PATH ensures that nothing stays the same. In this constantly changing world you are required to learn how to survive. You are compelled to compete with others. You want things to be easy and relaxed. Life demands constant attention. *The challenge is to accept this grown up world as being a big playground. It provides you with a constantly changing palette from which to express your visions.*

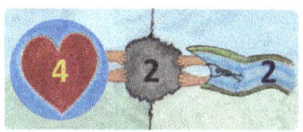
Your INNER FOUR likes to set goals and to work diligently toward their realization. Your TWO LIFE PATH always asks you to set aside your own desires and to be sensitive to those of others. You aren't allowed to plow straight forward, but are encouraged to pay attention to the timing that is necessary to successfully reach your goal. Learn patience. *The challenge is to accept that the most efficient way to get there is by listening carefully to the world's response, especially when it comes from those closest to you.*

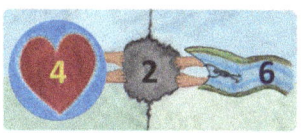
The INNER FOUR wants to set goals and to work methodically toward their realization. You enjoy doing the job yourself, partly because you have figured out just how it should be done. Your SIX LIFE PATH always brings other people into the mix. No matter how much you want your goal to be the main focus, you find that you are called to make the care of those you are working with your first priority. If you don't support them, then the job cannot be completed. *The challenge life is asking of you is to replace functionality with love, with a sense of belonging as your primary goal. Together we can do it.*

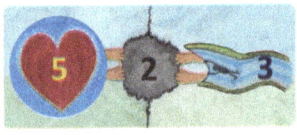
Your INNER FIVE is competitive, always wanting to perform well and to move forward as quickly as possible. Your THREE LIFE PATH tends to slow things down to encourage you to be expressive and creative. Life wants you to fully express who you are. There is no competition involved; there is only honest sensitivity. *The challenge is to take this as your job. Give up the race. Stop and smell the flowers.*

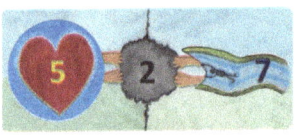
Your INNER FIVE wants to manipulate, change and improve everything. You want to get ahead in the world. Your SEVEN LIFE PATH forces you to take a large step out of this world that you wish to manipulate, so that you can look inside and find meaning. To make sure that this happens you experience extreme challenges that derail your progress. *The challenge is to deal with questions of faith and fear. The progress and change will come, and it will be spiritually directed.*

Your INNER SIX wants to be a part of a group and to help and be helped. Love and people come first. Your FOUR LIFE PATH keeps reminding you that you have other work to do. As much as you would like this work to be a cooperative group process, the bulk of it falls to you. You are busy, busy, busy, and often with seemingly repetitive tasks. You are being asked to build something solid and long-lasting. You are being led to discover truth. Others can be a part of this process, but if you try to place them in the center, you will be frustrated. *The challenge is to surrender to the process of the tasks life presents. You will find love there, too.*

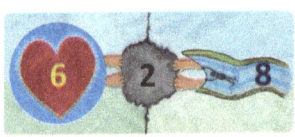
Your INNER SIX puts people first and wants to live and work in loving service. Your EIGHT LIFE PATH constantly reminds you that there is a bigger world out there for you to deal with. Your life becomes one of dealing with large institutions and the use and abuse of power. This is a culture that often lacks the warmth that you so much desire. Yet, there is no satisfactory way for you turn your back on the EIGHT energy. *The challenge is to learn how to unleash your inner power. You will find a way to serve and work with people in a loving way, but it will be from a place of power.*

Stress number between motivation and life path — TWO

Your INNER SEVEN wants isolation and the time to go deeply into things. Your FIVE LIFE PATH throws you into the very heart of the vibrating physical world. You are forced to deal with an ever-changing menu of changes and challenges — opportunities that pull you out of the quiet place you desire to be in. *The challenge is to learn to think on your feet rather than in a meditative space. You will be able to develop your special skills, but only in a way that helps the world be a better place — now.*

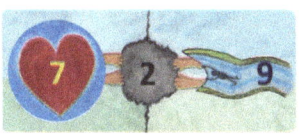

Your INNER SEVEN has a desire for solitude and the space to develop things on a deep level. Your NINE LIFE PATH pulls you more out into the drama of the world. You would prefer your own private laboratory, but life wants you to be involved with and to give selflessly to all. *The challenge is to develop the faith to let go and trust where life is taking you. There is a large spiritual purpose to your life. Find out what it is by following the treasure hunt that has been prepared for you.*

Your INNER EIGHT is ambitious and thinks big. Your SIX LIFE PATH asks you to serve others. You want to focus on the big picture, but life wants you to be more focused on the cares and concerns of those around you. You can try to run away from those responsibilities, but then you still find yourself unable to realize your big dreams. They lie on the other side of your service. *The challenge is to find your power In the midst of providing for others. Perhaps you will find yourself in a more hands on and a less executive position, but you will be pleased with the direction your power has taken.*

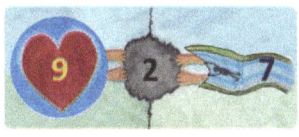

Your INNER NINE is idealistic, loving, and humanitarian. It is also not highly motivated to get out into the world and do something. Your SEVEN LIFE PATH would seem to be aligned, in that you are encouraged to follow a spiritual direction. However, a large part of that path is the experience of challenges and losses that require a deepening of faith and understanding. *The challenge is for you to face these moments of crisis, seemingly alone, though you wish for the support of others. You will want to share your lessons with the world, and you will. Your directionless-ness now has a purpose.*

When THREE is the STRESS NUMBER there is a friction between an even and an odd NUMBER. Since these NUMBERs are not adjacent the conflict is not as severe. However, there is still the conflict between an introverted and an extroverted VIBRATION. There can also be blocks on self-expression. *The challenge is connected to self-expression and freeing yourself up from whatever feels restricting. Lighten up.*

Your INNER ONE is inspired and wishes to charge off in a direction. Your FOUR LIFE PATH slows everything down; demanding that you work methodically and repetitively until something solid is created. You want to start something new, but life wants you to finish what you have started. Life is like a restrictive, demanding parent. Any attempt to run off to something new will likely fail. Let go of the tantrums. *The challenge is find a creative way to forge your new direction at the turtle's pace life delivers. When you learn to be relentless and disciplined you can create that new path.*

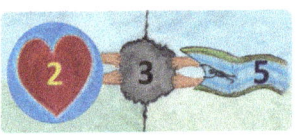

Your INNER TWO wants to be sensitive, to have peace, and to stay in the background. Your FIVE LIFE PATH throws you out into the heart of a vibrating, tumultuous world. You are forced to assert your place, to compete with others and with yourself in order to survive. You are not permitted to stay in the background, nor are you allowed to always consider others' desires first. *The challenge is to learn how to land on your feet and to use your sensitivity for determining which direction to turn. When you have mastered this for yourself, then you can use your adaptive skills to support others.*

Stress number between motivation and life path — THREE

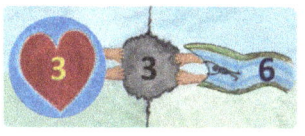
Your INNER THREE wants to play, have fun, and never grow up, but your SIX LIFE PATH requires you to take responsibility and to be of service. You will certainly try to run away from the maturity that is asked of you, but these endeavors will tend to self-destruct and you will find yourself back with a group or groups, where there is much for you to do. *The challenge is to learn to let your creativity express through a form that is supportive of the group's effort and helpful to others. Eventually you will find that the support you give is reciprocated and the group propels your creativity to new levels.*

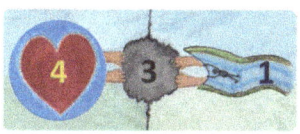
Your INNER FOUR plans carefully toward reaching a goal. You favor more conservative choices, following the tried and the true. Your ONE LIFE PATH insists that you go in an entirely new direction. Then, instead of giving you the time to develop your plan, life sweeps you off in yet another new direction. *The challenge is to learn how to be independent and fearless. This is to be realized before any plan can be effected. You will reach a goal, but not the one you originally set off for.*

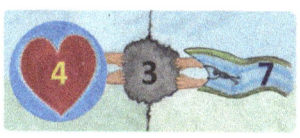
Your INNER FOUR likes to set goals and to reach them. Your SEVEN LIFE PATH always has a way of throwing a fly in the ointment, a really big fly. So, the goal isn't necessarily reached on any kind of timely basis. *The challenge is to consider just how important your goals are in the big picture of things and just why you are here, anyway. You love a challenge and seeking after truth, but without repriortizing, life may prove to be extremely frustrating. Then you can find yourself seeking after practical truths — answers that can be used in the physical world.*

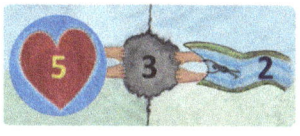
Your INNER FIVE is chomping at the bit for action and adventure. Your TWO LIFE PATH is asking you to always consider the wants of another before acting. You are also being taught how to flow with events and timing, rather than charging off at a moment's notice. Learn to channel your desire to manipulate the world around you into one where you use those skills to support others in their endeavors. *The challenge is to master listening and patience, as you wait for and support another to take action. Your changes will come, and they will prove to have been worth waiting for.*

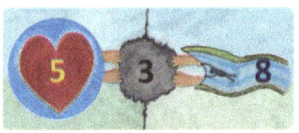
Your INNER FIVE wants movement, freedom, and experiences. Your EIGHT LIFE PATH confronts you with powerful organizations. You are sensitive to how power is used out of balance, but wish to take pot shots from the outside rather than really getting involved. This won't work for you very well. *The challenge is to let yourself get tied down to an organization; that is what you are being called to do. Organizations can change, and your persuasive hand can help to guide them.*

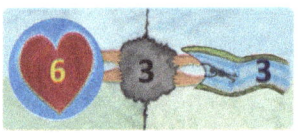
Your INNER SIX is very serious and caring and wishes to be responsible for others. Your THREE LIFE PATH lets you off the hook. There isn't so much that you are called to do for others. You are free to develop your creative expressive talents. You react in terror, looking for places to be of service. *The challenge is to face your terror that you are not truly creative and that your desire to serve others is in part an expression of this fear. The space will continue to present itself. As you allow your real creativity to rise to the surface, you will realize that it can be used in service to others.*

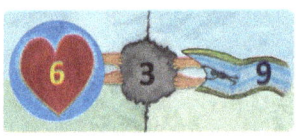
The combination of the SIX and the NINE are quite interesting, because they both are VIBRATIONs of love. Your INNER SIX desires a personal love that is very involved with family, friends, and colleagues while your NINE LIFE PATH leads you to a more selfless and universal love. You are asked to surrender attachment to your relationships. To assist you in learning how to do this, you lose one relationship after another. *The challenge is to move from your emotionally based heart to your spiritually based path. Let go of your neediness for others. Then you will have all the love you could want.*

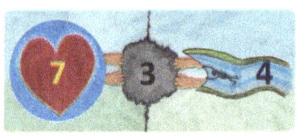
Your INNER SEVEN wishes to have a quiet space where you can think deeply about things and hone your special talents. Your FOUR LIFE PATH requires you to work hard at what you do. Results take longer than you would like and the results may seem less refined than you might wish them to be. Life is forcing you to be more practical. You will be spending more time working hard and less time theorizing. *The challenge is to let go of some of your ideals, but in return is the potential for more real world application of your dreams. A livable spirituality is something worth working for.*

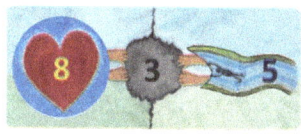

Your INNER EIGHT wants to be in charge and always thinks big. Your FIVE LIFE PATH makes it difficult for you to reach your aspirations because everything keeps shifting around you. Your primary job becomes one of learning how to deal with change. Become flexible, adventurous, and fast moving. Any attempt to hold things in place so that you can control the situation will likely prove disastrous. *The challenge is to learn that your power can only be expressed through your ability to adjust to the shifting sands. The end result is a greatly increased potential for expressing power to improve the world.*

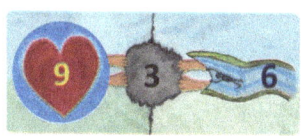

The combination of the SIX and the NINE are quite interesting, because they both are VIBRATIONs of love. Your INNER NINE is idealistic about love, not wanting to be mired down in the muck of needy, possessive relationships. Your SIX LIFE PATH leads you right into the messy day to day of living, loving, and working with others. Though you would prefer to keep things at a fairy tale like level and want to run away from the responsibilities of real life, that isn't in the cards for you. Your dance card is filled with people, relationships, and service. There are tears and there is laughter. *The challenge is to surrender to this intimate contact, and through it you learn to truly love others unconditionally so you can find the love you seek.*

Ascension Numerology

With the FOUR STRESS NUMBER the difficulties center on either a lack of discipline and follow through or a stifling rigidity. The answer is either in becoming more organized and finishing what is started, or in loosening up a little while realizing that the purpose of self-disciple is to help you in realizing a goal, not as an end in itself. There is also the danger of your being too hard on yourself and perhaps on others, also. *The challenge is to toughen up and face the truth.*

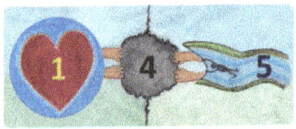

Your INNER ONE has a singleness of focus that wishes to go off in a new direction. Your FIVE LIFE PATH is leading you in five directions at once. You are frustrated by all of the tangents life takes as you try to sustain your singleness of purpose. You have no choice, short of crashing and burning, but to set your plan aside and deal with the many fires that are burning. You would like to throw yourself into just one flame, but another demands your attention…and then another. *The challenge is to learn how to place all of your attention in one direction and then to quickly release it to focus elsewhere. You will still be the innovator, but the direction will be honed by the realities of the world about you.*

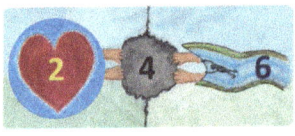

Your INNER TWO desires peace and places a great value upon the one-to-one relationship. You like to remain quietly in the background supporting another. Your SIX LIFE PATH throws you constantly into group situations where you find yourself dealing with many people at once instead of just one. There are so many diverse energies present that it is difficult for you to be sensitive to each one. You are forced to come more out of yourself and get involved with the give and take of expressing feelings and desires, even though you would rather just run away from the whole mess. *The challenge is to become more assertive in letting others know where you stand. You learn to offer help before it is asked for. Your sensitivity shines through.*

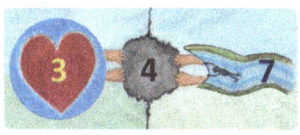
Your INNER THREE wants to have fun, to be in the moment, to be creative, and to postpone growing up indefinitely. Your SEVEN LIFE PATH asks you to become serious and to grow up quickly. You are faced with spiritually challenging situations that can't just be laughed off. You would love to find someone else who can take the weight from your shoulders, but you are forced to look deep within yourself for answers. *The challenge is that you have no choice but to develop a deep faith and understanding. As you find this inner strength you are able to share your treasures in inspiring, creative ways that help others to lighten their load.*

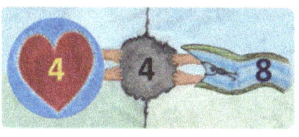
Your INNER FOUR has a drive for truth, hard work, and the setting and reaching of goals. Your EIGHT LIFE PATH asks you to step things up to the next level. The goals are to be bigger, as is the impact on society. Life won't let you just plug along with your own personal projects. Big power stands in your way. You are asked to go into the belly of the beast, even though you would rather just continue on in your own independent direction. Life won't let that work, though your stubbornness can make it difficult for you to accept defeat. *The challenge is to work with the out of balance power around you and redirect it to the truth. You have both the power and the fortitude to succeed.*

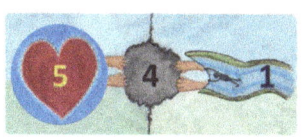
Your INNER FIVE wants to have the freedom to explore everything. Your ONE LIFE PATH constantly tries to narrow your focus down to one thing at a time. It demands that you become independent, that you become your own person. You are left on your own and don't have the freedom to follow every whim. *The challenge is to become strong and independent, the kind of person who follows your own inner voice. You now have the freedom to go anywhere and do anything, but you will narrow that down to the choice that matches your heart.*

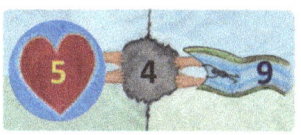
Your FIVE MOTIVATION is inwardly focused, wanting to try everything and to have the freedom to follow your desires. Your NINE LIFE PATH is asking you to let go of your personal desires and to work for the greater good. You are opportunistic and life is asking you to be selfless. You are competitive and want to create the best situation for yourself and life asks you to let go of everything. You try to fight this by trying to build something that will last. It doesn't. You learn to give without the expectation of return. *The challenge is to learn to go with what life brings you. You begin to make a big difference in changing things for the better for all.*

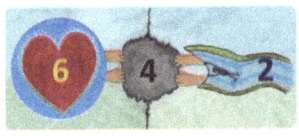
Your INNER SIX places the good of the group and service above all else. You love to be the teacher, the wise counselor, the trusted healer. Your TWO LIFE PATH asks you to take a step back from your desires to take such an active role in supporting others. Instead life asks you to be quieter and gentler. You are asked to pay attention, to be sensitive, and to wait for the right moment to act. Part of you would rather withdraw altogether than to play this role. But, this role is the one you have given yourself. *The challenge is to learn to wait until another is ready to receive what you have to offer. This help is always gladly received.*

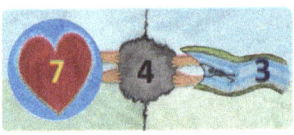
Your INNER SEVEN enjoys solitude and looks on the world in a serious and analytical manner. Your THREE LIFE PATH is constantly asking you to step out of your comfort zone and express yourself to the world. You are asked to express what is there now, not to wait a week or a month or a year or a decade until you feel that you have perfected the message. You want to be the researcher, but life wants you to be the artist. *The challenge is to release your self-restrictive ways and trust and flow with what presents itself in the now. You might try to hide yourself in a group, but you will be constantly thrust out into the limelight. Trust that truth will be channeled through you.*

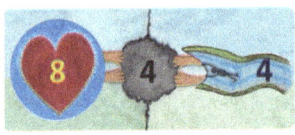
Your INNER EIGHT has big goals and wants everything to be big in your life. Your FOUR LIFE PATH demands that everything slow down. Where you would prefer to delegate, life asks you to do it yourself, to get your hands dirty. Work on the big plan one small step at a time. *The challenge is to resist trying to speed up the process, as any attempts to do so will likely blow up in your face and you will find yourself back to slow and steady. You can achieve your grandiose dreams, but first everything must pass the test of truth and practicality. Only repetitive effort and self-discipline will lead you to that place.*

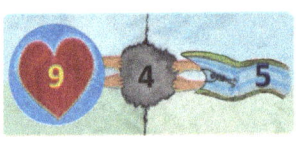
Your INNER NINE is humanitarian in its outlook, but can be unmotivated to follow any course of action. You are more likely to perceive an idealistic outcome than to have any idea of how to reach it. Your FIVE LIFE PATH throws you right out of your ivory tower and into the "real" world. You learn how to handle the myriad changes that come your way in order to survive. Dreaminess won't cut it. You want to slow the world down, perhaps so you can get off, but it maintains its dizzying speed. *The challenge is to learn to think on your feet and to make the most of the opportunities change brings with it. Life is giving you a big lesson on how to bring your idealistic dreams to fruition.*

The STRESS NUMBER FIVE is a challenge in flexibility. It may be a case of being blocked by routine and a fixed way of doing things, or it may be that there is too great a tendency to go with every whim or influence. There also may be a pattern of running away from situations rather than dealing with them. The balance comes through recognizing when change is necessary and when flexibility is important. *The challenge is the stress between an even NUMBER and an odd NUMBER, with the even NUMBER pushing more toward rigidity and the odd more for freedom. The importance of which of them falls on the MOTIVATION helps show in which direction you might be inclined to lean.*

Your INNER ONE knows what you want and does not want to be deterred. Your SIX LIFE PATH constantly denies your personal agenda for that of the group, whether the group consists of family, friends, or workmates. This is an extremely frustrating position for you. You are burning with energy and direction, while the group is slow to make decisions and it is unlikely that theirs will agree with yours. Life not only asks you to go along with the group but wants you to take care of others, when you would rather be taking care of your own desires. You planned it this way. *The challenge is to surrender to the group. Learn to love and be loved. It will change the direction in which you want to go. When you and the group are aligned, you will go off in your pioneering direction with their support.*

 Your INNER TWO cares more about partnership than anything else. You want to work closely with another in most situations. Your SEVEN LIFE PATH leads you to places of isolation. When you most want somebody to be there for you, there is nobody who can or will help. No matter how hard you look for a partner or friend to help you, you are left on your own to deal with your crisis – so you learn how to go inside of yourself. *The challenge is for you to develop a strong faith that can carry you through the troubling times that will continue to come. As each test makes you stronger, your ability to support others magnifies.*

 Your INNER THREE wants to remain a child and to express at will. Your EIGHT LIFE PATH places you in direct contact with powerful forces in the world. You are forced to grow up quickly and find your own power or you will feel overwhelmed. *The challenge is that though you would prefer to go off on your own, you have to agree to work within the system. You will help bring about valuable changes and you will use your creative expression to inspire others to join your cause.*

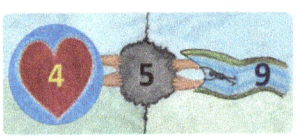 Your INNER FOUR wants to set goals and work toward their successful completion. Your NINE LIFE PATH asks you to let go of whatever you build, perhaps even to let go of the goal before it can be realized. This is very frustrating, but your determination keeps you plowing ahead. Life keeps demanding that you let go of the personal goals until you realize a more universal purpose. *The challenge is in doing what is given to you to do and giving up attachment to how the outcomes might look. You will create great successes built on truth that will bring change for many.*

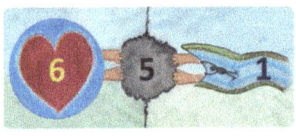 Your INNER SIX wants to belong, to be accepted, and to serve others. Your ONE LIFE PATH throws you out into the world on your own. You want to work together with others, but life provides you with no support system. Whatever group you have is more trouble than it is worth. Learn to stand on your own, to be strong and independent. The experience can at times be heartbreaking, but you grow strong. *The challenge is to transform your dependency on a group to support you into a sense of independence. Then you can attract others who look to you for leadership and you can use your great ability to help them from your position of strength.*

Your INNER SEVEN wants to be left alone to follow your deep interests. Your TWO LIFE PATH asks you to set aside your personal desires and to be there in support of another, usually a partner. You want to direct your energy in a specific manner, but life demands that you be sensitive to the energies and desires of those around you and to be guided by what life brings. You rebel and wish to hide in your own space, but life is not going to allow that to happen. *The challenge is to learn to flow with what is in the present instead of what you would like to be there. In the end you will be led to the perfect spot for you to work your magic. Wait patiently for the call.*

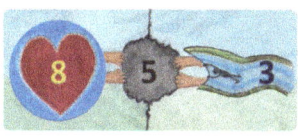
Your INNER EIGHT has large aspirations and wants to leave your mark upon the world. Your THREE LIFE PATH does not provide those opportunities. Instead you are given an extended childhood and the opportunity to develop and express your creative side. This terrifies you, because you want to accomplish big things, and you don't believe that you are creative. Perhaps you try to fill the space with serving others, but your soul is not fulfilled. *The challenge is to play with the space you are given, developing your creative abilities. It is your art that will create great things and bring about change in the world.*

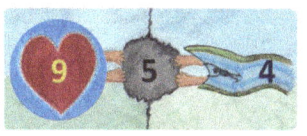
Your INNER NINE is idealistic and unfocused. Your FOUR LIFE PATH doesn't allow you to live in your idealized dreams. Life asks you to roll up your sleeves and to work hard. You don't see any purpose in it and look for a quicker way to get it all done. *The challenge is to do it over and over until you get it right, learning that the quick fix doesn't hold. Along the way you develop self-discipline and order. You learn how to get things done. Ultimately, it will be your idealistic dreams that you get done.*

The stress now is related to the pressures of the group. The stress is between likes, that is, between two odd NUMBERs or two even NUMBERs. You have only splits between the lower and higher VIBRATIONs. With STRESS NUMBER SIX the conflict centers on the extremes of either allowing yourself to be controlled by peer pressure or contrarily to avoid working with others altogether out of the fear of giving up autonomy. *The challenge is about working with others and having a sense of belonging.*

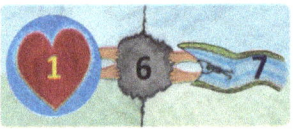

Your INNER ONE knows just where it wants to go. Your SEVEN LIFE PATH doesn't let you get there. Instead you are presented with crises and dark nights of the soul. You are on a spiritual path. If your direction is not aligned with this, you will continue to run into walls. Focus your intense drive toward your spiritual healing. *The challenge is to do this by yourself. You will draw strength and guidance from spiritual groups, but don't try to depend on any one person to be your guide. You will create your own path and it may help many others, though that will not be your intention.*

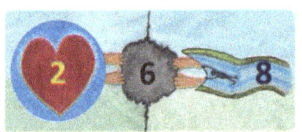

Your INNER TWO wants companionship, to be sensitive, and to be in a supportive position with others. Your EIGHT LIFE PATH asks you to step to the forefront and to be a leader. You are confronted with powerful energy that appears to be out of balance. It won't work for you to wait patiently for the right time to make subtle suggestions. It also won't work to walk away from the situation and go off on your own path. *The challenge is to stay, to learn to understand how power works, and to use your sensitivity to bring balance to the situation. When you become willing to take leadership in this action, you will find your peace.*

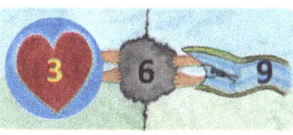

Your INNER THREE wants to be the eternal child, to play and be creative. Your NINE LIFE PATH removes all of the safety that your innocent childhood depends on. Your security blanket is gone. This is an enormous challenge for you. Continue to express as your stage becomes the entire world. If the focus of your creativity is not on unconditional love, universal acceptance, and humanitarianism, it will not find an audience. *The challenge is to learn to let go of all of your attachments and prejudices. Your potential is then awe-inspiring.*

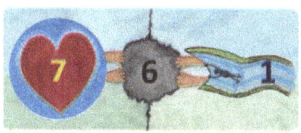

Your INNER SEVEN has a deep desire for perfection and spiritual growth. Your ONE LIFE PATH doesn't allow you the luxury of dwelling in the refined air you crave. You are forced by circumstance to learn how to stand strongly on your own. *The challenge is to develop integrity and courage. The existing paths and choices won't work for you. As you become independent, then you find yourself free to refine the talents that you have. Nothing will be able to stand in your way.*

Your INNER EIGHT wants to exert power in your environment. Your TWO LIFE PATH asks that you be patient, wait in the background, and be the supportive, rather than the leading energy. This is a tall order for you. You find yourself working with a partner, or with partners, where you are required to play the secondary role if things are to work out successfully. You try to take control, but that becomes a disaster. Perhaps you try to leave and find your own private place to develop the work. You will end up with a partner. *The challenge is for you to learn to listen, to develop your timing and your awareness of everything around you. When you can flow with life you will be able to realize all your big dreams.*

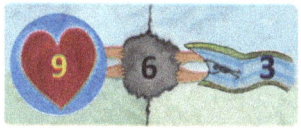

Your INNER NINE wants to make the world a better place, though you don't know how to go about doing it. Your THREE LIFE PATH gives you a wonderful space to develop your dreams, but no impetus for accomplishing anything. You are terrified with the enormity of the creative options open to you and may feel guilty about not accomplishing anything to help mankind. You may try to fill this space with service to others, but this is unfulfilling. *The challenge is to develop your expression. You have something to say to the world that will serve everyone. Begin by loving yourself and share your passions with the world.*

This STRESS NUMBER involves questions of faith and issues of perfectionism. There are only two pairings, each of a higher VIBRATION with a lower. *The challenge involves going more deeply inside and moving through fear. There may be issues of over-rationalizing things and being too much in the mind. The path to wholeness will come through an increase of faith — in self, in the unprovable, in intuition.*

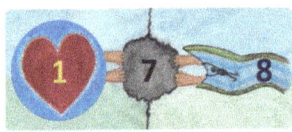

Your INNER ONE knows what you want and wishes to move unquestioningly in that direction. You want to be in charge of your fate, not having to be affected by the whims of others. Yet your EIGHT LIFE PATH has you dealing with the power of the collective, rather than your personal power. You can try in whatever ways possible — and you probably will do that — to go off on your own individual path, until you realize that never works out. *The challenge is to surrender to working within the organization, unable to bend it in the direction you choose unless your direction also supports the group. Ultimately you will realize that the two directions merge.*

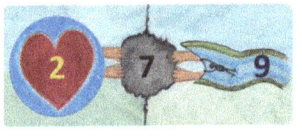

Your INNER TWO wants peace, cooperation, and partnership. Your NINE LIFE PATH asks you to let go of everything that you want. You can keep your sensitivity, but you will tend to lose your relationships. You find yourself in the middle of all types of human drama. Part of you feels it would be easier to just be alone, but life doesn't allow that either. *The challenge is to give up your attachments and your codependency. Operating from a higher level of intuitive sensitivity can make all of this easier. When you are no longer needy, you will have the fulfilling relationship you desire. You will also be a sensitive support to everyone you meet.*

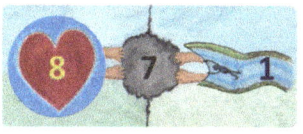

Your INNER EIGHT wishes to use your power to create a just and fair world. Your ONE LIFE PATH does not allow you to use your leadership abilities, because you are faced with the more immediate challenges to your ability to survive. You are forced by circumstance to learn how to take care of yourself. Become strong, independent, and courageous. You would like to find an organization to join where you can work with a team and develop your leadership skills, but you are left to fend for yourself, to build your own empire. *When you learn to stand on your own and have the courage to take on anything, you will look around and see others waiting to follow your orders.*

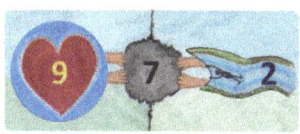

Your INNER NINE has big dreams and the desire for a better, more loving world, but you don't know how to begin to make this happen. Your TWO LIFE PATH doesn't seem to make things any easier. It does not push you in any particular direction, but asks you to be patient, to stay in the background, and to learn to be sensitive to the lives of others. You don't mind doing this, but you want to make a much bigger impact on the world. *The challenge is to develop your sensitivity and your intuitive nature. It is time to deepen your faith. The time for dramatic action will eventually be thrust upon you and you will be ready.*

Ascension Numerology

The STRESS NUMBER EIGHT brings challenges centered in the very use of power. Is it for good or evil, or is that even the highest questions to ask? *The challenge is in gaining an understanding of the true nature of power, which is central to unleashing one's tremendous personal power potential. Go back and read about the NUMBER EIGHT. Learn how manifestation truly takes place.*

With this pairing you have the alpha and the omega. Your INNER ONE is the beginning. You are guided to new creations, answering only to your own vision. Your NINE LIFE PATH doesn't let you follow that direction. You want to set the course, but life has other ideas. You are strong minded and get into a power struggle with life. It is a fight you cannot win. You chose to come here to learn selflessness, generosity, and to have a humanitarian spirit. *The challenge is to learn to let go and let God direct your life. You have the courage to do this. All that is lacking is the will. You will find your direction when you develop that, and you will love it.*

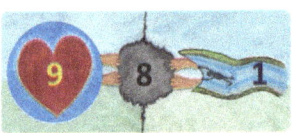

With this pairing you have the alpha and the omega. Your INNER NINE is always the idealistic dreamer, coming in with no agenda and a good deal of wisdom. Your ONE LIFE PATH does not let you focus your life in the service of others. Instead, you find that you are forced to look out for yourself. Others wish to control you, or perhaps you are abandoned. Either way life forces you to grow up in a hurry and become strong and independent. *The challenge is that there is a lot of confusion about how to deal with power in the world, but what works for you is to use your power to follow your own vision. Ultimately, when you are strong enough, you will use your strength in the loving service of mankind.*

Stress number between motivation and life path — EIGHT

There are different ways that you can relate STRESS NUMBERs to the LIFE PATH. The most important correlation is between the MOTIVATION and the LIFE PATH (see "COMPUTATIONS" on page 283). Here you are looking at the difference between what you would like to happen in life and what actually occurs.

The RELATIONSHIP between the PERSONALITY and the LIFE PATH is less significant and there is also less that you can do about it. Your PERSONALITY operates more or less autonomously, so there is not much to tinker with. You can think how your way of doing things might interact with the way things are happening. Mostly, it is a matter of having a greater awareness, so that you can surrender more fully to the LIFE PATH.

Finally, there also is little that you can do to adjust your INTEGRATED SELF to your LIFE PATH. By looking at the interaction they have, you can see how your LIFE PATH supports or works in another direction from the talent you are bringing. You can think about how the two VIBRATIONs work, separately and when added together. Each represents a half of you. The LIFE PATH shows in what way you are going to apply your INTEGRATED SELF's gifts.

If any of the NAME NUMBERs are same as the LIFE PATH, things are easier — but they are not easy. There is no direct conflict, but the life path is always a challenge.

The most important thing to remember is that there is nothing more important than learning to flow with your LIFE PATH. Use the STRESS NUMBERs to help figure out the best ways to do that.

CYCLE

SEASONS OF YOUR LIFE

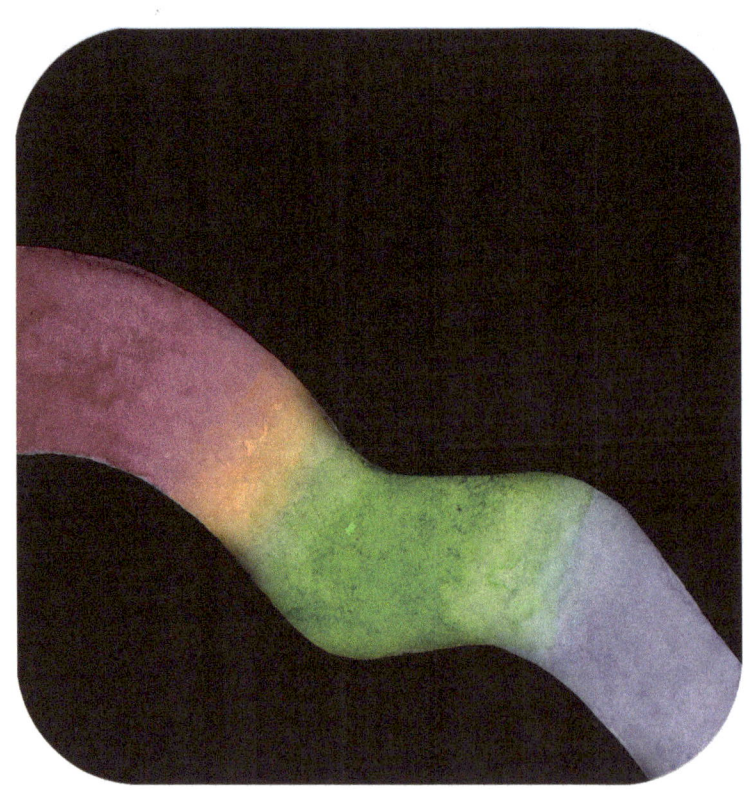

The CYCLE POSITION represents the way that life is acting upon you during a specific period. It works in a similar way to the LIFE PATH, but is more subtle and lasts for only a certain time. You are being asked to surrender to the energy of the CYCLE and to flow with it. The CYCLE is to be read in conjunction with the dominating influence of the LIFE PATH, showing a specific twist your path is taking at certain stages of your life. There are three CYCLEs in your life, the DEVELOPMENTAL, the PRODUCTIVE and the HARVEST. If your CYCLE NUMBER is KARMIC, this is a time when life really encourages you to balance that VIBRATION. *You will be better able to flow with your LIFE PATH when you are also surrendering to the energy of your current CYCLE.*

THE THREE CYCLES

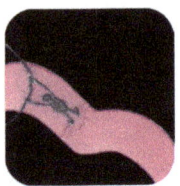

The FIRST CYCLE is called the DEVELOPMENTAL CYCLE. This CYCLE explains the particular influences on your childhood, adolescence, and early adult years. This tends to be your most challenging CYCLE.

The SECOND CYCLE is called the PRODUCTIVE CYCLE and shows the environment that is particular to the central period of your life where your career and the raising of children may take center stage.

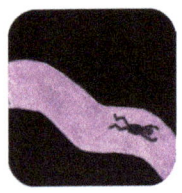

The THIRD CYCLE is called the HARVEST CYCLE and indicates the direction life is guiding you into in your years of wisdom and maturity. This tends to be the easiest CYCLE for you to flow with.

READINGS FOR THE CYCLES

The following NUMBER descriptions could appear on any of the three CYCLEs.

Life is encouraging you to develop the courage to be your own person. You are asked to use your power to follow your unique path. Though you may be tempted to work within larger organizations, that might not work well for you now. *Learn how to be independent.*

Life is encouraging you to be sensitive to the situations of others. It is not a time to push your own agenda, but rather one of listening to and supporting others, while being aware of the flow of events. When the time is right, you will be called. *Learn how to be a sensitive friend.*

Life is encouraging you to develop your creativity and your expression. You will have fewer responsibilities and more time to play. Try to avoid the temptation to fill this space with service to others. Your greatest service will come through your expression. *Learn to share your creativity with others.*

Life is encouraging you to become more disciplined, to work hard, and to face the truth. You may feel weighed down by all of this and wish to break free, but your greatest growth will come through facing head on what life is presenting. *Learn to become an immovable rock of determination.*

Life is encouraging you to learn how to roll with the punches and to land on your feet. You might wish for things to stand still for a while, but your greatest opportunities will come through unexpected changes. *Learn to adapt and how to persuade other people to join with you.*

 Life is encouraging you to put aside your personal desires in order to be of greater service to others. This is a busy time where you are given the opportunity to experience the joy of belonging. You may wish to take your ball and go home at times, but the love you will experience makes it all worthwhile. *Learn to enjoy being a team player.*

 Life is encouraging you to develop your faith. You may find yourself facing many challenges, with nobody there to support you when you most want help. This is also a time when you are encouraged to become an expert at something. *Learn to go inside to find the divinity within you.*

 Life is encouraging you to learn how to deal with power. You find yourself working with or being strongly affected by big organizations. You will be aware of how they are out of balance. Avoid the temptation to go off and work by yourself; be willing to go into the belly of the beast. *Learn the true nature of power.*

 Life is encouraging you to let go of the personal for the universal. Your horizons will be expanded. You will be asked to give up prejudices and possessiveness. You may be asked to surrender people, places, things, and ideas you value. *Learn to let go and to receive unexpected treasures that allow you to rise to a new level of experience.*

Your CYCLEs (see "COMPUTATIONS" on page 282) are elements of timing that are supplementary to the LIFE PATH. The transition from one CYCLE to the next is slow and gradual. You may begin to feel the SECOND CYCLE at age twenty-eight, but it won't fully kick in until you reach your next ONE PERSONAL YEAR. The same is true of your next transition. You may begin to feel the change at age fifty-five, but not the full effect until your next ONE PERSONAL YEAR. The higher the NUMBER you have in your LIFE PATH POSITION, the sooner your SECOND and THIRD CYCLEs fully take effect. In other words, lower LIFE PATHs are likely to have longer childhoods. If a CYCLE NUMBER repeats, you will be going through a deeper lesson in that VIBRATION the second time.

The way to read the CYCLE is similar to the reading of the LIFE PATH. In addition to looking at what is suggested above, you may wish to read the paragraph for a LIFE PATH of the same VIBRATION. Keep in mind that the CYCLE lasts for only a certain segment of your life. It is important to factor in which period of your life it is affecting. You want to pay attention to the STRESS NUMBER between your MOTIVATION and your CYCLE as well any KARMIC NUMBER that coincides with your CYCLE. You could read the comparable reading for the STRESS NUMBER between MOTIVATION and LIFE PATH for a suggestion. As always, bring your own intuition into the process. *Your first call with timing is to surrender to the LIFE PATH. The secondary voice to yield to is that of your CYCLE. It is always quieter, but still well worth paying attention to.*

PINNACLE

HELPING KEEP YOUR EYE ON THE PRIZE

The PINNACLE POSITION represents a "high point" of achievement under the influence of the CYCLEs. Think of a mountain peak. A PINNACLE suggests a mental attitude that you are likely to develop at a particular time of your life because of what is coming down around you. While the CYCLE indicates the environment you are experiencing, the PINNACLE is an indicator of the type of spiritual growth that might be taking place or the spiritual wisdom that might be acquired. You experience four different PINNACLEs. The energy of them is felt most strongly at the beginning and at the end of their appearance. If your PINNACLE is KARMIC you will feel a strong draw to balance the energy of that VIBRATION during this period. *Awareness of your current PINNACLE helps you to maximize your spiritual growth.*

THE FOUR PINNACLES

 The FIRST PINNACLE is the most personal. Everything refers back to the self. Because it is determined by the first two CYCLEs it not only picks up what is present, but also what is to come next. Every VIBRATION is more of a challenge when experienced in the FIRST PINNACLE.

 The SECOND PINNACLE represents foundation laying. This is a time where responsibilities and obligations begin to kick in. Because it is determined by the SECOND and THIRD CYCLEs it picks up on not only what is happening, but also on what is still to come.

 The THIRD PINNACLE is a time for broadening and for a slowing of the pace. It is a time for by-paths. This is the first PINNACLE to contain all of the CYCLEs, so it reaches out into all dimensions of time.

 The FOURTH PINNACLE is a time of beginnings and endings. It can be a second childhood, but it also represents the repository of wisdom and retrospection, as well as a vision of the future. This is an active, though more relaxed time.

READINGS FOR THE PINNACLES

The following NUMBER descriptions could appear on any of the four PINNACLEs.

You find yourself becoming more independent and are learning how to stand up for yourself. It is a time where you go into uncharted waters, starting things that are new to you as well as to others. *It is a time where you will overcome repression and become your own person.*

You find yourself working with others. You become more sensitive and patient. Your diplomatic skills increase as does your desire for harmony in your life. *It is a time when you will develop a feeling for details and for accuracy and precision in your work, as well as patience and sensitivity.*

You learn to develop your expression. You allow yourself to experience a greater enjoyment of life. You open yourself to receiving encouragement and give yourself the space for creative endeavors. *It is a time of friends and of becoming more gregarious. This is your time to be on stage.*

You find yourself bringing more order, system, and practicality into your life. This is a serious time where you look to build something and to achieve concrete results. *This is a time where you lay a good foundation for yourself and are relentless in the search for truth.*

You find yourself becoming more active and willing to try things and live a more public life. You take the freedom to come and go and to make many changes in your life, as well as changes affecting others. *This is a time of progress where you are learning that you will always land on your feet.*

Ascension Numerology

 You find yourself wanting to help, serve, or teach others. You choose to take many duties and responsibilities during this period, most likely to your family. *This is a time of rich rewards for you in love, self-satisfaction, and a sense of home and belonging.*

 You seek quieter places in life with the purpose of soul development. You wish to strengthen your faith and trust. You are drawn to study, to going deeper into things. *This is a time when you go within yourself to perfect and augment your spirituality.*

 You choose to get more involved with the business world, or other organizations, and seek opportunities for leadership. You find that material manifestation flows well for you. *This is a busy time where you find yourself feeling more ambitious and learn to deal with a power in a more balanced way.*

 You find yourself developing your senses of compassion, tolerance, and humanitarianism. You want to grow and to leave behind the "small" parts of yourself. *This is a time where you gain richness from travel, broadening experiences, and human interactions that expand your spiritual consciousness.*

MORE ABOUT

The PINNACLEs are very much connected to the energy of the CYCLEs. As with the CYCLEs, the SECOND PINNACLE begins later when the LIFE PATH NUMBER is smaller (see "COMPUTATIONS"). PINNACLEs represent the essence of the CYCLEs through a uniting or overlapping of their energies. They show the types of reactions you are likely to encounter as a result of your interaction with the CYCLEs. PINNACLEs both use the experiences of the past and help to plan the future. The PINNACLE energy is highly prophetic. PINNACLEs show testing times and indicate the subjective handling of a situation. The crossover time between PINNACLEs can be traumatic, particularly the transition from the FIRST PINNACLE to the SECOND PINNACLE. This is true even if the VIBRATION remains the same. If a pinnacle number repeats, you will be going through a deeper growth in that vibration the second time. PINNACLEs show when and how major changes may come into your life. Here are a few examples:

- If your MOTIVATION is the same as a PINNACLE, you ought to be well pleased and doing what you like best.
- If your PERSONALITY is the same as a PINNACLE, you are instinctively able to carry out the requirements of that VIBRATION; things come easily.
- If your INTEGRATED SELF is the same as your PINNACLE, you are doing what you do best. Much can be accomplished.
- If the LIFE PATH VIBRATION is the same as a PINNACLE, it is a time when you are fully prepared to meet the demands of those lessons.

To read your PINNACLE, begin by looking at the suggestion at the beginning of this chapter. You can also read the general description for the NUMBER in your PINNACLE POSITION. Look to see in what other POSITIONs that NUMBER appears in your CHART. Those areas will be connected to what you experience with your PINNACLE. Read and think about which of the four PINNACLE POSITIONs you are experiencing. Finally, think about your current CYCLE as well as your LIFE PATH VIBRATION. Listen to your inner guidance. *Though the PINNACLE may be experienced as a challenge, there will be a sense of growth and accomplishment attached to it. The PINNACLE always takes you higher.*

PERSONAL YEAR

FLOWING WITH YOUR LIFE

The PERSONAL YEAR POSITION represents a cyclical energy in your LIFE PATH where a particular VIBRATION is felt more strongly for a year. The effect is similar, though secondary, to that of the LIFE PATH and CYCLE. Each PERSONAL YEAR lasts for just one year, progressing VIBRATION by VIBRATION from a ONE PERSONAL YEAR through a NINE PERSONAL YEAR, and then repeating that NINE YEAR CYCLE over and over. This brings a natural flow to your life. The PERSONAL YEAR transition occurs on your birthday. *Paying attention to the PERSONAL YEAR helps you understand and flow with events more smoothly. It can also guide your choice of actions. It is like Jacob's ladder. Every round takes you higher, higher.*

This is a time for new beginnings. Hopefully, you left a good deal of the past behind you last year (in your NINE PERSONAL YEAR), so you have a relatively clean slate. This year, life encourages you to be more ONE than you normally are. Start something new. Plant some seeds. Allow yourself to be more singularly focused. Be courageous. Don't listen to others, unless they are supporting what your heart is telling you. You never know during the ONE PERSONAL YEAR, itself, where all of this is going to end up. Pioneers never have that kind of information. If they did, they would be following a well-worn path rather than this new one. The most important thing this year is to have integrity, to be true to yourself. ONE represents archetypal masculine energy. *Start in a new direction.*

Now that you have planted your seeds in the ONE PERSONAL YEAR, it is time to cultivate them. This requires attention and patience. It is no longer the right time to force issues, but rather to flow smoothly with the events that life brings. The TWO PERSONAL YEAR is a period for bringing balance back into your life. The direction has been set and it cannot now be altered. It is too soon to know where everything is going to lead, so the best you can do is bring peace and harmony into your everyday life. You may not have been overly attentive to your relationships last year, but now is the time to mend fences and nurture those around you. This is a make or break year for intimate relationships. TWO represents archetypal feminine energy. *Bring your life into balance.*

The last two years have been enjoyable, but intensive. Now it is time to relax a bit. If the ONE is the father and the TWO is the mother, then the THREE PERSONAL YEAR is the child. This is a year for having more free time and for playing. THREE is the VIBRATION of creativity. The laboratory that breeds creativity is the relaxed mind and open heart. Your job this year is to visualize the future, to see the big picture. In the ONE year you were shown a direction, but now you are shown a possible place that road might lead to. This expression is not something that can be rushed or forced. Enjoy your time. Follow your heart and express what is there to those around you. Trust what comes to you and follow that dream. Enjoy this playground while it lasts. *Visualize your future.*

Personal year

Roll up your sleeves and get ready to go to work. You did a wonderful job in the THREE PERSONAL YEAR visualizing your future. Now it is time to begin to build it. Your "family" is ready for a home. You build it from the ground up. The work can't really be delegated at this point, for only you have the vision. It is your job in your FOUR PERSONAL YEAR to stay busy (aren't you glad for last year's vacation?). Stay true to the vision. Build your foundation slowly and steadily. There will be time to rest later, but now is the time to be dedicated and relentless. Face reality and be honest with yourself and others. Drive yourself hard; you can take it. This structure you are building is going to serve you for a long time. There are no shortcuts. You may take great pride in your accomplishments; others may not be aware of them yet. Not to worry. *Build your dream.*

Take a deep breath and let it go. The foundation is built and now you can dance on it. Notice how you have been skipping back and forth from even NUMBERs to odd ones. The odd NUMBERs give you more space to express yourself. The FIVE PERSONAL YEAR is the time for movement and progress. Now you can utilize others and manipulate whatever you can to maximize the usefulness of what you built in the FOUR year. Travel will likely be a part of your plans. Everything seems to move ahead more quickly and with less effort. You are glad you paid your dues last year. You make many small to medium size adjustments to the plan. You are getting good at thinking on your feet. The year may be as busy as the FOUR PERSONAL YEAR, but it seems easier. You are firing on all cylinders. *Enjoy and improve what you have built.*

You have been a bit of a workaholic the past two years. Now it is time to take care of family and friends. In fact, this year it seems like everybody fits into one of those two categories. This is your year for service and your "family" is growing. The structure you have built can roll on without your total focus now. It is the people who call out for attention. Listen to them; love them; give them what will help. Let your SIX PERSONAL YEAR be filled with love. If you have a business, it is staff development time. Whatever your business, it is hands on people-service time. Your family and relationships are all pulling at you. Surrender to the call. This is a year to enjoy all the people in your life. This is a time to feel the difference you make for them and to feel yourself to be a part of the team. *Find yourself in loving company and service.*

It is time for a well-deserved rest. The past three years have seen a flurry of activity. Now you have reached the "Sabbath" of your NINE YEAR CYCLE. The SEVEN PERSONAL YEAR is a time for reflection; it is a time to look back over the past six years and to ask yourself questions like, "What has this all been about?" or "Why am I here?" This is not a period for play and expression as it was in the THREE; this is the season of inner searching, of finding faith and meaning. Life is not going on as usual. It is a time where you are more likely to go it alone. The close connections of the SIX are not so easily grasped, now. When you most feel a need for others, you find that life encourages you to instead depend upon yourself. You may have reached many of the goals you set, but it is not enough. This is the year of finding a higher reason for your life. *Step back from the world and take care of your spiritual life.*

You have come down from the mountain. You have realized that your purpose is much bigger than you thought it was. The EIGHT PERSONAL YEAR is about fully realizing your power. This is the year where you take the impetus of the ONE year, the balancing of the TWO, the dreaming of the THREE, the hard work of the FOUR, the progress of the FIVE, the loving service of the SIX, and the soul searching discoveries of the SEVEN and create heaven on earth. This is a tall order, but you are well prepared. This is not about personal power; it is about channeling the love you feel within yourself to manifest your biggest dreams. This will mean as much to the planet as it does to you. You have not just been working for this for the past seven years, you have been preparing all your life and for lifetimes before that. However, the completion of this NINE YEAR CYCLE does not come until the NINE PERSONAL YEAR. *Reach for the heavens; the sky is your limit.*

Now it is done. You have completed what you wanted to achieve in this NINE YEAR CYCLE. The NINE PERSONAL YEAR is time to let go, to give everything up. If there is anything that will be of use for your next NINE YEAR CYCLE, you don't need to worry about it; it will hang around. Give up your attachments. Give up your ego. Expand and float upward. This is the time to see everything around you. It's the time to see the drama of life without personal involvement. You are to give up all judgments and love unconditionally. There is another rung for you to climb, but now is not the time to think of it. Don't start anything new; it will probably leave before the year is out. Clean everything out on every plane. The only thing to hold on to this year is your heart. Weed with loving care. There is no hurry; but the more space you create in your life, the less there will be standing in the way for your coming ONE PERSONAL YEAR. *Let go freely; lighten your load so you can rise to the next level.*

The last of the timing POSITIONs, though not the least, is the PERSONAL YEAR (see "COMPUTATIONS" on page 285). This VIBRATION shows your personal rhythm with the life around you, and it is something you share with everyone. Whereas the LIFE PATH is yours alone (shared with eleven percent of your fellow travelers), everyone goes through the NINE YEAR CYCLE from ONE to NINE. Your timing is further individualized by the CYCLE you're in and the PINNACLE that is lifting you up. Against this backdrop you traverse your NINE YEAR CYCLE.

NINE YEAR CYCLE

Your life is somewhat neatly packaged into nine year periods. Each period begins with a ONE year and ends with a NINE year. Each year within that NINE YEAR CYCLE has its own influence. An understanding of your PERSONAL YEAR can help you flow more easily with your life as it unfolds. Each NINE YEAR CYCLE spirals higher, building upon the one before it. *As you read the descriptions of the PERSONAL YEARS in the NINE YEAR CYCLE, keep in mind that life will be presenting you with opportunities; the italicized suggestions are there to encourage you to receive what happens in your life as gifts and flow with them in the highest way.*

FURTHER CONSIDERATIONS

There are aspects of each PERSONAL YEAR that have been introduced in the descriptions above, but there are also some general things for you to look at. Here are a few to consider:

- The PERSONAL YEAR that corresponds with your LIFE PATH is the most important single year in your NINE YEAR CYCLE. It is a year where you have no choice but to fully surrender to your LIFE PATH. Big things are going to happen; it is easier if you go willingly.
- The year of your ASCENSION NUMBER becomes more important each successive NINE YEAR CYCLE, as you are growing spiritually. Eventually it can outshine your LIFE PATH year in the significance of its impact.
- The PERSONAL YEAR that matches your current CYCLE is of secondary importance.
- A PERSONAL YEAR that matches a KARMIC NUMBER is always a particular challenge, but is a valuable learning time.
- A PERSONAL YEAR that aligns with your PINNACLE will show leaps of growth toward the possibilities of that VIBRATION.
- You are more likely to enjoy the experiences during a PERSONAL YEAR that matches your MOTIVATION.
- Each successive NINE YEAR CYCLE brings you to a higher level of understanding for the requirements of each of the nine VIBRATIONs.

Your PERSONAL YEAR has its maximum impact at three times during your year: 1) your birthday, which is the time of transition to the new PERSONAL YEAR, 2) a ONE PERSONAL MONTH when the new energy really start to kick in, and 3) September, which always has the same PERSONAL MONTH VIBRATION as your PERSONAL YEAR.

Look at the description of the VIBRATION matching your current PERSONAL YEAR (in Chapter 4) to get more of a feeling for what that VIBRATION is about. Likewise, read the description for the LIFE PATH that matches your current PERSONAL YEAR to get an idea of what might be in store for you. Remember, you are getting a much smaller dose of the energy than you would if that were your LIFE PATH. Finally, the descriptions for the PERSONAL YEAR that have been given demonstrate the highest potential for them. Don't be concerned if your experience seems to fall short. Each NINE YEAR CYCLE you will experience more and more alignment with this picture.

PERSONAL MONTH
Fine tuning your path

The PERSONAL MONTH POSITION represents an energy similar to the PERSONAL YEAR, but much diluted. It cycles from ONE through NINE month by month (with the exception of the transition at the end of the year between December and January, where it jumps back two). Knowing your PERSONAL MONTH can help you be sensitive to more subtle aspects of timing. *Awareness of the PERSONAL MONTH can help you to really be here now.*

 Look for a clear sense of the meaning of the year to be shown. Time to get on track.

 Try to flow with things and pay attention. Is there something or someone you're not being sensitive to?

 Get a bigger picture of where you are going. Enjoy!

 Stay busy. Organize something. Face facts.

 Pick up the pace. Vary your schedule. Travel.

 People come first. Help somebody. Be a team player.

 Take a step back. You might benefit from some down time. Face your fears.

 Don't hold back. Give it everything you've got. Make your year happen.

 Let go. You have done what you can. Give it up to a higher place. Forgive.

MORE ABOUT

Okay, so I wasn't totally accurate when I said that the PERSONAL YEAR was the last timing POSITION. The PERSONAL MONTH (see "COMPUTATIONS" on page 285) is far less significant in its influence than is the PERSONAL YEAR, but it is worth taking a look at. Here are some things to consider with the PERSONAL MONTH:

- You want to examine your PERSONAL MONTH in the context of the PERSONAL YEAR. That is to say that the PERSONAL MONTH helps you to see the timing of how the PERSONAL YEAR unfolds.
- You will change PERSONAL MONTH (and PERSONAL YEAR) mid-month at your birthday, with both increasing by one. This is a powerful transition moment for you, even though the full affects are still to come. Otherwise, your PERSONAL MONTH changes with the calendar on the first of the month.
- You may really begin to feel your PERSONAL YEAR kick in when you reach your ONE PERSONAL MONTH.
- In September, your PERSONAL MONTH and PERSONAL YEAR will always be the same, so there is a strong impetus for that VIBRATION.
- The most significant PERSONAL MONTH is the one that coincides with your PERSONAL YEAR.
- Keep in mind the coincidence of your PERSONAL MONTH with other significant POSITIONs in your CHART, and think about how that might affect your month.

PERSONAL DAY
Delivered fresh to your door

If you think things are getting a little ridiculous at this point, you are at least half right. This is mostly for fun. It is not a big deal to be aware of your PERSONAL DAY (see "COMPUTATION" on page 285), whereas you definitely want to know what PERSONAL YEAR you are in and knowing the PERSONAL MONTH is also helpful. The PERSONAL DAY cycles from ONE through NINE, except for jumps between months and at your birthday.

ASCENSION NUMBER

THE VANISHING POINT

The ASCENSION NUMBER POSITION represents the ultimate potential to realize your divinity, for which you designed this incarnation. Like the vanishing point in a drawing, all roads in your life point to the ASCENSION NUMBER, however, you cannot go directly there. First you balance your MOTIVATION and PERSONALITY to unveil your true talents through your INTEGRATED SELF. Then you surrender fully to your LIFE PATH, to learn to co-create with the divine presence of love. *It is through the ASCENSION NUMBER that you realize your own divinity, and it is upon realizing your personal ASCENSION that your greatest service to humanity manifests.*

Ascension Numerology

You are absolutely independent. You answer to nobody but your own divinity. You know that you are one with all, but your connectedness comes through your personal relationship with your higher self. No one else can show you the path you came to walk. You are fearless as you walk into the unknown. You are the originator for what newness is important for the planet. You are the inspiration for others when they seek to have courage, when they want to trust their own inner guidance, and when it is time to stand up for themselves.

You are the agent for peace and harmony on the planet. You feel everything that goes on around you. You read the hearts of others. You are empathetic without buying into the people's fears. You can see their true divinity behind the illusions they project. You know exactly what move to make to support others in finding their divine balance. You know this in a way that is far beyond conscious thinking. You seek nothing for yourself, yet all is drawn to your field of energy. When others seek inner or outer peace they are inspired by your presence. Your presence alone is sufficient for healing to take place.

You are the light of the world. You see the divine potential in every person and every situation and you express those possibilities for all to see. Your smile covers the sky and your creativity knows no bounds. You are a fountain of youth. You allow whatever you channel to flow through you without filters. You are equally comfortable playing the fool or the sage. You see no difference between them. You help others to unblock their own creativity and release their inhibitions. You demonstrate the unlimited potential of the creator, inspiring others to unleash their inner artist and prophet.

You are the absolute rock of truth. You can and do build anything you choose. You are indomitable, a force that cannot be stopped once you have set your course. This is because the absolute divine truth of the universe is always your compass. You understand that love is truth and fear is illusion on an innate level. You inspire others to build their dreams. You give them the toughness to face their fears and to persevere. They can always count on you for the truth. You lay the foundation stone for building heaven on earth. You are the most practical of dreamers.

You are the divine agent for change in the world. Your feet are planted firmly on the earth or at least you will land with them that way. Everything can be improved by you. You created the world in order to experience it in its totality. You love life. When others find themselves stuck, they turn to you for the inspiration to move on. You progress fearlessly, neither holding on to the past nor leaping blindly. You are the gilded tongued Pied Piper [1] from heaven, convincing one and all that life can be more for them than they have been willing to allow. Ultimately, you realize that nothing that can change is divine.

You give loving service to the planet. You care deeply about people and want to help through teaching, counseling, feeding, clothing, housing, and listening to them. You are at home wherever you go and show others that real joy comes from working together and loving each other. You see that we are all one and the greatest joy you can give yourself is to give of yourself to another. You inspire others to open up their hearts and share. You make them feel wanted. You feel love from everyone. Your life is a "pay it forward" that brings divine love and brotherhood to the entire planet.

---

1) The Pied Piper is a legendary pipe player whose beautiful playing could only be heard from by children, who gaily followed him away.

You are the beacon of faith and trust for the world. Your deep inner connection to the divine has brought you a wisdom that others will lean on. But you are not here to be their support; you are here to guide them to their own inner strength. All recognize the purity of your spirit, but few can get truly close to you. Your happiness comes most deeply in your time alone with the divine. There you are never alone. You see the divine in every aspect of earthly life and are able to show that to others. Where they experience problems, you see divine gifts that exist to help them open up to their spiritual treasures.

You are the channel for power on earth. You understand the laws of manifestation. You have no desire for material accumulation because you create what is of use to you in the moment. You see the divine potential in all people and can show them how to uncover it. You are doing what you came here to do, and you have the ability to guide others to realize their divine purpose. Your head is in the clouds, but your feet are placed solidly on the earth. You understand that scarcity exists only in the mind and that there are no true limits. Others are drawn to your power, but they come away empowered themselves.

Ascension Numerology

You love unconditionally and are the divine, but humble servant of the whole planet. There is nothing you wish for yourself, not even a sense of belonging or gratitude from others. You watch the great human drama unfold, but do not take part. When people are ready to let go of their old fear-based stories, they come to you. You are free of judgment and everybody feels safe with you. You are the loving spiritual parent they have dreamed of. But, you will not be just their parent; your job is to help them grow up and become a spiritual adult. Your absolute freedom from attachment and discrimination opens the doors of humanitarianism to all.

MORE ABOUT

Your ASCENSION NUMBER is the combination of your INTEGRATED SELF and your LIFE PATH (see "COMPUTATIONS" on page 285). It is the totality of what is within you added to the totality of what is happening outside of you. Your task is to realize that you are one with creation. Your job is to fully express your divinity while completely surrendering to the gifts that are being presented to you from the universe. As you are doing that, you want to be sure you're focusing on any KARMIC NUMBERs, bringing those into balance in your life. Be aware of your STRESS NUMBER BETWEEN MOTIVATION AND PERSONALITY, fine-tuning that relationship. At the same time, your attention is riveted to your LIFE PATH, consciously choosing it while avoiding the temptation of the ANTI-NUMBER. Likewise, you are also sensitive to your NINE YEAR CYCLE, your CYCLE, and your PINNACLE. Until all of this is moving into an order and fluidity, any attempt to focus on the ASCENSION NUMBER would be fruitless; you would be, at best, spinning your wheels. So, feel free to read this now. Use it as a source of inspiration, as the light at the end of the tunnel. This is where you are headed. You will get there.

While you cannot successfully focus solely on your ASCENSION NUMBER during the early years, it is still constantly present in subtle ways. Here are some places to pay attention to. As you get closer to the time for a more focused pursuance of your ASCENSION NUMBER, these hints will be of increasing importance; but it is never harmful to be aware of them. Look for the following correlations in your CHART:

- If your ASCENSION NUMBER is the same as either your INTEGRATED SELF or your LIFE PATH (which requires that the other of the two VIBRATIONs is a NINE), your ASCENSION NUMBER will take things to an entirely new level. That being said, there is an obvious and significant connection between that other VIBRATION and your ASCENSION NUMBER.

- When the ASCENSION NUMBER falls on your PERSONAL YEAR it will be a vital year and have more influence on your future than any other year in that NINE YEAR CYCLE with the possible exception of your LIFE PATH year.
- If your ASCENSION NUMBER falls upon a PINNACLE that time will likewise be most important to your spiritual development and your future. Here is a great opportunity to develop the powers and energies that lead to realizing your ASCENSION.
- If the ASCENSION NUMBER does not appear on a PINNACLE, the development will take place more gradually and be, perhaps, more delayed in its realization.

Here are some connections between your ASCENSION NUMBER and another person's NAME NUMBERs:

- When another's MOTIVATION is the same as your ASCENSION NUMBER there will be a deep, interesting, mutual attraction. There can be an immediate understanding.
- When another's PERSONALITY is the same as your ASCENSION NUMBER there will not be as deep an attraction, but you will be drawn by this person's manner or appearance.
- When another's INTEGRATED SELF is the same as your ASCENSION NUMBER there is a deep past life link. This relationship can be subtle and not always deeply harmonious, but much can be attained and worked out together. This could be a lifelong relationship. The other person's INTEGRATED SELF will take the lead and support the development of your ASCENSION NUMBER. The teacher will likely be strict and the student may prove difficult.
- When another's ASCENSION NUMBER is the same as yours there is an interesting attraction. You have much in common. The tie may be unusual and can last throughout the life if spiritual growth is equal. You provide each other with mutual support even though you are of seemingly different natures. There is a great sympathy and a satisfaction in the relationship. Much potential good can come of it.

It is not important to focus on your ASCENSION NUMBER. Everything in your life is pointing you in this direction. Take care of today, let go of your resistance, and the universe will handle everything else.

TABLE OF INTENSIFICATION

WHERE ARE YOUR PASSIONS?

The TABLE OF INTENSIFICATION is not a POSITION. However, it shows you where your KARMIC NUMBERs lie. It also shows the relative strengths and weaknesses you came in with for the non-KARMIC VIBRATIONs. The NUMBERs in the TABLE are derived from the letters of your name. If you have a NUMBER represented in the letters of your name at least once, you were born with a basic ability to work with that VIBRATION. You may not love it or excel at it, but when life calls on you to use it, you can do it. *When you have a high number of a VIBRATION then that indicates a passion for you.*

MORE ABOUT THE TABLE OF INTENSIFICATION

There are only 729 different combinations of NAME NUMBERs and LIFE PATHs. Of course KARMIC NUMBERs, CYCLEs, and PINNACLEs bring in more diversity. The true uniqueness of you becomes more obvious as we look at the TABLE OF INTENSIFICATION and the PLANEs OF EXPRESSION.

If you have one or more zeros in your TABLE OF INTENSIFICATION, those indicate your KARMIC NUMBERs. For the rest of the VIBRATIONs you want to look at the relative strength that is shown in the table below. The more of a VIBRATION you have, the more natural ability you have with it. High NUMBERs show passions. This is likely an area that you did significant work with in a previous lifetime. Even if the VIBRATION is not significant in your name numbers, it is a source of strength for you. You will also feel a connection with others who are strong in that VIBRATION. Low NUMBERs show indifference or even some aversion to the VIBRATION. However, even if the value in your TABLE matching your MOTIVATION is low, that VIBRATION is still a passion with you. That doesn't mean that you necessarily deal with it well to begin with, but you want to follow its energy.

AVERAGE DISTRIBUTION OF NUMBERS

Here is an average amount for each NUMBER in your TABLE OF INTENSIFICATION (see "COMPUTATIONS" on page 286):

1	2	3	4	5	6	7	8	9
3-4	1	1	1	4-5	1	0-1	0-1	3

Notice that ONES, FIVES, and NINES are the most commonly found VIBRATIONs in names. They are rarely found as KARMIC NUMBERs. SEVENS and EIGHTS, on the other hand are often KARMIC NUMBERs, with a majority of CHARTs probably having a KARMIC EIGHT.

RELATIVE STRENGTH OF A VIBRATION

In the sample TABLE below, having a "2" under 8 shows more relative strength than having a "2" under 5, since "2" would be an above average number of EIGHTS while "2" would be a below average number of FIVES.

It is not significant to look at the quality of the digit you have for each NUMBER VIBRATION. In other words, the numerological qualities of "TWO" don't matter when you have "2" under EIGHT; what matters is that it is a relatively high quantity of EIGHTS.

BALANCE AND TEMPERAMENT

You can see the balance in your own temperament in the TABLE OF INTENSIFICATION. Having a sizable difference between your high and low NUMBERs in your TABLE OF INTENSIFICATION or having a significant variation between your NUMBERs and the average frequency for that NUMBER can indicate extremities of mood. Having a more balanced and average distribution shows a more even-tempered personality.

PLANE OF EXPRESSION

YOUR DAY TO DAY DIALOGUE WITH LIFE

The PLANEs OF EXPRESSION POSITIONs show your day to day relationship with life. Whereas the NAME NUMBERs show your overall direction and energies, the PLANEs OF EXPRESSION show how you operate in the here and now. They are a natural and automatic part of you, somewhat as is the PERSONALITY. You simply act with the energies they indicate. You operate simultaneously on the PHYSICAL, EMOTIONAL, MENTAL, and INTUITIVE PLANEs.

THE FOUR PLANES OF EXPRESSION

PHYSICAL PLANE deals with your physical body, your day to day dialogue with life, the type of work you might do, your basic instincts, and your relationship with the tangible three-dimensional life style. It deals with form and common sense, rather than fancy or high logic. A high NUMBER indicates a practical nature and an abundance of energy.

EMOTIONAL PLANE deals with the heart, feelings, imagination, creativity, and sex life. It deals with emotion over logic, with the heart of mankind. A high NUMBER indicates an artist of some sort.

MENTAL PLANE deals with how you analyze things or how you put things together. It represents your willpower and your determination. It stands for facts over imagination. A high NUMBER indicates you are very cerebral.

INTUITIVE PLANE deals with the spiritual realm, intuition, ESP, universal intelligence, and divine knowing. It goes beyond learning and brings reverence and worship. It includes compassion, tolerance, invention, prophecy, and an inner guidance that "quickens" all other levels. A high NUMBER indicates a comfort in working on non-physical levels.

PLANES OF EXPRESSION

Begin by noticing what NUMBER you have on each of the four PLANEs. The commentary begins with a general statements that apply to all PLANEs having that particular NUMBER. This is followed by a specific text for each PLANE.

You have an independent streak and can have a one-track mind. You have courage and integrity. People usually know where you stand. There are few areas of gray for you.

PHYSICAL: You are not a physically oriented person, though you are capable of amazing energy in short bursts. Mostly, your focus is on other PLANEs. You have the courage to begin things alone.
EMOTIONAL: It is all about you. In relationships others may find they meet you way more than half way. You are relentless in the pursuit of a relationship and can only have one at a time and few in a lifetime, as it will take a long time for you to change your focus. You can be a lone wolf.
MENTAL: Deep thinking is not your forte. You make up your mind quickly and then are off in other directions. You always decide things for yourself. Unless EMOTIONAL VIBRATIONs are strong elsewhere, you usually don't take others' wishes into consideration. Though a low NUMBER, ONE is in its home court and can act powerfully.
INTUITIVE: You consider yourself to be more practical than spiritual, but intuitive blasts come to you like a bolt out of the sky. Then you take it to another PLANE and work with it there. You are not the meditative type.

You are sensitive to everyone and everything around you. Your presence increases the peacefulness in any setting. You try to be supportive of others' efforts.

PHYSICAL: Physical endurance is not your domain and your body can be sensitive to sickness or injury. Pay attention. Take it easy. Physically, you are a comfort to be around and you prefer to do any activity with somebody else.
EMOTIONAL: Your TWO is on its own turf. Though your focus is mostly on your other higher-numbered PLANEs, you can be very sensitive to others, particularly in one-to-one relationships. You are more comfortable having a primary relationship. You enjoy sharing your experiences.

MENTAL: You are indecisive. You can always see the other side of the story. You tend to go along with the prevailing idea. You don't think deeply about things, but can be a collector of information. It will be up to somebody else to analyze the data and put it to use.

INTUITIVE: You have a strong spiritual intuition about things, and particularly about people. Though you don't spend a lot of time on this PLANE, you can use your hunches in the real world.

There is something eternally young and playful about you. You are fun to be with. You can always be counted on to have a creative or humorous take on things. Part of you seeks an audience.

PHYSICAL: You have lots of energy for things that are fun, but tire easily at more burdensome tasks. You always look younger than your age and bring a creative influence into every activity. You are not structured and can jump from thing to thing rather than completing activities.

EMOTIONAL: You are at home on the EMOTIONAL PLANE. Even though THREE is a somewhat low VIBRATION, you have a lot of emotional strength. Though emotional commitment is not your long suit, you love to play with others, are great fun to be with, and are very creative.

MENTAL: You are a creative thinker, one who lives outside the box. You express your opinions freely. Your thinking is not logical nor are your mental pursuits disciplined. You are the idea person. Others will flesh things out.

INTUITIVE: You have the gift of prophecy. You have a sense for how things will turn out. You are also divinely inspired to say the right thing to the right person at the right time. Otherwise, you probably don't think of yourself as a deeply spiritual person.

You are an honest and dependable person. People can count on you. You are slow and steady, determined and unstoppable. You can be quite disciplined.

PHYSICAL: You have a physical VIBRATION on the PHYSICAL PLANE making you very grounded in the world. Though your physical energy is not boundless, you have enough to finish the job. You start a task slowly, but develop a system that allows you to increase your productivity.

EMOTIONAL: You are a loyal friend and lover. You are not one to change horses easily or freely. You prefer to work on familiar ground with proven allies. Trust is very important to you. Forgiveness does not come easily to you for one who has deceived you. That's when you might search for a replacement.

MENTAL: You are an orderly and logical thinker. You don't easily make large mental leaps. You operate best taking ideas step by step. Once you grasp a concept you can work well with it. You have little use for theoretical ideas. You want results and the application of ideas.

INTUITIVE: You are not drawn to the "woo woo" side of spirituality. Your spiritual beliefs function when they bear real life fruit. Given that, ritual is important to your spiritual process. You like having a form that can be repeated. You are much stronger spiritually than might be evident to others.

You have a spirit of adventure and are always open to new things. You are quick with things and are often a step ahead of others. You can be persuasive. Change is important to you and you do a good job of landing on your feet.

PHYSICAL: This is home territory for your PHYSICAL FIVE and you have lots of energy. You make many changes in your work and activities, displaying much flexibility. Even if you maintain the same work for a long period of time, you will constantly be bringing in new approaches or taking on different tasks. You are an adventurer.

EMOTIONAL: Commitment doesn't come easily to you because you have so many interests and don't want to be tied down. Your partner will be someone with varied interests and a spirit of adventure. You have a pragmatic rather than a romantic nature. You are in love with life itself.

MENTAL: You are a fast thinker. You grasp concepts quickly and jump ahead, not following any orthodox pattern. You are a natural salesperson, able to share your excitement about something with others. You are curious about everything, though you will likely jump to something new rather than to plunge deeper.

INTUITIVE: You are intuitive about things in a way that seems to be second nature to you. Though you may not consider yourself psychic, you make practical use out of intuitive awareness. This quality doubles if you also have a PHYSICAL FIVE. You, however, are not the meditative type, nor are rituals of importance to you.

 You are a service oriented person. You naturally help those around you. People are important to you. You can set aside your personal desires for the good of the group. You like the feeling of belonging.

PHYSICAL: People feel nurtured by your presence. Your work likely involves helping others, perhaps as a teacher, health care worker, or counselor. You have lots of physical energy and enjoy the physical presence of others. It feels good to be of assistance.
EMOTIONAL: Your SIX is in its natural home on the EMOTIONAL PLANE. You love people and want to be surrounded by a warm loving family. You love to take care of those who are close to you and you stand by them and behind them. You are a cheerleader for them — a tireless advocate.
MENTAL: You spend a lot of time thinking about others and their situations. Be careful not to carry the weight of the world on your shoulders. Your goals often are for others, or, if for yourself, include others.
INTUITIVE: You have a great deal of power on the INTUITIVE PLANE. You want to use this to help others, so you would operate well as a minister or in another capacity where you use spiritual energy to support others in handling their lives.

 You go deeply into things and require a certain amount of space and privacy in order to do that. There is a spiritual touch for you on all PLANEs. You always have one foot pulled out of the day to day world.

PHYSICAL: You have much energy and work best alone. You are a specialist in your field and become an expert in whatever you do. You may not mix easily socially, though this is not from discomfort. You simply have little need to share your thoughts with others. You will talk at length about what you know.
EMOTIONAL: You are emotionally strong, but tend to be private with your feelings. It can be difficult for you and others to feel deep emotional connections, as you remain somewhat aloof. Still you can bring spiritual insight into the problems of others and be a source of support.
MENTAL: You are analytical and think deeply about things. You are a perfectionist. Your reasoning is not only influenced by facts, but also by a deeper spiritual knowing. You are capable of writing and doing research. This is a powerful PLANE for you.

INTUITIVE: Your SEVEN is in its home territory on the INTUITIVE PLANE. You are a deeply spiritual person. Meditation and communion with the infinite are comfortable places for you. While this spiritual wealth can be shared with others, it is something you access by yourself.

You are a powerful person and others automatically respond to your leadership. You work in a large fashion with the world, never choosing to do things in small ways. There is something royal in your bearing.

PHYSICAL: Your physical presence tends to dominate in any environment. Others feel your power and turn to you for leadership. You have seemingly unlimited energy and can accomplish much. You manifest whatever material things are necessary to accomplish your goals.
EMOTIONAL: You control any group or relationship emotionally. This is not the most ideal place for such power if your desire is for intimacy. However, you are wonderful at getting others to deal with their emotional problems in a constructive way. You are fearless with your feelings.
MENTAL: Your EIGHT is on its home turf on the MENTAL PLANE. Your will is powerful and indomitable. You think in managerial ways: how to delegate, how to get the most production out of others, and how to support the development of others.
INTUITIVE: You are a spiritual leader. You show people how to fish rather than feeding them for today. You have tapped your spiritual power and you work to share that knowledge with others. You and the infinite are a powerful team.

Part of you is not quite on this earth plane and it is a powerful part. You are an impractical idealist and have a dramatic effect on all who come into contact with you. You are free of prejudices and love all people. There is a flair for drama in all that you do.

PHYSICAL: You have the talent to be a great actor. You can play any role, but you will always be noticed. Your presence is enormous wherever you are. You use your power to help those who are experiencing difficulties. You are charismatic.
EMOTIONAL: You feel an enormous love for everyone. Your emotional energy is pulled in so many ways that it is difficult for you to give too much to a single relationship. You have great creative talent that wishes to express itself.

MENTAL: You are a broad thinker. Your mind not only thinks outside the box, you aren't even aware that the box exists. You see the universality of the human race and can see the divine potential in all. You could express this through writing, speaking, or dramatic presentation.

INTUITIVE: Your NINE is very much at its home on the SPIRITUAL PLANE. You are a spiritual leader for the masses. Your message of unconditional love and non-attachment will be heard by many. You are not bound by dogmas; your teaching is the gospel of love.

Though the CIPHER (zero) is not considered to be a NUMBER, it can appear on a PLANE OF EXPRESSION, though it is a rare occurrence. It would seem that there would be no energy on that PLANE and that you who have the CIPHER on a PLANE would have little competency in that realm. Yet, an interesting situation is apt to develop. Because of the magnetic energy of KARMIC NUMBERs for balance, there will tend to be a great deal of energy drawn to this PLANE. However, there is likely to be a corresponding amount of confusion. You may find this PLANE impacting strongly upon your life's work, which is truly getting on-the-job training. Though you might seem to succeed, it could be at great cost if you don't find a way to balance the karma. Also, look at your CHART and see where else your KARMIC VIBRATIONs show up. They may already be playing an important role for you. It is even more critical that you be aware of the challenges of your KARMIC VIBRATIONs on this PLANE. Regardless, you will be on a crash course for correction.

Plane of expression

Each PLANE OF EXPRESSION is considered to be a MAJOR POSITION in your CHART (see "COMPUTATIONS" on page 287). There is much to say about their operation, so let's begin with some general observations:

- A high NUMBER on any PLANE indicates a place of power or strength for you and can be considered vocationally important. Numbers from ten up, though they reduce to low NUMBERs, are considered high on the PLANEs. They are read in their reduced form, but they act in a highly powerful manner. It is a place where you focus much energy.

- A low NUMBER on a PLANE might indicate a weakness or vulnerability. It mostly indicates that you don't tend to spend much time there. The labels "high" and "low" are relative. Longer names will tend to have higher NUMBERs. "High" or "low" do not mean good or bad.

- Look at the variations within your PLANES. An even spread of numbers among your PLANES, say, for example, there is a difference of no more than one or two between the highest and lowest number, indicates a balanced temperament. If the spread is great, say you have a difference of six or more between the highest and lowest number, then you are more likely to find yourself on an emotional roller coaster. This is neither good nor bad, but simply how you experience things, whether on an even keel or with highs and lows. Remember that you cannot have highs without lows, so the down periods are necessary parts of the cycle. Knowing that can help you to flow with and accept these down times. Moderate spreads between the high and low numbers indicate more moderate swings of temperament.

- The type of VIBRATION on your PLANE is also significant. Is the number in its natural sphere, for example a PHYSICAL number on the PHYSICAL PLANE? Think about what it might mean to have, for example, a MENTAL number on the EMO-

TIONAL PLANE. You might tend to deal with your emotions in a willful way. The reverse pattern of having an EMOTIONAL number on the MENTAL PLANE indicates your thinking may be people oriented and affected by your feelings. How these manifest will be shown more precisely by the actual number you have on that PLANE.

- You also want to look at all your PLANES together. If you have two or more values on your CHART's PLANES OF EXPRESSION that come from the same PLANE, for example a TWO on one PLANE and a SIX on another (both EMOTIONAL numbers) your day to day behavior will be much influenced by emotions. If three or four of your CHART's PLANES come from a single PLANE (say the EMOTIONAL), this influence is correspondingly stronger. If, say, you have three PHYSICAL VIBRATIONs on your PLANES, your day to day relationship to life is very practical. If you have no PHYSICAL or MENTAL numbers on your PLANES, your day to day activities may seem to be quite impractical. Look at your particular combination and accept it. This is how you designed yourself to operate. Notice that this day to day relationship with life might be far different from what is indicated by your NAME NUMBERS. Your MOTIVATION still shows the way that you want to be, but the PLANES show how you actually carry this out in the moment.

- If you have higher total numbers on the PHYSICAL and MENTAL PLANES (combined value), you are a more practical person. If you have more numbers on the EMOTIONAL and INTUITIVE PLANES, you are a more artistic person.

- If you have a KARMIC NUMBER on a PLANE, you have added help in bringing this VIBRATION into balance through your natural daily use of it. It does, however, remain a bit of an Achilles heel while you are sorting things out. Eventually it becomes a fountain of strength.

- If your MOTIVATION appears on a PLANE you will tend to like the way you operate on that PLANE. This could be a challenge to your ego. If the MOTIVATION is on your PHYSICAL PLANE, you may like the way you look. If the MOTIVATION appears on your MENTAL PLANE, you may think highly of yourself. If the MOTIVATION appears on your EMOTIONAL PLANE, you may be pleased with your love life. If the MOTIVATION appears on your INTUITIVE PLANE, you may be pleased with your spiritual development. If your INTEGRATED SELF appears on a PLANE, there is an added impetus and ability to what might be accomplished.

- Check also to see other places where the VIBRATIONs on your PLANES connect to your CHART. If, for example, you have a PHYSICAL FIVE, where else does FIVE appear in your CHART? If it corresponds to a period of timing, you will have a specifically physical response to that period.

- You can also look at the relationship between your PLANES and the PLANES of those you interact with closely, whether through a primary relationship, family, friendship, or work. Two people who share a VIBRATION on any PLANE (it need not be the same PLANE) have a comfort in being around each other. If the shared VIBRATION is on the same PLANE, the closeness and comfort intensify and are focused on that particular PLANE. Two or more shared PLANES increase the comfort zone, again magnifying if the shared VIBRATIONs are on the same PLANE. So, even if the NAME NUMBERs and LIFE PATHs are quite different, you will really enjoy hanging out with that person. The more VIBRATIONs you share, the more compatible you will feel.

- The PLANES bring a variety and individuation to your CHART. You share your name numbers with one out of 81 people, but it would be quite rare to find someone who also shares all your PLANES. Thus the PLANES help to reflect your individuality as a person. Again, understanding your PLANES can help you to more fully accept and express the uniqueness of who you are.

With the readings suggested for each of the four POSITIONs, remember, as always, that these are but suggestions and represent a starting point for your own intuitive guidance. *Paying attention to your four PLANEs helps you to understand and to accept many of the nuances of your character. Allow yourself to be fully you.*

MORE ABOUT

FOURs and FIVEs are the PHYSICAL VIBRATIONs:
- The FOURS represent the worker, builder, practical, economic, sense of form side of the PHYSICAL PLANE.
- The FIVES represent the curious, flexible, change oriented, experiential side.

In the average CHART the FIVES will outweigh the FOURS by a factor of 3 to 1. If your values are significantly different from this, you can see in which direction you lean.

An average NUMBER on the PHYSICAL PLANE might be FOUR or FIVE. Notice that these are both PHYSICAL NUMBERs, so having an average NUMBER indicates a strong grounding in the physical world. From SIX on up would be considered high on the PHYSICAL PLANE. Remember that even though ten acts like a ONE, it has the power of ten on a PLANE (likewise for eleven, twelve, and so on).

A high NUMBER on the PHYSICAL PLANE indicates you have fine endurance and the ability to withstand hard conditions. You are the type who can always pull through. You have strong positive opinions and a cautious, practical nature. You have a demand for things of the world including the substantial and the comfortable. You have an ability to keep and maintain order and systems. You are able to apply yourself and to concentrate. If FOURS are relatively lacking, there may be less concentration, but more of a demand for things.

A low NUMBER on the PHYSICAL PLANE, between ONE and THREE, shows that your practical side is not dependable or you may have a lack of caution. You also may have little endurance for hard physical work. When reading for a ten (one), eleven (two), twelve (three) or higher ignore any statements that were made about less energy or focus on this plane. You are very powerful here, still acting in the manner described above.

MORE ABOUT

TWOs, THREEs and SIXes are the EMOTIONAL VIBRATIONs
- The TWOS represent feelings and sensitivity.
- The THREES represent creativity and imagination.
- The SIXES represent love, caring, and directing of human affairs.

In the average CHART there would be a balance between the three VIBRATIONs with one of each. If one or more of these VIBRATIONs outweigh the other(s) you can see where your emotional energy tilts.

An average NUMBER on the EMOTIONAL PLANE would be FOUR or FIVE. This would show a basic ability to deal with emotional situations. A KARMIC NUMBER in one or more VIBRATIONs would throw a crimp into that area.

From SIX up would be considered high on the EMOTIONAL PLANE. A high NUMBER on the EMOTIONAL PLANE shows that your heart and affections rule over your logic and reason, unless your practical PLANEs are equally high or higher. You have a happy disposition and a love of beauty. You have a sympathetic nature and possess artistic feeling and talent. A SIX shows a high EMOTIONAL VIBRATION on the EMOTIONAL PLANE. SEVEN, EIGHT, NINE, and ten—while all high VIBRATIONs—are MENTAL or INTUITIVE VIBRATIONs, pulling somewhat away from the pure emotionality and adding a more rational or spiritual aspect.

A low NUMBER on the EMOTIONAL PLANE, between ONE and THREE shows a limited ability to express emotions, or they simply might not appear to be that important. With a TWO you have an EMOTIONAL VIBRATION on the EMOTIONAL PLANE. Though not powerful in expression, there is deep sensitivity. A THREE would also give you an EMOTIONAL VIBRATION on the EMOTIONAL PLANE. Since TWO and THREE are at home, an emotional nature is shown, even though more focus may be placed on other PLANEs. What you end up with in this case, assuming no KARMIC NUMBERs, is a situation where you are competent on the EMOTIONAL PLANE, but probably tend to hang out more on other PLANEs. When reading for a ten (one), eleven (two), twelve (three) or higher ignore any statements that were made about less energy or focus on this plane. You are very powerful here, still acting in the manner described above.

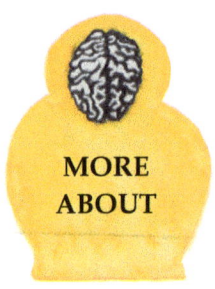

MORE ABOUT

ONEs and EIGHTs are the MENTAL VIBRATIONs:
- The ONES represent strong will and determination with touches of imagination based on mental facts.
- The EIGHTS represent the power of the mind, logical deduction, efficiency, and control of the practical and the emotional. Reason predominates.

In the average CHART the ONES will outweigh the EIGHTS by a factor of 3 to 1. If your values are significantly different from this, you can see in which direction you lean.

An average NUMBER on the MENTAL PLANE would be FOUR or FIVE. This would show you to be fully competent in dealing with mental issues.

From SIX and up would be considered high on the MENTAL PLANE. A high NUMBER on the MENTAL PLANE shows that you have fine reasoning powers. You are determined and have a strong will and executive ability. You want to have the facts before you are ready to act. Your reason may rule over your heart, even though love and sentiment are in your nature. You have the ability to push things through to their logical conclusion. You are not easily deterred. This is particularly true when the MENTAL VIBRATION of EIGHT is located on the MENTAL PLANE.

A low NUMBER on the MENTAL PLANE, from ONE to THREE, shows that you don't reason confidently. You may favor fancy over fact; your mind does not work in logical patterns. You are not a particularly cerebral person. You are not a natural leader. The curious exception is with the VIBRATION of ONE. Since it is a MENTAL VIBRATION, it is in its natural home. With a ONE you are forceful, but you don't spend much time thinking about things. You make up your mind quickly and then act. When reading for a ten (one), eleven (two), twelve (three) or higher ignore any statements that were made about less energy or focus on this plane. You are very powerful here, still acting in the manner described above.

Plane of expression

MORE ABOUT

SEVENs and NINEs are the INTUITIVE VIBRATIONs:
- The SEVENS represent analysis and technical facts, delving into the unknown and hidden, faith, and using inner guidance to gain your goal.
- The NINES represent not being influenced by reason or sentiment but by the heart of the universe. It is abstract and impressionable, deeply sensitive, and imaginative—being touched by a higher plane.

In the average CHART the NINES will outweigh the SEVENS by a factor of three to one. If your values are significantly different from this, you can see in which direction you lean.

An average NUMBER on the INTUITIVE PLANE would be THREE or FOUR. This would show a depth of feeling and an ability to understand mankind and humanity without too much personal feeling.

From FIVE and up would be considered high on the INTUITIVE PLANE. A high NUMBER on the INTUITIVE PLANE shows that you have a spiritual sensitiveness. You may have a great dramatic talent in literature, religion, prophecy, or invention, but not in accordance with the normal ways of thinking and acting. SEVEN and NINE are powerful on their own on any CHART, but here they are in their natural place and show you have a profound spiritual power.

A low NUMBER on the SPIRITUAL PLANE, primarily ONE or TWO, shows that you spend little time on the SPIRITUAL PLANE. A low NUMBER on a PLANE never suggests incompetence, you might act very clearly while you are there, it simply indicates that your energy is primarily focused on other PLANEs. When reading for a ten (one), eleven (two), twelve (three) or higher ignore any statements that were made about less energy or focus on this plane. You are very powerful here, still acting in the manner described above.

NOW WHAT?

TYING IT TOGETHER AND MOVING FORWARD

Your LOVE LETTER FROM YOUR HIGHER SELF is not a one-time gift. It is not intended to feed you just for today. This is a present that has the potential to reap rewards for you indefinitely. On the following pages are some suggestions for how this can work for you. These are not listed in any particular order of importance. See which one jumps out at you and follow that first.

REVIEW

Yeah, I know. That sounds like a homework assignment, but this might be particularly pertinent for those of you with significant FOURS, who either enjoy working at things until you get them right or else have a path that suggests that for you. I will also mention you SEVENS who like to go deeply into things and perfect your abilities, or may be compelled by your path to deal with these spiritual issues. For all of you who want to deepen your experience, go back over everything. Because the readings offered for the different POSITIONs are minimalistic, you will find yourself adding to them from your own understanding and intuition each time you revisit your CHART. Meditation, taking and reading notes, and discussions with others can all expand your experience. It isn't necessary to look at everything. Maybe one aspect of your CHART comes to mind, so you drag it out along with the book and give it a second (or third, or fourth, or…) look to see what insights come. Michael has been dealing with his CHART for over 35 years, and he still comes up with new inspirations (all right, he does have both FOURS and a SEVEN operating). If you were doing this with a group, you might wish to get the gang back together once every month or two and do the review. Helping others, whether from your group or outside of it, is a great way for you to develop your understanding of NUMEROLOGY.

YOUR BIRTHDAY

Focusing on your LOVE LETTER FROM YOUR HIGHER SELF is a wonderful birthday present that you can give yourself each year. Because your PERSONAL YEAR is changing (along with perhaps even a PINNACLE, or a PINNACLE and a CYCLE) this is a perfect time to give your LOVE LETTER another look. What energy will the new PERSONAL YEAR bring for you? How does that connect with your LIFE PATH and your ASCENSION NUMBER? While you are at it, this is a perfect time for a complete tune up. Check out your NAME NUMBERs and look at how things are going with your STRESS NUMBER. Got any KARMIC NUMBERs? How is your progress with balancing them going? And what about your LIFE PATH? Perhaps a renewed commitment to surrendering to it is in order. It is also always helpful to revisit your PLANEs OF EXPRESSION. Focus on accepting and loving who you are. You are a divine and unique treasure. Oh, and Happy Birthday!

E-OPTIONS

You might wish to get your personal NUMBERs calculated for you. Check it out on our website: www.channelswithoutborders.com. You will find more e-options on the site.

A PERSONAL READING WITH SANHIA

You can arrange to have a personal reading with me (Sanhia). This can be done in Järna, Sweden if that is possible for you, or at a site where Michael and Ulla and I are traveling. You can check the website: www.channelswithoutborders.com for those dates and locations. The website also has a variety of resources for supporting your spiritual quest, including a process called Spiritual Alchemy (or *the five-step process*) and a collection of monthly messages on a variety of topics. For those of you unable to arrange a personal session in a timely manner, it is possible to set up a Skype or a phone appointment. You can also accomplish this on the website. The reading will take ninety minutes. It is suggested that you make a recording of it. If you do not have a copy of your CHART, it will be emailed to you.

You may be asking yourself why you might want to get a reading from me when I have already put your information in the book. That is an excellent question. The answer most likely would be because you feel guided to do so. You have probably worked already with your NUMBERs and have received your own intuitive guidance, along with the suggestions I have given you. When I give you a reading I follow what comes intuitively to me at the time we are talking. This is not intended to replace what comes to you, but rather to supplement it. Your best use of the CHART is one where you take ownership of it and become your own numerologist. This doesn't mean that you might not want to bring in an outside expert now and then.

A LAST WORD

I am glad that you have decided to open this present from your higher self. It is always my wish that your trip be as expedient as possible. Spiritual growth is inherently painful, as is life. This book is not offered as a way to avoid the pain, but rather as an encouragement to go right into the heart of it and to find your truth and love. NUMEROLOGY is a great tool for doing just that. Bon voyage!

COMPUTATIONS

HOW TO FIGURE OUT WHICH NUMBERS TO USE

This chapter contains clear and simple step-by-step instructions for filling in your NUMEROLOGY CHART. It also contains a model chart as an example for how to complete the task. We chose Gandhi for the model because he is familiar to a great number of people. As you become more comfortable with numerology, you may wish to see how what you know about Gandhi correlates with his CHART (see page 288). The math necessary to compute your CHART is minimal, nothing more than simple addition and subtraction is involved, but—as with math—you might want to work with a pencil and an eraser. If you experience any confusion, take a deep breath, relax, and reread the direction. Look at the example of the model chart of Gandhi to see how that step was performed for his CHART. If you are still confused, ask your inner guidance for help. You will get there. Filling in your CHART yourself can give a broader perspective on the POSITIONs and their RELATIONSHIPs. Out of this can come a deeper self-awareness and acceptance. As you begin to know the NUMBER equivalents for each letter, you may find yourself applying what you know about NUMBERs to other people, places, or things in your daily life. *Relax and have fun with it.*

YOUR NAME

What's in a name? Everything. Your parents went through a lot trying to figure out what to name you. In the end they were guided to choose the name that best supported you to know yourself. Your parents had whatever reasons and went through whatever dynamics they used to justify the choice. You are who you are, and you attracted the name that helps you to understand yourself.

For the purposes of your NUMEROLOGY CHART, you wish to use your full birth name as it appears on your birth certificate. Include all middle names. Do not include any confirmation names or nicknames. Do not include titles, such as Junior, the Third, and so on. The name that you were given at birth is the important one, even if you identify more with another name, even if you detest your birth name. If there is confusion about the original name, here are some suggestions. If there is a clerical mistake on the document, go with your parents' intention. If there is no document and there was a disagreement between your parents, go with your mother's intention. If you were adopted, go by the name you were given by your birth mother/parents. If there is simply no information about the birth name, say from an adoption situation, and you have done the best research that you can do—use the first full name that you are aware of.

A word of caution. It is not suggested that you try to create a "perfect name" for your child, or for anything or anyone else you might choose to give a name. There are too many variables for you to have any realistic expectation of control. If you want to play God, listen to your intuition and choose what feels good. On the other hand, it is not possible to do harm with your choice. Remember that there is no such thing as a good name or a bad name. The name that is attracted is the perfect name.

LETTERS AND NUMBERS

Names are made up of letters. We deal only with those languages that use the twenty-six letter alphabet. Accents and diacritical marks are not considered, so, for example, the Swedish "å" is treated as an "a". We will also be dealing with the nine NUMBER VIBRATIONs, that is, the numerals from ONE through NINE. Zero, the CIPHER, comes into play only rarely, as do the NUMBERs higher than NINE. Those situations will be dealt with as they come up. There are three aspects to your CHART: NUMBER, POSITION, and RELATIONSHIP. Again there are but nine NUMBERs, but there are a multiplicity of POSITIONs those NUMBERs can take.

Computations

CONVERTING LETTERS TO NUMBERS

Before we can proceed further, it is helpful to understand the relationship between letters and NUMBERs. It is quite simple, logical, and straight-forward. A is the first letter, so it has the value of ONE. B is the second letter and therefore has the value of TWO. We're providing a table to make things even easier (see page 279).

SIMPLIFICATION OF NUMBERS

When we reach the tenth letter, J, we give it the value of ONE (1). This is done because we like to keep things simple. NUMEROLOGY is not a tool reserved for great mathematical minds. A calculator isn't really necessary, though I don't mind one bit if you use one. You simplify all compound NUMBERs, that is, NUMBERs with more than one digit. You accomplish this by adding the component parts together. So with ten (10) we add 1 + 0 and get 1. Fifteen (15) would simplify as follows: 1 + 5 = 6. One hundred eighty-six (186) would require two steps as follows: 1 + 8 + 6 = 15, 1 + 5 = 6. That's all there is to it.

COMPUTING YOUR CHART

Now you have all of the background information necessary to get started with computing your chart. Just follow the steps in order. Each step is identified by a white number, embedded in a black circle. That same numbered circle is located in the portion of the Gandhi chart that precedes the section of the directions you are reading. In that way, you can find where to enter that step on your own chart, as well as see how the calculation is carried out for Gandhi. A few of the numbers are red rather than white. This indicates that they are not to be found on the Gandhi chart. The directions are printed on a colored background, so that they stand out. The line after each direction contains the NUMBERs and the calculation for the Gandhi CHART. If you are having any confusion about what to do, please study that example. Some of the steps are then followed by additional information in italics. This is another place to check if you are experiencing any confusion.

If you wish to have your chart calculated for you, go to the website: www.channelswithoutborders.com.

Computations

LETTERS TO NUMBERS TABLE

A	J	S	1
B	K	T	2
C	L	U	3
D	M	V	4
E	N	W	5
F	O	X	6
G	P	Y	7
H	Q	Z	8
I	R		9

COMPUTING YOUR NAME NUMBERS

1 Print a blank CHART from the website: www.channelswithoutborders.com or copy it from this book.

We will be using the CHART of Gandhi, the great Indian leader, as a model. For the full chart see page 288.

LOVE LETTER from YOUR HIGHER SELF

3 | 6 | 1 | | 1 | | 1 | 1 | | 1 | | 1 | | 9 | | | | | **5**
21

2 M O H A N D A S K A R A M C H A N D G A N D H I

81

4 | 4 | 8 | 5 4 | 1 | 2 | 9 | 4 3 8 | 5 4 | 7 | 5 4 8 | | **7**

Hearts: 3, 6, 9, 11, 13, 12; Other: 6, 3, 9, 8, 3, 9

2 Print your full birth name, leaving a space between names. Begin with your first name and end with your last name.

MOHANDAS KARAMCHAND GANDHI

3 Assign a NUMBER value to each vowel (using the "LETTERS TO NUMBERS TABLE" on page 279).

6 1   1 1 1 1 1 9
O A   A A A A A I

The vowels are A, E, I, O, U, and Y – when there is no other vowel in the syllable (in Cary – "y" is a vowel because there is no other vowel in the second syllable, in Carey – "y" is a consonant because the "e" acts as a vowel in the second syllable). Any diacritical marks (e.g. å, ä) are to be ignored.

4 Assign and write the consonant values.

M H N D S K R M C H N D G N D H
4 8 5 4 1 2 9 4 3 8 5 4 7 5 4 8

5 Add up all the vowel values in your name and write that NUMBER.

6 + 1 + 1 + 1 +1 + 1 + 1 + 9 = 21

6 Simplify the NUMBER from field 5 to a single digit and write this NUMBER.

21: 2 + 1 = 3

Simplify by adding the digits together until they equal a NUMBER from ONE to NINE (see "SIMPLIFICATION OF NUMBERS" on page 278 for more assistance). This is your MOTIVATION.

7 Add up all the consonant values in your name and write that NUMBER.

4 + 8 + 5 + 4 + 1 + 2 + 9 + 4 + 3 + 8 + 5 + 4 + 7 + 5 + 4 + 8 = 81

8 Simplify the NUMBER from field 7 and write the NUMBER.

81: 8 + 1 = 9

This is your PERSONALITY.

9 Add together the NUMBER from field 6 (MOTIVATION) and the NUMBER from field 8 (PERSONALITY), simplify, and write this NUMBER.

3 + 9 = 12, 1 + 2 = 3

This is your INTEGRATED SELF.

10 Double check everything, by seeing that you have recorded the correct NUMBER for each letter and that all of your additions and simplifications are correct.

The MOTIVATION, PERSONALITY, AND INTEGRATED SELF are called your NAME NUMBERs.

COMPUTING YOUR STRESS NUMBER BETWEEN MOTIVATION AND PERSONALITY

11 Write the NUMBER from field 6 (MOTIVATION).

3

12 Write the NUMBER from field 8 (PERSONALITY).

9

13 Subtract the lower of the two NUMBERs from the higher NUMBER, and write the answer.

9 - 3 = 6

This is your STRESS NUMBER BETWEEN MOTIVATION AND PERSONALITY.

Ascension Numerology

COMPUTING YOUR BIRTH NUMBERS

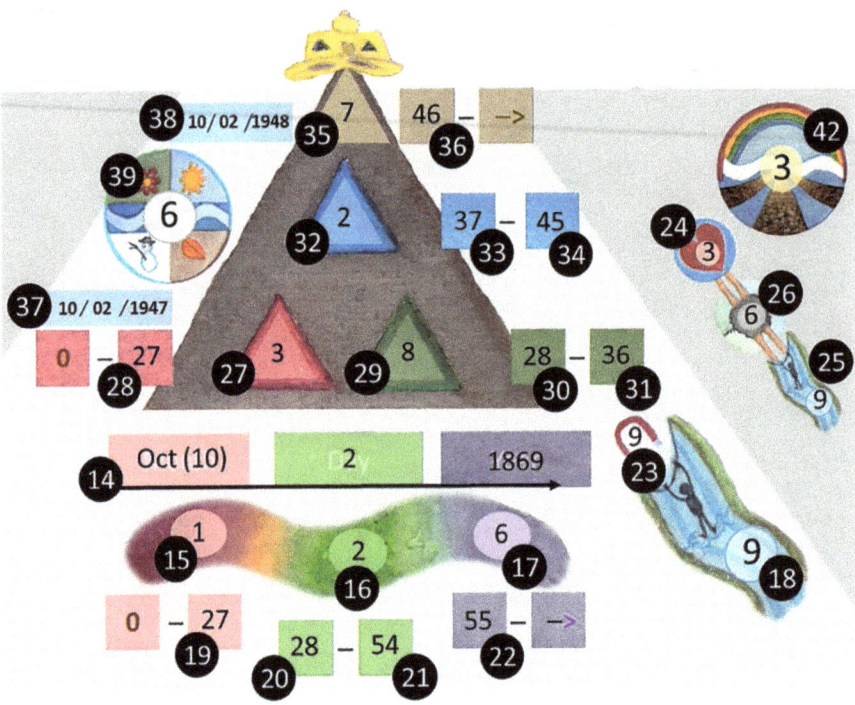

COMPUTING YOUR LIFE PATH AND CYCLES

14 Write your birth date out in the American style.
Oct (10) 2 1869

15 Simplify the month NUMBER from field 14 and write this NUMBER.
1 + 0 = 1
This is your FIRST (DEVELOPMENTAL) CYCLE.

16 Simplify the day NUMBER from field 14 and write this NUMBER.
2
This is your SECOND (PRODUCTIVE) CYCLE

17 Simplify the year NUMBER from field 14 and write this NUMBER.
1 + 8 + 6 + 9 = 24,   2 + 4 = 6
This is your THIRD (HARVEST) CYCLE

18 Total fields 15, 16 and 17 (CYCLEs), simplify and write this NUMBER.
1 + 2 + 6 = 9
This is your LIFE PATH.

(19) Subtract field 18 (LIFE PATH) from 36 and write that age.

36 − 9 = 27

This is your age during the last year of your FIRST CYCLE. The first pink squares is already filled in with a "0" which indicates that your FIRST CYCLE begins at birth.

(20) Add 1 to your age in the box 19 and write that age.

27 + 1 = 28

This is your age the first year of your SECOND CYCLE.

(21) Add 26 to your age in the box 20 and write that age.

28 + 26 = 54

This is your age during the last year of your SECOND CYCLE.

(22) Add 1 to your age in the box 21 and write that age.

54 + 1 = 55

This is your age the first year of your THIRD CYCLE. The arrow in the second purple box indicates that the THIRD CYCLE lasts as long as you do.

ANTI-NUMBER

(23) Subtract field 18 (LIFE PATH) from nine (9) and write this NUMBER.

9 − 9 = 0 ---> 0 becomes 9

This is your ANTI-NUMBER.
If your number is the CIPHER, your ANTI-NUMBER becomes NINE.

STRESS NUMBER BETWEEN MOTIVATION AND LIFE PATH

(24) Write the NUMBER from field 6 (MOTIVATION).

3

(25) Write the NUMBER from field 18 (LIFE PATH).

9

(26) Subtract the lower of the two NUMBERs from the higher NUMBER and write the answer.

9 − 3 = 6

This is your STRESS NUMBER BETWEEN MOTIVATION AND LIFE PATH.

COMPUTING THE PINNACLES

27 Add together fields 15 and 16, simplify, and write that NUMBER.
1 + 2 = 3
This is your FIRST PINNACLE.

28 Write your age from box 19.
27
Your FIRST CYCLE and your FIRST PINNACLE end at the same age. The 0 in the first dark pink box to its left shows that your FIRST PINNACLE also begins at birth.

29 Add together fields 16 and 17, simplify, and write that NUMBER.
6 + 2 = 8
This is your SECOND PINNACLE.

30 Write the age from box 20.
28
Your SECOND PINNACLE and your SECOND CYCLE begin at the same age.

31 Add 8 to box 30 and write that age.
28 + 8 = 36
This is your ending age for your SECOND PINNACLE.

32 Add together boxes 27 and 29, simplify, and write that NUMBER.
3 + 8 = 11, 1 + 1 = 2
This is your THIRD PINNACLE.

33 Add 1 to box 31 and write that age.
36 + 1 = 37
This is your starting age for your THIRD PINNACLE.

34 Add 8 to box 33 and write that age.
37 + 8 = 45
This is your ending age for your THIRD PINNACLE.

35 Add together fields 15 and 17, simplify, and write that NUMBER.
1 + 6 = 7
This is your FOURTH PINNACLE.

36 Add 1 to box 34 and write that age.
45 + 1 = 46
This is your starting age for your FOURTH PINNACLE. The arrow in the second beige box indicates that the FOURTH PINNACLE lasts as long as you do.

CALCULATING YOUR PERSONAL YEAR

37 Write the date of your last birthday (month/day/year)

10 / 2 / 1947

For Gandhi, we are using the PERSONAL YEAR when he was assassinated (January 13, 1948).

38 Write the date of your next birthday (month/day/year)

10 / 2 / 1948

This shows the span of your PERSONAL YEAR.

39 Add the month, day and year from field 37 (your last birthday), simplify and write this NUMBER.

1 + 0 + 2 + 1 + 9 + 4 + 7 = 24   2 + 4 = 6

This is your PERSONAL YEAR. Notice that your PERSONAL YEAR changes at your birthday, not on January 1st. A shortcut for this calculation: Add the year from field 37 to field 27 (FIRST PINNACLE).
1 + 9 + 4 + 7 + 3 = 24   2 + 4 = 6

CALCULATING YOUR PERSONAL MONTH

40 Add together the value from field 39 (PERSONAL YEAR) and the value for the present month and simplify.

6 (from PERSONAL YEAR) +1 (from "January") = 7

This is your PERSONAL MONTH. It is not included in your CHART because it changes frequently. For Gandhi, we have calculated the PERSONAL MONTH when he was assassinated.

CALCULATING YOUR PERSONAL DAY

41 Add together the value for your PERSONAL MONTH plus today's date and simplify.

7 (PERSONAL MONTH) + 13 (13th day of the month) = 20   2 + 0 = 2

This is your PERSONAL DAY. It is not included in your CHART because it changes daily. For Gandhi, we have calculated the PERSONAL DAY when he was assassinated.

COMPUTING THE ASCENSION NUMBER

42 Add together fields 9 and 18, simplify, and write this NUMBER.

3 + 9 = 12, 1 + 2 = 3

This is your ASCENSION NUMBER.

Ascension Numerology

COMPUTING THE TABLE OF INTENSIFICATION AND PLANES OF EXPRESSION

CALCULATING THE TABLE AND FINDING YOUR KARMIC NUMBERS

43 Count the number of "1"s in fields 3 and 4 and write that total.
No of 1´s = 7

44 Do the same thing for the NUMBERs "2" through "9".
2's = 1, 3's = 1, 4's = 5, 5's = 3. 6's = 1, 7's = 1, 8's = 3, 9's = 2

This is your TABLE OF INTENSIFICATION.

45 Count the number of letters in your name in field 2. It should be equal to the sum of the values in the circles 43 and 44. If the values are not equal, double check your figures in circles 43 and 44.

46 Write each NUMBER that has a "0" in the circles in fields 43 and 44.

Gandhi had no KARMIC NUMBERs, so nothing is shown.

These are your KARMIC NUMBERs. There is a circle for three KARMIC NUMBERs. If you have a four or more, write the other(s) in the space at the bottom center of the icon.

COMPUTING PLANES OF EXPRESSION

(47) Add together the NUMBER of FOURS and FIVES (green icons) from field 44 (TABLE OF INTENSIFICATION) and write the total.

5 + 3 = 8

This is your PHYSICAL PLANE. FOUR and FIVE are PHYSICAL VIBRATIONs.

(48) Add together the NUMBER of TWOS, THREES, and SIXES (pink icons) from field 44 (TABLE OF INTENSIFICATION) and write the total.

1 + 1 + 1 = 3

This is your EMOTIONAL PLANE. TWO, THREE, and SIX are EMOTIONAL VIBRATIONs.

(49) Add together the NUMBER of ONES and EIGHTS (yellow icons) from fields 43-44 (TABLE OF INTENSIFICATION) and write the total.

7 + 3 = 10

This is your MENTAL PLANE. ONE and EIGHT are MENTAL VIBRATIONs.

(50) Add together the NUMBER of SEVENS and NINES (PURPLE icons) from field 44 (TABLE OF INTENSIFICATION) and write the total.

1 + 2 = 3

This is your INTUITIVE PLANE. SEVEN and NINE are INTUITIVE VIBRATIONs.

GANDHI'S CHART

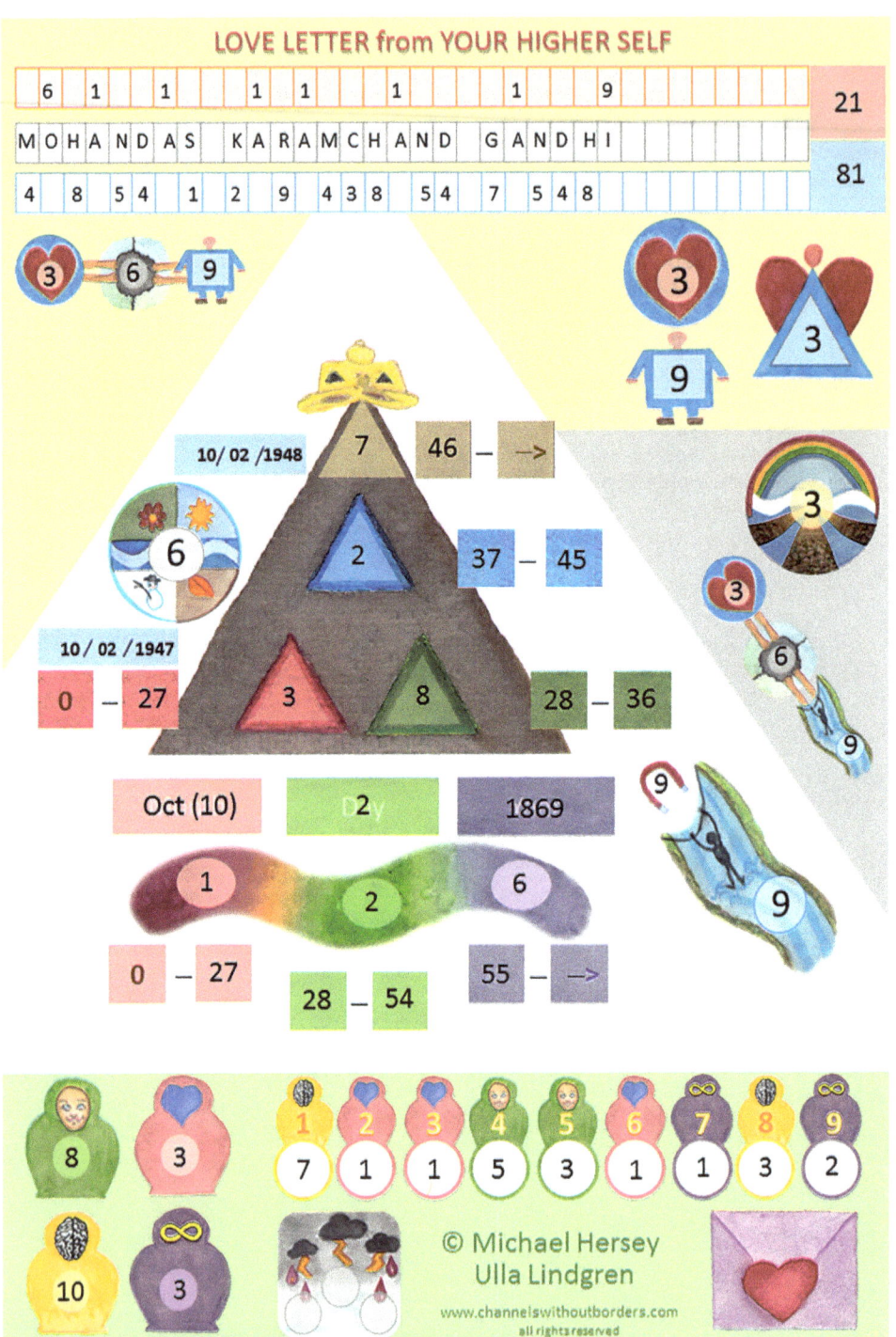

If you are reading this, you and I may be the only ones doing so—other than those being acknowledged. My INNER and OUTER FOURs always want to be thorough; while my NINE LIFE PATH seeks completion. My MENTAL SEVEN is also curious and wishes to go as deeply as possible into whatever is of interest. Whatever your reason for making it this far might be, welcome! It has been a joy to put this book together with the assistance of wonderful friends. The focus has always been dual: to create a quality product while enjoying the process and our time together.

I can't think of a logical place to begin, so I'm just going to wing this. I will start by thanking my wife, life partner, co-worker, and illustrator—Ulla Lindgren. Ulla is a relative late-comer to NUMEROLOGY, but she is a quick study, has a deep spiritual awareness, a highly developed intuition, and an unshakable devotion to her own ASCENSION process. Though NUMBERs are highly symbolic, little attention has been given to the expression of VIBRATION through shape and color in most of the NUMEROLOGY books I have seen. Ulla and I would kick around ideas until something jelled for both of us. The process was curious as we often ended someplace far away from where we started. Like the words, the graphics are not meant to be the final word (or picture), but are intended as a beginning of a dialog that you will continue. Ulla was also of great assistance in reading the text and offering suggestions, both large and small. We spent many hours discussing the book from many different vantage points. Of highest importance, she has kept the focus on ASCENSION throughout the book. Ulla has been a tremendous support on all four PLANEs.

Next, I want to give thanks to my publisher and digital designer, Marie Örnesved. I had just begun the book when I met Marie. Her excitement about it and her vision for what it could be were instrumental in the creation of what you have before you. She saw it not only as a book, but as an interactive experience. The next stage of the process will be an interactive process designed for your electronic devices. We are still involved in finding out just what that creation will look like. Marie also helped me to set up a test group to see just how usable the information was for novice numerologists. This has inspired a good deal of testing and tinkering. Marie has also been irreplaceable as a text reader and editor. Last, but not least, her computer skills, especially in the area of graphics were of great assistance in transferring Ulla's designs into the formats used in this book and in laying out the pages. Like Ulla, Marie has brought an unrelenting positive attitude to the product. The three of us always looked forward to getting together to work.

I can't go on from here without mentioning Sanhia. He asked me not to place him first in these appreciations, but the book simply would not have come to being without him. Sanhia led me to NUMEROLOGY; then, years later, showed me the potential for how a reading could be done, has been my spiritual teacher (consciously) for thirty years, and wrote most of this book through me. He left the nuts and bolts to the team, while making sure that the spirit and the direction stayed clear and pure. He appointed Ulla as his assistant there, and she was willingly and joyfully up to the task. Back to Sanhia, all I can say is that everyone should have such a friend. (He just said that you all do. Just ask.)

Next, I would like to give appreciations to my wonderful editor, Stella Hansen. My friendship with Stella goes back thirty-five years. She has been a student of NUMEROLOGY all of that time, and also developed a relationship with Sanhia not long after I began channeling. Several years ago, Stella offered to edit the monthly messages from Sanhia (see www.channelswithoutborders.com). She has done an outstanding job with them and was my first choice as an editor for the book. Not only is the editing work top-notch, but Stella has also unknowingly taken on the role of my conscience. Anything that I have had a second thought about but left in the draft, she has caught and questioned me on. Her depth of understanding of both the NUMBERs and Sanhia have made her an irreplaceable part of the whole that has created this book. I couldn't have found a better editor.

I also wish to give thanks to fellow numerologist Brett Simpson. It was Brett who initially encouraged me to write this book. As I mentioned in INTRODUCTIONS, I was less than enthusiastic about the project. Brett gave me clear reasons why he thought it was important that the book be written. He offered feedback on the text—not only from a technical and grammatical standpoint, but also with the depth of understanding that only years spent with the numbers can provide.

Now, I want to go back in time to and acknowledge those who were a part of the seed energy for the project. First, I want to thank Jacqueline Robertson-Swann for not only being my teacher, but for inspiring me to take up NUMEROLOGY through the power of her gift. She selflessly helped me get started by answering my numerous questions and then pointing me to the best books to read. Those books included ones by authors Florence Campbell and Juno Jordan, but the deepest influence came from Lynn Buess, who introduced the concept of the STRESS NUMBER and brought a more fully spiritual approach to the NUMBERs.

Next I want to thank my mother, BB Hersey, who introduced me to NUMEROLOGY and to Jacquie in 1977. For years we were co-conspirators on the spiritual path. BB and I rarely had a conversation that didn't include the discussion of somebody's CHART. We shared a NINE LIFE PATH and took turns being each other's teacher. I know that she is enjoying watching this come to fruition.

While we are back in the good old days, thanks go to my friends in West Virginia who were willing to receive a reading from a stumbling, uncertain novice—and especially to Blue Conopask who convinced me that I had some ability and organized my first class of students. A big smile also goes to Sister Elizabeth Reis who was my first paying numerology client, became my student, and then organized my first professional numerology class.

I would like to express gratitude to Sylvia Powell (and her husband George) for years of support. Sylvia got me back on the horse when I had gone into seclusion with this work. Sylvia is a great organizer and an enthusiastic Sanhia supporter, who brought many people to talk with me and with Sanhia in McAllen and Mission, Texas. Thanks to George for always making me feel welcome in their home and for hours of fascinating conversation.

I also wish to thank Joyce Hug for organizing many NUMEROLOGY classes at Sacred Waters in Mishawaka, Indiana, for being a great supporter, and for stretching her beautiful spiritual energy to accept and welcome Sanhia.

Up the road in Kalamazoo, Michigan, my cousin Mary Grace also did a wonderful job of promoting Sanhia, me, and NUMEROLOGY at her Unwindings center. We've had many interesting NUMBER related conversations about our shared family. Thanks also to her husband Jim for being a good sport and a welcoming host.

I wish to thank Patricia Hersey for years of support and a shared interest in the NUMBERs and in Sanhia. It was important for me to be able to share this passion on a day to day level through our marriage.

I want to thank the many people who have come to me for readings and classes. Each one made me a better numerologist. It took me a long time to develop and, more importantly, to trust my intuitive side. Your feedback was always helpful for me in realizing that. My KARMIC TWO provided innumerable barriers to my just getting out of the way and trusting what came. Thank you all for your patience and trust.

Finally, I want to acknowledge myself for my years of devotion to NUMEROLOGY, to Sanhia, and to my spiritual path. It wasn't always easy, but my FOURness kept picking myself up off the floor and trying again. It was my job to hold the constant vision and integrity for the book as others showered me with their ideas. Their involvement made this book so much more than it started out to be, But, Sanhia left it to me to keep its aim true. The writing of the book wasn't too hard. The groundwork had already been done. I enjoyed the writing process and the many rewrites. I regret that I have to stop somewhere so that the publishing can take place, because I keep finding things that can be changed and improved. I guess that is a good metaphor for life. Ulla and I love the book as it is and hope that you might take the time to let it truly work in your life.

BIOGRAPHIES

ULLA LINDGREN

Ulla's inner spiritual guidance is the most precious gift in her life. Her childhood was colored by large and unforgettable spiritual communications. When she was 20 she started to meditate regularly, and that slowly transformed her childhood spiritual experiences into a divine guidance for her grown-up life. Ulla expanded her intuitive and creative abilities through her more than 35 years of teaching drama and theater. At the same time she developed and refined aspects of her spiritual leadership through conducting Re-evaluation Counseling self-help groups and building support networks. Her own crises and difficulties have been her best and sharpest masters. They have crystallized her light channel and cleared her spiritual vision. Since 2013 she has co-led Spiritual Alchemy groups with Michael.

MICHAEL HERSEY

Michael Hersey has been working personally with his own ascension process since the early '70s. He was guided to study numerology and then to establish a practice in 1979. Michael also developed a workshop program which supported others to give up their fears about money and do the work they came here to do. He began channeling ascended master Sanhia in 1985, and has channeled for numerous groups and individuals throughout the United States and Sweden. Since 2013 he has co-led Spiritual Alchemy groups with Ulla. The focus of all the work is on realizing your personal divinity.

SANHIA

Ascended master Sanhia's final lifetime was as an Apache Indian. During the life of Jesus, Sanhia incarnated as the disciple known as Thomas. His service now is to support those who have chosen an ascension path. Sanhia models and teaches unconditional love and forgiveness. He has a gentle, humorous manner, but tells people exactly what they need to hear in that moment. Sanhia encourages people to take full responsibility for everything in their experience and to understand the perfection of their creations. He teaches people how to live more in the present moment and encourages them to discover their personal divinity.

The authors can be contacted at www.channelswithoutborders.com. You will find additional information and resources on the site.

INDEX

Bold numbers reference computation instructions

A

ANTI-NUMBER 41, 170, **283**
ASCENSION 28
ASCENSION NUMBER 40, 232, **285**

B

BIRTH NUMBER 40, 168, **282**

C

CHART (NUMEROLOGY CHART) 37, 38, 276, **277**
COMPUTATIONS **274**
CYCLE 40, 204, **282**

E

EIGHT 70
EMOTIONAL PLANE 41, 252, **287**

F

FIRST (DEVELOPMENTAL) CYCLE 206, **282**
FIRST PINNACLE 214, **284**
FIVE 64
FOUR 62
FOURTH PINNACLE 214, **284**

G

GANDHI'S CHART **288**

I

INNER VIBRATION (or INNER) 81
INTEGRATED SELF 40, 138, **281**
INTUITIVE PLANE 41, 252, **287**

K

KARMIC NUMBER 41, 86, **286**

L

LETTERS TO NUMBERS TABLE **279**
LIFE PATH 40, 162, **282**

M

MAJOR POSITION 40
MENTAL PLANE 41, 252, **287**
MINOR POSITION 41
MOTIVATION 40, 76, **281**

N

NAME NUMBER 39, 40, **280**
NINE 72
NINE YEAR CYCLE 225
NUMBER 52
NUMEROLOGY 36

O

ONE 56
OUTER VIBRATION (or OUTER) 101

P

PERSONAL DAY 41, 229, **285**
PERSONALITY 40, 96, **281**
PERSONAL MONTH 41, 227, **285**
PERSONAL YEAR 40, 220, **285**
PHYSICAL PLANE 41, 252, **287**
PINNACLE 40, 212, **284**
PLANE OF EXPRESSION 41, 250, **287**
POSITION 38

S

SECOND PINNACLE 214, **284**
SECOND (PRODUCTIVE) CYCLE 206, **282**
SEVEN 68
SIX 66
SPECIAL RELATIONSHIP 41
STRESS NUMBER 41, 104, 174
STRESS NUMBER BETWEEN MOTIVATION AND LIFE PATH 174, **283**
STRESS NUMBER BETWEEN MOTIVATION AND PERSONALITY 104, **281**

T

TABLE OF INTENSIFICATION 41, 244, **286**
THIRD (HARVEST) CYCLE 206, **282**
THIRD PINNACLE 214, **284**
THREE 60
TWO 58

V

VIBRATION 38, 53

making **messages** from
loving hearts
available to a **global** audience

cocreators @lightspira.com
www.lightspira.com

www.ingramcontent.com/pod-product-compliance
Lightning Source LLC
Chambersburg PA
CBHW061357010526
44107CB00012B/966